EAST AFRICAN CAMPAIGN
1940-41

**OFFICIAL HISTORY OF THE INDIAN ARMED FORCES
IN THE SECOND WORLD WAR
1939-45**

EAST AFRICAN CAMPAIGN
1940-41

The Naval & Military Press Ltd

Published by

The Naval & Military Press Ltd
Unit 5 Riverside, Brambleside
Bellbrook Industrial Estate
Uckfield, East Sussex
TN22 1QQ England

Tel: +44 (0)1825 749494

www.naval-military-press.com
www.nmarchive.com

In reprinting in facsimile from the original, any imperfections are inevitably reproduced and the quality may fall short of modern type and cartographic standards.

ADVISORY COMMITTEE

Chairman

SECRETARY, MINISTRY OF DEFENCE, INDIA

Members

DR. TARA CHAND
PROF. K. A. NILAKANTA SASTRI
PROF. MOHAMMAD HABIB
DR. R. C. MAJUMDAR
GENERAL K. S. THIMAYYA
LIEUT-GENERAL SIR DUDLEY RUSSELL
LIEUT-GENERAL S. P. P. THORAT
MILITARY ADVISER TO THE HIGH COMMISSIONER FOR PAKISTAN IN INDIA

Secretary

DR. BISHESHWAR PRASAD

CAMPAIGNS IN THE WESTERN THEATRE

NORTH AFRICAN CAMPAIGN 1940—43
CAMPAIGN IN WESTERN ASIA
CAMPAIGN IN ITALY 1943—45
EAST AFRICAN CAMPAIGN 1940—41

TO ALL WHO SERVED

PREFACE

This volume is the fourteenth to be published in the series "Official History of the Indian Armed Forces in the Second World War." The story relates to the Western Theatre and is a fitting companion to our earlier publication Campaign in North Africa. It describes the fighting with the Italian forces in East Africa. The regions covered are Eritrea and Ethiopia where the two Indian Infantry Divisions, the 4th and the 5th, played a distinguished role. A shattering blow was inflicted on the Italians in East Africa by a giant pincer movement on a large scale, the northern arm of which was formed by British and Indian forces operating from the Sudan and the southern arm by the forces advancing through Kenya. The Indian forces from the north conquered Eritrea and broke the back of Italian resistance in East Africa at Keren; the forces from the south conquered Italian Somaliland and opened Addis Ababa for the return of the Ethiopian Emperor. As the jaws of the pincer closed the army of the Duke of Aosta was pinned between the two forces and he surrendered at Amba Alagi in May 1941. This meant the military and political collapse of Italian East Africa.

The Government of India set up an organisation before the termination of the Second World War to gather material for writing an objective and authentic account of the operations in which the Indian armed forces had participated. This organisation grew into the War Department Historical Section, which on the partition of India in 1947 was designated as the Combined Inter-Services Historical Section, India and Pakistan, and was to work as the joint venture of the two Governments. This organisation was commissioned to produce a history of military operations and organisational activities relating to war. This official history has been planned into three series, viz., the campaigns in the western theatre; the campaigns in the eastern theatre; and the activities pertaining to organisation and administration. The present volume is the last of the series dealing with the Campaigns in the Western Theatre. The material for this volume was initially compiled by Major N. A. Qureshi. More information was subsequently added and the draft of the history prepared by Dr. Dharm Pal, which was revised and rewritten in parts by Dr. K. N. Pandey. All these officers at one time or the other belonged to the Historical Section. To them my thanks are due. The maps for this volume as for others were prepared by Shri T. D. Sharma to whom I am grateful. I am also grateful to Shri P. N. Khera for reading the narrative and seeing it through the Press.

The narrative has been read and approved by Prof. K. A. Nilakanta Sastri and Lieut-General S. P. P. Thorat, DSO, both members of the Advisory Committee to whom I am grateful.

In conclusion, I acknowledge with thanks the unstinting co-operation and encouragement I have received from the Ministries of Defence of India and Pakistan.

New Delhi
March 1963   BISHESHWAR PRASAD

CONTENTS

		Page
INTRODUCTION		xix

CHAPTER

I	THE BACKGROUND	1
II	TOPOGRAPHY	12
III	THE FIRST ENCOUNTERS	24
IV	ITALIANS ON THE RETREAT	40
V	THE FIRST ASSAULT ON KEREN	50
VI	THE ADVANCE DOWN THE RED SEA COAST	72
VII	PLAN FOR THE FINAL ATTACK ON KEREN	81
VIII	THE BATTLE OF KEREN	92
IX	THE ADVANCE CONTINUES	122
X	THE CAPTURE OF AMBA ALAGI	132
XI	CONCLUSION	153
APPENDICES		157
BIBLIOGRAPHY		173
INDEX		175

APPENDICES

I. Order of Battle of 5th Indian Division (on 27 September 1940)

II. Order of Battle Gazelle Force on Being Formed on 16 October 1940

III. Order of Battle—Troops in the Sudan as on 20 January 1941

IV. Estimated Order of Battle of Italian Northern Army on 10 April 1941

MAPS

Facing page

1. East Africa 13
2. Eritrea (Communications) 17
3. Northern Ethiopia 21
4. Gallabat—Metemma Area 31
5. The Advance—Kassala to Keren, Part I 41
6. The Advance—Kassala to Keren, Part II 45
7. Operations in Om Ager Area 47
8. Keren—The First Attack, Part I 51
9. Keren—The First Attack, Part II 69
10. Operations by 7th Indian Infantry Brigade Part I . . 75
11. Operations by 7th Indian Infantry Brigade Part II . . 79
12. Operations by 7th Indian Infantry Brigade north of Keren . . . . *page* 96

Facing page

13. Keren—The Final Battle 115
14. The Pursuit by 5th Indian Division, Keren to Asmara . . 123
15. Advance to Massawa 127
16. Battle of Massawa 131
17. The Pursuit, southward from Asmara 133
18. The Area north of Amba Alagi 135
19. The Features north of the Falaga Pass . . . . *page* 140
20. The Battle of Amba Alagi . . . . . . *Facing page* 145

ILLUSTRATIONS

(between pages 24 and 25)

1. Captain Premindra Singh Bhagat, V.C., Royal Bombay Sappers and Miners
2. Subedar Richpal Ram, V. C., 4/6 Rajputana Rifles
3. General Sir Archibald P. Wavell
4. Lt.-Gen. Sir William Platt
5. Maj.-Gen. A. G. O. Mayne
6. Maj.-Gens. L. M. Heath and N. M. de la P. Beresford-Peirse
7. Ethiopian Patroits on the march
8. Captured Italian war material at Agordat

(between pages 56 and 57)

9. One of the fine thoroughfares in Asmara
10. Lt.-Gen. W. Platt inspects his guard of honour at the Governor's Palace at Asmara
11. Sappers and Miners of the Indian Army clearing a road block between Asmara and Massawa
12. The sign post showing Massawa
13. Men of the 4/10 Baluch march into Asmara
14. Indian troops manning an A.A. post at Tessenei
15. A view of the deserted Laquatat Fortress near Agordat
16. Captured Italian war material at Agordat

(between pages 62 and 63)

17. Captured Italian war material at Agordat
18. Punjabi soldiers in position on a hill top between Tessenei and Barentu
19. A Bren-gun carrier section of the Garhwalis about to move off on reconnaissance somewhere in Eritrea
20. A panorama of the mountains around Keren
21. Supplies for the troops by the mules in Keren Hills
22. Supplies for troops in Keren—unloading provisions and stores at the dumps
23. In the 'dug out' office of the G. O. C. of an Indian Division at the foot of the Keren Hills
24. A view of Keren

(*between pages 84 and 85*)

25. Signalmen operate the field telephone at Battalion Hq. on top of one of the Keren Hills
26. Men of the Central India Horse in action in the front line in the Keren Hills
27. Bren-gun carriers of 4/11 Sikh Regiment coming into action around Keren
28. Keren at last
29. These Punjabis in Eritrea with an anti-tank gun are ready for all comers
30. Men of 4/16 Punjab Regt. in action with their 3" mortars in Eritrean highlands
31. Indian troops constructing a road in Eritrea
32. Some of the Bren-gun carriers of a famous Indian Cavalry Regiment in the mountains of Ethiopia

(*between pages 102 and 103*)

33. A despatch riders section in the Amba Alagi area
34. A truck of a mechanised column of an Indian Cavalry Regiment about to start off on a patrol in the Amba Alagi area
35. A Bren-gunner and a rifleman in a stone sangar at an observation post, Ethiopia
36. A squadron section post and observation post beyond Amba Alagi
37. Road block partly cleared for the trucks to carry supplies to the forward troops in Ethiopia
38. Panorama of the country on the southern side of the Falaga Pass in Ethiopia
39. Members of the Jammu and Kashmir Mountain Battery at work camouflaging their guns
40. With bayonets fixed a platoon of the Sikhs attack an Italian position up a mountain in Ethiopia

(*between pages 142 and 143*)

41. A 25-pounder gun in action against Amba Alagi
42. On the level top of the hill men take their next advance at the double, during an atack on a mountain feature in Amba Alagi area
43. Italian motor transport in Fort Toselli captured by Allied troops

44. The prisoners of war in Enda Medani Alem make a huge dump of arms
45. Indian troops on guard over what was left of Fort Toselli
46. The Duke of Aosta, after his surrender, with British Generals and Staff Officers leaving the former Italian stronghold at Amba Alagi
47. Maj.-Gen. Mayne with some officers after the Amba Alagi victory
48. Italian prisoners of war march down from Toselli Fort to the bottom of Toselli Pass at Enda Medani Alem.

ABBREVIATIONS

R.H.A. (A.T.)	Royal Horsed Artillery (Animal transport)
R.A.	Royal Artillery
MMG Group	Motor Machine-Gun Group or Medium Machine Gun Group
SDF	Sudan Defence Force
SR	Sudan Regiment
pdrs.	pounders

INTRODUCTION

The East African theatre of war was not a primary theatre of operations, but the campaign there had immense significance in determining the fortunes of the Allies and extricating the British military power from a difficult situation. With the entry of Italy into the war in June 1940, when France had ceased to be a reckonable force in the Anglo-German hostilities, Africa had developed as a scene of armed conflict. The British Government was faced with a major threat to its communications through the Mediterranean Sea and the Suez Canal. The security of Egypt and exclusion of any foreign control over that state had been a cardinal point of British policy. The Treaty of 1936 had ensured permanent alliance between the two powers and its military clauses had provided for the maintenance of British troops in the Suez Canal zone and for the construction of roads and other means of communication for use by military forces. The Suez Canal was the major artery of imperial communications and with the dependence of the British Navy on the oil from Iran and Iraq, the defence of the eastern Mediterranean coast and the Red Sea passage was vital for the existence of the British Empire. The rising power of Italy in Africa, both in Libya in the north and Eritrea in the east, under the Fascist regime, had created a danger to British interests. The conquest of Ethiopia had further aggravated it, for now the Sudan was threatened on its east by the Italian empire. With this new accretion of power to Italy in eastern Africa, even Egyptian security was menaced, for it faced the prospect of a two-pronged threat from Libya in the west and Italian East African Empire in the south. Italy was even striving to find a direct contact between its northern and eastern possessions by joining Libya with Ethiopia. The growing naval and air strength of Italy posed a big threat to the British naval communications through the Mediterranean. The alternative rotue via the Cape of Good Hope to the eastern dominions was also threatened by Italian possessions in Somalia and Eritrea. Thus with the conclusion of the Ethiopian affair, and the entry of Italy into the Rome-Berlin Axis, the British Government had become aware of a major danger to its vital imperial interests and security.

The Middle East had been a zone of peculiar interest to the United Kingdom, where it had maintained throughout the 19th century a position of predominance. It was threatened by the competition of Germany and Russia, but with the end of the First World War, for a time both these rival powers had been eliminated from the contest, and the post-war settlement after 1919 had assured her a status of pre-eminence. The Turkish Empire had disintegrated and Iraq, Syria and Palestine were handed over to the United Kingdom or France to be held as Mandated territories. Turkey, shorn of its vast Asian provinces, was engaged on a programme of radical social and economic reconstruction and the Government there was pacific and friendly to the western powers. With Iran, the British Government had treaties and in its southern part British oil companies were busy extracting oil which became the chief source of supply to Great Britain. In Iraq while the mandate had been concluded, a treaty bound that kingdom to provide facilities for British air force to establish a base, and the oil of that state was used for the British navy. The pipeline ran to two ports on the eastern Mediterranean, which involved control over Palestine and the kingdom of Trans-Jordan. In Yemen, which provided hinterland to Aden, British influence was operative over the Imam. Thus the Middle East, a rich source of oil supplies, and controlling the main air route to India and Australia, was a zone of British influence, any interference with which by a hostile foreign power was bound to meet with stiff resistance. The Persian Gulf, the Red Sea, the Suez Canal and the eastern Mediterranean were the natural outlets for the region and therefore of vital importance to the British. Any danger to free communication through these sea passages would be a blow to the security of the British Empire.

Italy under Mussolini became interested in the Middle East, and after her victories in Ethiopia her credit in the region started to rise. Her propaganda was active and her agents were trying to exploit the fast growing Arab nationalism in her favour. As far east as Afghanistan, Italian interest was developing. The Mufti of Jerusalem was inclined to favour the Axis Powers whom he wished to employ as instruments for the realisation of Arab aspirations of independence from foreign control. In Iraq and Iran, Italian agents were striving to gain a foothold. These activities in the Middle East countries at a time when Italy had annexed Ethiopia to her dominion and was strengthening militarily her possessions in Eritrea and Somaliland, which flanked the Red Sea and the Indian Ocean, caused great concern in Britain. The Italian ports of Assab and Massawa were well sited to threaten British ships passing through the Red Sea. Similarly Kisamayu and Mogadishu in Italian Somaliland, on the Indian Ocean, could easily harass the ships bringing supplies from the east or by way of the Cape of Good Hope. From Eritrea or Ethiopia land-based aircraft posed another and greater danger to the shipping in that area. The prestige which Italy had acquired, the military and political power which it had gained and the strategic situation of its east African possessions, had no little effect on the attitude of the Arab nations of the Middle East which was definitely adverse to British hold over that region. Possibility of German control over the Balkans and subsequent thrust through Turkey or Syria into Iraq and Iran as well as Italian aggressiveness in the Red Sea area or against Egypt were appreciated as a threat not only to British interests in the Persian Gulf region but also as a danger ultimately to the defences of India. On that basis the Chatfield Committee had urged the necessity of India undertaking the responsibility of the joint defence of Egypt, Persian Gulf area, Iraq, Aden and East Africa. These regions were defined as zones of India's external defence, in the integrity of which lay inherent the security of India's western frontiers and extensive coastline. India did send forces to the Persian Gulf oilfields, Egypt and the Sudan before the war commenced in 1939.

After 1936 it was clear that Mussolini would join his forces with those of Hitler against the Western Powers. British strategic planning had taken note of this contingency and it was rightly presumed by the British General Staff that owing to her military weakness, Italy would provide early opportunity for dealing decisively with this Mediterranean power and utilising the country for launching air attacks on Southern Germany and Austria. For the defeat of Italy, Egypt and the northern African coast provided the only ground for assault. But this strategy was frustrated by Mussolini's keeping out of the ring in the initial stages of the war. The only policy then for the British Government was to keep Italy neutral as long as possible so that the Mediterranean might remain open for their shipping and the Royal Navy might continue to have its sway there. The British Chiefs of Staff wrote : "Italian neutrality would appreciably reduce our military commitments and military risks, in particular the Mediterranean would remain open as a line of communications.... the longer Italy remained neutral, even if her neutrality showed benevolence towards Germany, the better it would be for the Allies, and only if her neutrality were strained to an extreme point would it be to their interest to antagonise her." On this basis, the British did nothing to offend Italy even though it at times meant delaying defence preparations in Africa. But this attitude did not prevent Italy from adopting an increasingly hostile mien towards the Western allies, particularly anti-British propaganda had been whipped up further. Mussolini met Ribbentrop on 10 March 1940 and learnt about Germany's future military plans. This was followed by a Hitler-Mussolini meeting at the Brenner Pass, where the Duce was convinced of German military supremacy as also of her south-eastern designs. Both these convinced Mussolini that the time was ripe for him to enter the war on the side of his Axis friends and gather the fruits of victory. His Balkan ambitions and the hope of success in Africa whetted his appetite for war, and when France succumbed and the British had to evacuate their expeditionary force from Dunkirk and leave Norway to the Nazis, Italy declared war on the United Kingdom and France on 10 June 1940.

This declaration of belligerency by Italy when the United Kingdom was left almost isolated to face the determined Axis opposition created a difficult situation for the British. Hitler had launched his *blitzkrieg* on Great Britain and was at the same time making preparations for a thrust down the Balkans. The situation in western Asia was not free from anxiety. Syria had declared for Vichy France, and in Iraq and Iran Axis influence was active. The Soviet Union was still dubious about its attitude to war, and the United States was not yet prepared to convert its benevolent neutrality into a state of open belligerency. To the British the problem was one of existence, and for that the maintenance of their hold over Egypt and the security of the Persian Gulf and Red Sea routes were extremely vital. The supremacy on the sea and contact with India and the eastern Dominions were important for British stability and survival. Any blow to British position in the Mediterranean region and the Middle East would affect adversely the existence of Britain itself. Hence Italian threat had to be encountered and that was most likely to arise in Africa.

The British military strength in Egypt and its neighbourhood was not overwhelming; none the less it was adequate enough to resist the Italian attacks. Despite the increasing pressure on the home island, nothing was done to reduce the force in the Middle East Command, rather every spare unit, whether of land forces or air forces, was certainly despatched there as reinforcement. India, Australia and New Zealand came forward to meet the requirements of fighting forces in the Middle East. Even before the War, India had accepted the commitment to supply up to one well-equipped infantry division for service in that area. Later another division was raised and sent to Egypt. This was besides the troops maintained in the Persian Gulf region or Aden. General Wavell had in Egypt

36,000 troops, in the Sudan 9,000, in Kenya 8,500, in British Somaliland 1,475, in Palestine 27,500 and in Aden 2,500. Against this force, the Italians had a total of 415,000 divided between Libya and East Africa, and had enough of navy and air force in the Mediterranean and the Red Sea to interfere with British shipping in these waters.

Hitler had failed to grasp the shift in the centre of gravity in the war with the entry of Italy into it. He maintained pressure on England much longer before realising the futility of that step; for England's strength lay in her domination of the seas. The Middle East was like Achilles's heel for the British and their expulsion from Egypt would have repercussions on the whole course of their war effort. But while Italy maintained fitful pressure on Egypt in the first few months after joining the war, Germany afforded her no assistance. The result was that the Italian forces failed to make any deep impression on Egypt, and in the Ethiopian region beyond the occupation of Kassala and Gallabat on the frontiers of the Sudan or Somaliland, the southern Italian army did not proceed to expel the small British army from the Sudan. At the end of the year Wavell mounted an offensive invasion of Lybia and in spite of the numerically superior Grazziani's army, pushed the Italians back up to Benghazi within a period of two months. Two divisions on the British side had almost liquidated four corps of the Italian army and had taken 130,000 prisoners and a rich booty in armour and equipment. Wavell could not push farther because he had at the time to send troops to Greece to contain the German invasion and had also decided to undertake a campaign in East Africa, where a strong Italian army was stationed to strike in his rear. It was in this situation that the campaign in East Africa commenced.

The story of this brief campaign has been narrated in the present volume. It is a tale of audacity and efficient organisation on the part of the British Command, and lack of spirit and poor morale on the side of the Italians. The plan eventually culminated in a pincer from Nairobi in Kenya in the south and Khartoum in the north, the two bases being nearly 1200 air miles apart. The northern force included two Indian divisions, the 4th and the 5th, while the southern had one South African and two African divisions. The southern force moved into Italian Somaliland and then pierced through Ethiopia, and met the northern force at Amba Alagi. The main task for the Indian divisions was to open the route to Massawa and drive the Italians out of Eritrea. The Indian force had its toughest task at Keren and when that important well-fortified position was captured, the move to Asmara and beyond, leading to the final collapse and capitulation of the Duke of Aosta was an easy affair. The campaign added fresh laurels to the achievements of these two Indian divisions but more than that it freed the Red Sea and the Indian Ocean from any further threat and opened this route for the mounting rush of supplies to Egypt and the Soviet Union, which made for the security of the Middle East, defence of India and the eventual collapse of Italy and Germany.

BISHESHWAR PRASAD

CHAPTER I

The Background

The end of the first world war brought disappointment to Italy. She had hoped to gain much from her participation in it but the peace settlement left her bitter and sore, with a feeling that the sacrifices had been made in vain. Nonetheless, it was not Italy but Japan who first threatened international peace by committing aggression against Manchuria in 1931. In January 1933 Adolf Hitler came to power in Germany, taking office as Chancellor. His advent marked a new epoch in the history of Europe and brought the spectre of a second war nearer. In October 1935 Italy attacked Ethiopia thus putting the League of Nations to a crucial test. It was a clear violation of the Covenant of the League of Nations and constituted a challenge to it. Other nations with the possible exception of the United Kingdom were slow in waking up to the danger, and when the League of Nations decided on a policy of limited economic sanctions against Italy it was enforced half-heartedly, and was consequently ineffective in compelling her to abide by the League's decision. "A large number of commodities, some of which were war materials, were prohibited from entering Italy, and an imposing schedule was drawn up but oil, without which the campaign in Abyssinia could not have been maintained, continued to enter freely, because it was understood that to stop it meant war".[1] "Not a ship, not a machine, not a man had been moved by any other member state," said Sir Samuel Hoare in the House of Commons on 19 December 1935.[2] Italy got away with her defiance of the League of Nations and conveniently annexed Ethiopia. A little earlier in March 1936 German troops had marched into the Rhineland, thus showing that Germany too poured scorn on the European settlement as effected by the Treaty of Versailles. The League could do nothing. The Ethiopian Emperor, Haille Selassie, fled from his country. The crisis revealed clearly that the League of Nations, by itself, lacked power to enforce respect for its decisions, its authority might be flouted with impunity and that aggression might be rewarding. As events showed the experiment of Mussolini was not lost on Hitler.

---

[1] Churchill, W.S., *The Second World War*, Vol. 1 *The Gathering Storm*, p. 175.
[2] Playfair, I. S. O., *The Mediterranean and Middle East*, Vol. 1, p. 2 (footnote)

The annexation of Ethiopia showed the weakness of the League of Nations. It also drew British attention to their interests in the Mediterranean region and the Middle East, the defence of which was closely linked to the security of the line of supply to India, Australia and the Far East. The developments in North Africa and the Mediterranean concerned Britain vitally. Apart from the possibility of Italy endangering her interests there, she was disturbed by the growing menace of Nazi Germany. Even greater was the danger from a combination of hostile Germany and Italy. Though danger was anticipated, the British Government continued to look on the bright side of the picture and hope for the best. But the signs were too clear on the wall to be mistaken. In the situation that was developing the Chiefs of Staff of the three services warned the British Government of the danger of a simultaneous hostility of Germany, Japan and Italy. The last occupied an important position in the Mediterranean and was well placed to cut off British communications with the east. It was considered therefore important to be on friendly terms with her, at any rate outwardly, and to take such military precautions unobtrusively by sea, land and air as were feasible, without raising an alarm. In the meantime, the British Government also set about improving its diplomatic relations with the other powers. A treaty was signed with Egypt which was ratified on 26 May 1937. It provided for the termination of the military occupation of Egypt and for the stationing of British forces in the canal zone for the security of the Suez Canal. The British Government was to help in training and equipping the Egyptian army and air force. The treaty made Egypt responsible for her own defence.

Meanwhile, the Spanish Civil War broke out in 1936. The efforts of the British and French Governments were directed to prevent it from spreading beyond the Spanish frontiers. Both, therefore, advocated a policy of non-intervention. Germany and Italy however failed to abide by their undertakings not to intervene in the Spanish affairs and sent men and material to Spain and gave General Franco their active support. Before long Italy also started developing the Balearic Islands. In November both Germany and Italy had accorded recognition to General Franco's government. They were now showing a common outlook. For some time Italy had been suspicious of German designs on Austria and that had stood in the way of co-operation between these two powers. But now Italy was diverting her attention from the Danube and thinking in terms of expanding in the Mediterranean zone. Events in Ethiopia and Central Europe had clearly shown that the two powers might gain mutually by sticking to one another. It was not surprising therefore that their unity of interest was formally expressed by the formation of the Rome-Berlin Axis.[3]

On the other hand, elements of irritation and friction between the United Kingdom and Italy were not wanting. The Anglo-Egyptian Treaty was not well received by the latter, who could not but resent, observed the *Giornale d' Italia*, the strengthening of British influence in a region where Italy had her own interests to safeguard. Britain yet hoped for the restoration of friendly relations with Italy in the interest of peace in the Mediterranean, the importance of which was again stressed by the Chiefs of Staff. There was a gleam of hope for amiability when the Anglo-Italian Joint Declaration (popularly known as the Gentlemen's Agreement) was signed on 2 January 1937. It had the effect of reducing tension momentarily between the two countries. By this agreement the two powers recognised freedom of movement in the Mediterranean Sea as vital to the interests of both of them. Both of them disclaimed any desire to modify or see modified the national sovereignty of any country in the Mediterranean area. But the Gentlemen's Agreement failed to achieve any lasting improvement in the relations of the two powers. On the contrary, tension tended to increase. Mussolini felt that his ambitions would succeed only at the expense of British interests in the Mediterranean, Red Sea and the Indian Ocean. He started hostile propaganda against her. The Italian press fed public opinion with unfavourable references to the British. Broadcasts were made in Arabic to undermine British influence in the Middle East countries. This propaganda became more offensive in tone and content with the passage of time. In a broadcast to the Arabs of Libya, Mussolini was even extolled as the protector of Islam. The harbours of Massawa and Assab in the Red Sea were developed and the African army in Ethiopia increased. The British Government viewed these developments with concern and in July 1937 the British Cabinet felt that Italy could no longer be regarded as a reliable friend. Precautionary measures were adopted to improve the defences of the Mediterranean and the Red Sea ports. Nonetheless, it was Germany which constituted the main danger, and it was desirable that no action should be taken which might alienate Italy and provoke her hostility.[4]

---

[3] Hitler in his *Mein Kampf* had expressed the idea that Italy could become an ally of Germany.

[4] Playfair, *op. cit.* pp.7-8.

Meanwhile events elsewhere added to the tension. In November 1937 Italy joined Germany and Japan in their Anti-Comintern Pact. Then came Italian withdrawal from the League of Nations. The British Chiefs of Staff found the situation "fraught with greater risk than at any time in living memory, apart from the war years." The German menace was also casting its ugly shadows. Hitler had set his eyes on Austria. On the first page of *Mein Kampf* he had written, "German-Austria must be restored to the great German Motherland...people of the same blood should be in the same Reich."[5] He was resolved to achieve it. The Austrian republic succumbed to German intimidation and in March 1938 German forces marched into Austria and Hitler entered Vienna in triumph. He had made a bloodless conquest. Things were now heading for a climax. It appeared almost certain that before long Hitler would strike his next blow at Czechoslovakia. Munich Settlement which sealed the fate of Czechoslovakia was signed on 30 September. According to it the Sudetenland was to be evacuated in five stages starting from 1 October. Thus the British Prime Minister, Mr. Neville Chamberlain who had thrice flown to Germany and believed that he had brought "peace with honour" had allowed himself to be outwitted by Hitler.

Early in February 1939, the British Cabinet decided to approach the French Government with the suggestion that staff conversations might take place on the basis of defence against Germany and Italy who might possibly be joined later by Japan. They were to cover all possible fields of operations, especially the Mediterranean and the Middle East. These conversations were held at the end of March 1939. The Allied strategy was conceived in terms of a long war. It was appreciated that Germany would start her offensive on land in Europe; Italy would strike principally by land from Libya and Ethiopia and would menace British supply route through the Mediterranean Sea.[6] In April 1939 Italy invaded Albania. It was followed by the conclusion of a political and military agreement between Italy and Germany. The situation soon deteriorated steadily. In March 1939 Hitler invaded Czechoslovakia. He denounced the naval agreement with Britain and the non-aggression treaty of 1934 with Poland. On 23 August the Non-Aggression Pact was signed between Russia and Germany. It was a prelude to the invasion of Poland on 1 September and the entry into the war of France and Great Britain. On 3 September

---

[5] *Mein Kampf,* Translated by James Murphy (London, 1939)
[6] Playfair, *op. cit.* p. 23.

1939, they declared war on Germany on the strength of their alliance with Poland. Australia and New Zealand declared war on Germany the same day. The Second World War had thus begun.

On the outbreak of war with Germany the Middle East Command assumed operational control over the troops in Egypt, Palestine and the Sudan.[7] The British forces at the time in those countries were:—

In Egypt,
- (i) The 7th Armoured Division—
  Two armoured brigades (each of two regiments only)
  One armoured car regiment
  One motor battalion.
- (ii) The 4th Indian Division—
  One regiment of artillery
  One infantry brigade.
- (iii) Royal Artillery Group—
  7 Medium Regiment
  3 Regiment R. H. A. (A. T.)
  4 Regiment R. H. A.
  31 Field Regiment R. A.
- (iv) Eight British infantry battalions.

In Palestine,
- (i) The 8th Division—
  Two brigades-each of three British battalions.
- (ii) Two British cavalry regiments.
- (iii) Four additional British battalions (less one company of one battalion in Cyprus)

In the Sudan,
- (i) Three British battalions
- (ii) Sudan Defence Force consisting of twenty companies in all, the greater part of which was employed on internal security.

In British Somaliland,
> The headquarters and three companies of Camel Corps.

The above forces in the Middle East and East Africa were not complete formations. There were in all twenty-one battalions

---

[7] British Somaliland came under operational control on 13 January 1940.

of infantry, but only 64 field guns and there were only 48 anti-tank and 8 anti-aircraft guns[8].

When the war with Germany had commenced the possibility of Italy's joining in was kept in view by the Allied Governments and precautionary measures were taken against a possible surprise attack by the latter. The plans for the defence of the western frontier were brought into execution and the security of the Suez Canal was a matter of primary consideration in view of the danger of sabotage by Italian ships going up and down the canal. With Poland eliminated and secure on her eastern frontier by the Soviet-German Non-Aggression Pact, Germany was free to strike either west or south through the Balkans towards Egypt. The chances of Italy participating in this venture had thus increased.

General Sir Archibald Wavell[9], who was responsible for the conduct of operations in all African theatres, in the ensuing months established relations with the French commanders in Syria, in North Africa and in French Somaliland with the object of co-ordinating Allied plans and efforts. Later he made contacts with the military authorities in Turkey also when she had signed the Treaty of Alliance on 29 October 1939. In the winter of 1939-1940 there took place tripartite discussions between the French in Syria, the British and the Turks on the means of carrying out the military clauses of that treaty.

But Mussolini hesitated to strike, and meanwhile by March 1940, the British position had also somewhat improved by the arrival of reinforcements. A second Indian infantry brigade (the 5th) had arrived from India in October. An unattached battalion had arrived from China by the end of February. The 1st Cavalry Division had arrived in Palestine from England in the third week of March. The 16th Australian Infantry Brigade and a portion of the 6th Australian Division arrived in February. Also the 4th New Zealand Infantry Brigade and some of the Divisional troops of the 1st New Zealand Division arrived soon after. Although these reinforcements totalled 20,000 men in all they did not add greatly to the

---

[8] Wavell's Despatch on Operations in the Middle East from August 1939 to November 1940.

[9] He was appointed General Officer Commanding-in-Chief in June 1939, when the war clouds were gathering and a crisis appeared to be not very far off. From 15 February 1940 his title was changed to "Commander-in-Chief Middle East". This gave him wider powers of decision without having to refer to the home authorities and also placed him in a better position to collaborate with the French authorities.

fighting strength of the Allies. Only the Indian Infantry Brigade was complete, though with obsolescent equipment, and fit for fighting. Other formations were not fully trained and lacked equipment especially of the latest type.

Meanwhile events were taking shape which indicated that Italy would show her hand soon. Hitler and Mussolini had met on the Brenner Pass on 18 March 1940 and, from the information that leaked out, it appeared that Mussolini had made up his mind now to hurl Italy into the fight. By early May the situation was serious enough and orders were issued for the forward troops to reoccupy positions which they had held in the previous August. It was definite now that Italy had for some time been preparing for war. Her navy was in a state of preparations as also the air force. The army had been in the process of mobilisation since 10 May. Her army in Libya, Albania and the Dodecanese had received reinforcements. The balance of evidence indicated that, in spite of deficiency of material in the fighting services and strained finances, Italy might throw her weight on the side of Germany.

On 10 May German armies invaded Holland, Belgium and Luxembourg. A few days later German forces crossed the line of the Meuse. With the military collapse of France the tempo of war had greatly increased. At the end of three weeks France contemplated capitulation. These events which followed in rapid succession had a great psychological effect on the people in the Balkans, Turkey and the Middle East. Every German success confirmed Nazi military strength and created doubts about the ability of the Allies to win the war. With Germany triumphant in Europe it was certain that Italy would join the winning side and she had not long to wait. It appeared to Mussolini that Germany had already won the war and that he had everything to gain and little to risk by aligning Italy with Germany. Hence on 10 June the General Headquarters Middle East was warned that France was on the point of collapse and that Italy was certain to come into the war on the opposite side. It proved true and at 1645 hours the same day the British ambassador in Rome was informed that at one minute past midnight Italy would be at war with the United Kingdom. Her decision to enter the lists did not come as a surprise as for sometime it had been anticipated.[10]

We may now review the situation in East Africa where the British forces were opposed by an Italian army of which the Duke of Aosta,

---

[10] Playfair, *op. cit.* p. 109.

as Viceroy and Commander-in-Chief of Italian East Africa, was the head, and General Frusci in actual command. In that zone British troops were organised in three subordinate commands; the Sudan, Kenya and British Somaliland and the forces were scattered and not numerous. In the Sudan, with a long and vulnerable frontier of 1,200 miles, were three British battalions and Sudan Defence Force which, together with the police and irregular formations, totalled about 9,000 men. In Kenya, which had a frontier of 850 miles, were two East African brigades and two light battalions or some 8,500 men. British Somaliland had one battalion of the King's African Rifles and five companies of the Somaliland Camel Corps, in all about 1,475 men.[11] The British garrison there was inadequate for the defence of British Somaliland and reinforcements were not in sight. Hence the co-operation of the French was considered essential for the defence of this territory. Aden was garrisoned by two Indian battalions.

The exact strength of the Italian forces in Italian East Africa at the time was not known with certainty. There were assumed to be, on the Sudan frontier, eleven brigades of African troops and twelve *Blackshirt* battalions with 200 guns; in Southern Ethiopia about 7,000 African and 1,000 white troops; in Italian Somaliland 7,000 African troops and 4,000 levies. A metropolitan division was at Addis Ababa and six African brigades at Dire Dawa and Harar. The total was estimated at 30,000 white and 100,000 African troops with 400 guns, 200 light tanks and 20,000 lorries. Thus the Italians were far superior to British in numbers.[12]

As far as air force was concerned the Italians in East Africa, exclusive of reserves, were believed to have 36 modern bombers and 114 of Colonial types; 45 modern fighters, and 18 others; a total of 213 aircraft. They suffered from one disadvantage, however, that as long as the Allied blockade by land and sea was complete Italian stocks of fuel, ammunition and other items, could not be increased. On the British side, in the Sudan, there were three bomber squadrons (Wellesley) and one fighter flight (Gladiator). "Excluding the aircraft of the Rhodesian squadron and the Kenya Auxiliary flights, there were, by the outbreak of war, some 85 Wellesleys and Blenheims, 9 Vincents, 24 Hartbeests, 15 Junkers 86, and 30 Gladiators and Furies in Aden, Kenya and the Sudan."[13]

---

[11] Ibid. p. 94.
[12] Ibid. p. 93.
[13] Ibid. p. 96.

The entry of Italy into the war was likely to have far-reaching effects on British imperial interests, in general, and on the military situation in the Middle East, in particular. The British depended for easy communication with their outstretched possessions and the Dominions of the Commonwealth on the sea route of the Mediterranean. The shift of Italy into the Axis camp and her declaration of war against the United Kingdom inevitably affected the utilisation of this route and thereby prejudiced the transportation of men, equipment and war supplies to the eastern theatres of war and India. The Italian navy, by no means negligible, having turned hostile, the whole balance of naval power in Mediterranean waters was upset. For, by operating from its home bases, the Italian Fleet could, at least for sometime, close the Mediterranean to the Allied shipping. Even with the help of the French Fleet it was not possible to keep the ordinary sea routes through the Mediterranean open. With the collapse of France the situation grew even more critical. The closing of the Mediterranean sea route, it was feared, would greatly delay the arrival of reinforcements from the United Kingdom. A voyage which had averaged two weeks was expected to take six times that number by the route of Cape of Good Hope. This also required a large amount of additional shipping, and ships were in short supply—which meant that the arrival of reinforcements to the Middle East would be further delayed.

The defence of the Suez Canal was another factor to be considered. The problem of its defence against mine-dropping by aircraft was very difficult. Another problem was the effect of the French surrender on the personnel of the canal since the technical staff in charge of it had been largely French from the early days of its construction. Their withdrawal from the operation of the canal was likely to create a critical situation.

Lastly, there was the Red Sea route the safety of which was more important than before for the success of operations in East Africa and the Middle East. With the closing of the Mediterranean as a supply route British forces in East Africa and the Middle East could receive reinforcements both from the United Kingdom and India only through this route. General Wavell considered the Red Sea his real life-line and he had been anxious for the defence of Port Sudan and Jibouti from the beginning. The principal danger in the Red Sea came from eight Italian submarines and seven fleet destroyers which were based on Massawa, in addition to other vessels for local defence. If properly used they could menace the Allied shipping in that area. There was, however, a counterbalancing factor as Massawa was cut off and could not receive supplies and reinforcements from Italy and her threat was expected to grow progressively weaker.

To meet the new danger, the Allied strategy at the outset was generally defensive. Egypt, Palestine and Syria were to be defended. The Suez Canal and the sea communications to French Africa were to be kept intact and the Red Sea route was to be maintained as a safe supply line. In the Sudan the plan approved by General Wavell was that the key towns of Khartoum, Atbara and Port Sudan were to be defended firmly by the three British battalions there. The Sudan Defence Force companies were to harass an Italian advance, inflict casualties and exploit the natural difficulties to the full. It was realized that it would not be possible to hold Kassala or Gallabat and these would probably have to be given up. In any case a fighting withdrawal was envisaged which was to be made as expensive for the Italians and as cheap for the Allies as was possible.

This then was the general background against which the campaign in Italian East Africa was conducted.[14] The situation for the Allies was far from pleasant, the Italians being vastly superior in numbers. But this was offset to some extent by other factors which favoured the Allies. It was apparent that with the declaration of war the Italian army in East Africa would be cut off from its supplies and would not be able to hold on indefinitely. The second factor was the internal situation of Ethiopia. Here the activity of the Patriots could not but undermine Italian position, who were to be hard put to keep internal order by suppressing the Patriots and at the same time to defend Ethiopia from external attack. The

---

[14] For the campaign in British Somaliland and Indian participation therein please refer to Playfair, *The Mediterranean and Middle East*, Vol. 1, pp. 171-9, 417-8.

At the time of Italian invasion British Somaliland had the following forces: 1st Battalion Northern Rhodes Regiment, 2nd Battalion King's African Rifles, 1st East African Light Battery from Kenya, 1/2 Punjab Regiment from Aden, 3/15 Punjab Regiment diverted from Aden and the Somaliland Camel Corps.

The Italians invaded Somaliland from Ethiopia early in August 1940 and the small British force was compelled by overwhelming numbers to withdraw after a brief stand at the Tug Argan pass. On evacuation units were taken into Aden. From there the two Indian battalions returned to land at Berbera in March 1941. With the aid of Royal Navy, Indian Navy and Royal Air Force the reoccupation of Berbera and its hinterland was accomplished against slight opposition. Thereafter, Berbera became the base for the South African forces which were now advancing into south-eastern Ethiopia.

British were naturally expected to exploit the situation and ensure that Patriot revolt was festered and supported by all means at their disposal.[15] An Ethiopian rising while Italian forces fought in Ethiopia was to become General Frusci's worst fear.

---

[15] Even before the war had begun the British and French staff delegations in laying down 'the broad strategic policy for the conduct of the war' had agreed on the need of taking "adequate measures to raise the tribes in Ethiopia..........
Butler, J. R. M., *Grand Strategy*, Vol. II, p. 10.

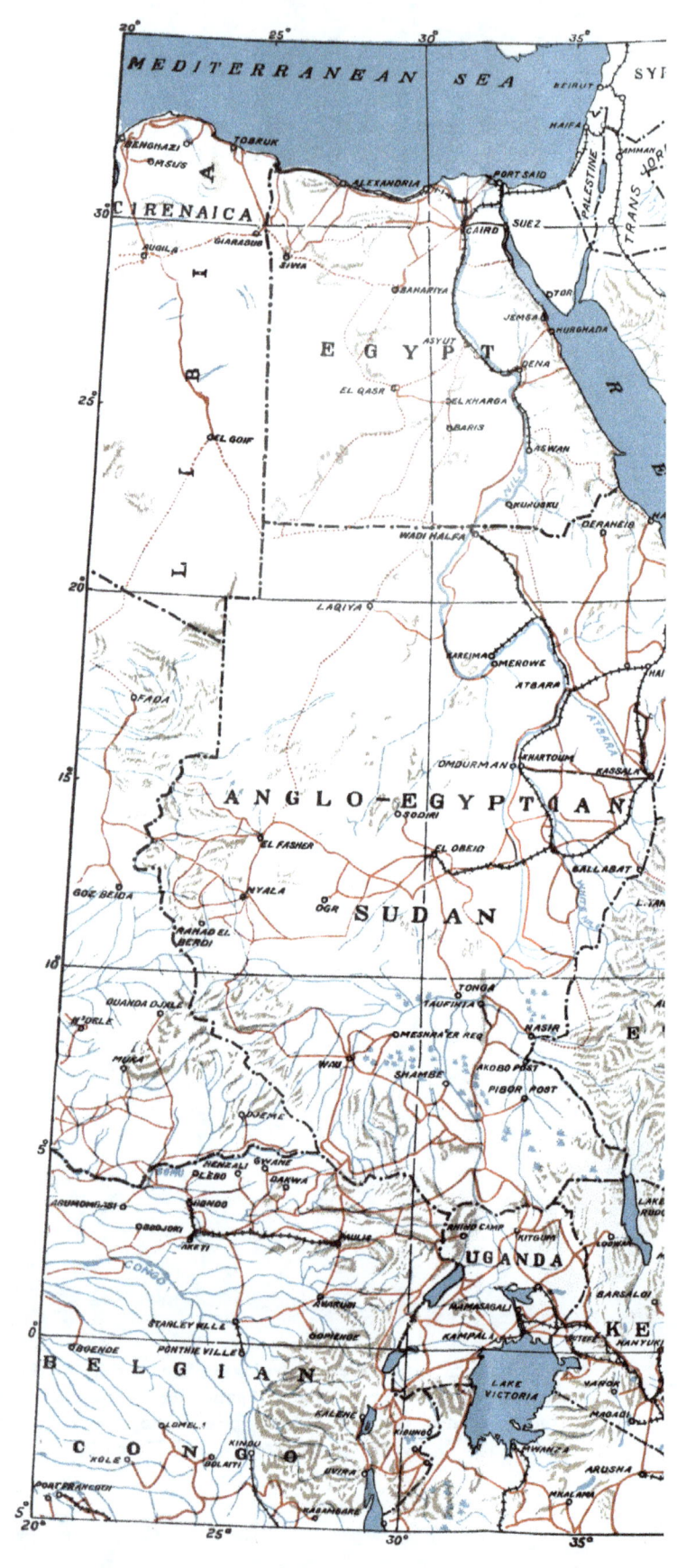

CHAPTER II

Topography

The area of operations in East Africa in which the Indian armed forces took an active part comprised the political divisions of the Eastern Sudan (east of the rivers Nile and Blue Nile), Eritrea, and Northern Ethiopia. The geographical and topographical aspects of these regions are given below separately.

EASTERN SUDAN

Anglo-Egyptian Sudan was a British protectorate which flanked the Italian possessions of Eritrea and Ethiopia. Geographically Eastern Sudan may be divided into three areas, the coast region, the northern region lying between the coastal region and the Nile and Atbara rivers as far south as Gallabat, where the Atbara crosses the frontier into Ethiopia, and the south-eastern region lying between the Atbara, the Blue Nile and the Ethiopian frontier.

The Coast Region

The coast region is a belt of sandy plain, frequently covered with low scrub, stretching inland from ten to twenty miles and traversed by Khors (water courses), generally dry, with ill-defined, shifting channels. Beyond this plain rise the mountain ranges with their slopes often bearing a considerable amount of vegetation. The climate of this area is generally hot and humid. There is occasional rainfall between August and January. The hottest month is July, when the maximum temperature at Port Sudan rises to 106° F, and the coldest month is February with a minimum temperature of 66° F.

Wind conditions in the Baraka Delta need special mention as they were likely to hamper operations in the area. With the exception of September, winds varying in speed from 40 miles per hour to 80 miles per hour normally blow during the day. The worst period is from mid-June to August when a wind, called "Baboob" blows from the south-west at 80 miles or more per hour. It blows continuously day and night making visibility almost impossible.

The Northern Region

In the north-east, bordering on the coast region, the Ethiopian plateau stretches northwards through Eritrea, with a steep eastern face and a gradual fall, in a series of terraces, to the west. In the north-west, this plateau yields place to small hilly ranges which are separated by wide valleys. The hills are between two and three thousand feet high. The valleys very often contain stretches of cotton soil in the wider parts, but they are rocky in the proximity of the hills. East of these hills is the plain watered by the inland river Gash. Farther south, a dry plain continues as far as the point where the Atbara crosses the frontier into Ethiopia. It is formed of cracked cotton soil, which is overgrown with high elephant grass. It is generally wooded with a few open spaces here and there.

The climate on the plateau is temperate and pleasant but the plains are hot and dry. The rainfall on the plains is generally very meagre, the southern parts getting comparatively more than the north. Kassala, in the Gash Delta, in the south, has an average annual rainfall of 13 inches. It is spread over the period from June to October. Water is to be found in the beds of Khors and in wells. The area of the Gash Delta tends to be highly malarious from July to October.

The South-Eastern Region

In the extreme north of this region there is a sand-stone plateau which is generally bare and level. Further south and to the west, the land is little more suitable for cultivation, though, here too, cultivation is practised in the valleys only. The remainder of this region is a huge plain, open and flat. During the rains it is used as a vast grazing ground. The rains last from June to October and there is a considerable difference in the average annual rainfall between the north and the south. This is illustrated by the following table :—

Place	Latitude	Average rainfall
Atbara	17° 40′	2.9 inches
Khartoum	15° 36′	6.5 inches
Wad Medani	14° 24′	15.9 inches
Gedaref	14° 02′	27.0 inches
Gallabat	12° 58′	35.2 inches
Roseires	11° 51′	30.2 inches

Except during the rains, the climate is dry. The summer temperature is high and even in winter the days are relatively hot. The maximum and minimum temperatures of Khartoum are tabulated below (F) :—

	Jan.	Feb.	Mar.	Apr.	May	June
Maximum	86°	89°	96°	103°	107°	107°
Minimum	59°	61°	65°	72°	77°	79°

	July	Aug.	Sep.	Oct.	Nov.	Dec.
Maximum	102°	99°	102°	103°	94°	88°
Minimum	77°	76°	77°	75°	68°	61°

Except towards the end of the rains the climate is generally healthy. The banks of the river Atbara are generally highly malarious during the period following the rains.

In the south and east very tall grass grows which makes visibility difficult.

COMMUNICATIONS

Ports

Port Sudan opens out on the Red Sea which provides it access to the world outside. But the coast line is neither extensive nor suited to the development of many ports. There were only two ports worth mentioning when the war started, Port Sudan and Suakin. The first was opened in 1908 and had a good average depth of ten to fourteen fathoms. It had five quays for berthing vessels and all the modern port machinery. The second, Suakin, was the old port of the Sudan. Its channel of entrance was gradually closing in owing to the growth of coral, and therefore it was not of much use.

Waterways

In the interior an important means of communication is the river Nile. Out of its total length of 3,526 miles, 2,130 miles lie in the Sudan. The nine hundred and sixty miles of the river in Egypt, from Damietta to Wadi Halfa is navigable. Of this the portion between Aswan and Shallal, is navigable through the Aswan Dam lock. The portion from Wadi Halfa to Khartoum in the Sudan, however, though navigable at high water, offers difficulties and is not free from risk. From Khartoum to Rejaf for over one thousand miles the river is navigable. The next hundred miles from Rejaf to Nimule do not admit of navigation.

Within the Sudan the Nile system of rivers consists of two elements. Firstly the flood rivers descending from the Ethiopian plateau, *viz.*, the Blue Nile, the Atbara and the Sobat, which bring down a great volume of water during the rains, but little during the dry season. The Blue Nile is navigable from Khartoum to Sennar, a distance of two hundred and twenty-three miles, from June to December. At Sennar, the Dam had no lock, therefore through service was not possible. South of Sennar the river is navigable for about six months, as far as Reseires, a distance of about one hundred and seventy miles. Above Roseires the river was not navigable. The two tributaries of the Blue Nile, the Rahad and the Dinder, had been navigated in the past, but there was no regular traffic on them. The river Atbara, which flows into the Nile at Atbara, about two hundred miles to the north of Khartoum, is not navigable except for small barges from mid-June to October as far as Sarsareib. The river Sobat, a tributary of the White Nile, is normally navigable from the beginning of April to the end of January.

The other element in the Nile system of rivers consists of the swamp rivers of the south and the south-west, namely, the Bahr-el-Jebel (the name generally given to the continuation of the White Nile south of Lake No), the Bahr-el-Ghazal and their tributaries, which contribute a comparatively small but constant volume of water throughout the year. The Bahr-el-Jebel is navigable as far as Rejaf throughout the year. The Bahr-el-Ghazal is navigable throughout the year, for about one hundred and fifty miles above Lake No where it joins the Bahr-el-Jebel. The Sobat, which joins the White Nile south of Malakal is navigable from April to January.

Railways

The railway system in the Sudan was a single line 3 ft. 6 in. gauge having one or more loop lines or sidings at every station. The main line began at Wadi Halfa, crossed the Nubian desert to Abu Hamed and then followed the right bank of the Nile to Khartoum via Atbara. South of Khartoum it followed the west bank of the Blue Nile to Sennar and then turned sharply to the west across the Gezira[1] to Kosti, where it crossed the White Nile. From Kosti it took a more or less westerly direction to El Obeid. From Wadi Halfa to Khartoum is a distance of five hundred and seventy-four miles, and from Khartoum to El Obeid four hundred and twenty-eight miles.[2]

From this main line forked the following branches :—

(i) From No. 10 station, sixteen miles north of Abu Hamed, a line ran south-west along the north bank of the Nile to Kareima. This line was about 138 miles long.

---

[1] Gezira consisted of the area between the Blue Nile and the White Nile.
[2] *Handbook of Topographical Intelligence., The Anglo-Egyptian Sudan*, p. 143.

(ii) From Atbara a line ran north-east to Port Sudan, first across the desert and then over the Red Sea hills. This was the most important section of the line in the Sudan, as almost the entire export and import trade of the country passed along it. It was two hundred and ninety-five miles long. The average time taken by passenger trains over this line was twenty-three and a half hours from Khartoum to Port Sudan and twenty-five hours in the opposite direction.

(iii) From Haiya Junction, on the Atbara-Port Sudan line, a line ran south to Kassala and thence south-west to Gedaref and west to Sennar, where it was connected with the main line. This line was four hundred and ninety-eight miles long. From Haiya Junction to Kassala the journey took eleven hours and the return journey about an hour longer. From Kassala to Sennar or back was a run of twenty hours.

(iv) From Sallom Junction, on the Atbara-Port Sudan line, a short length of line ran south to Suakin, which was the chief port of the Sudan before Port Sudan was built. The distance was twenty-eight miles and trains took about one hour and a quarter to cover it.

Not connected with the main railway system was the Tokar-Trinkitat light railway. It was nearly 18 miles long and the guage was two feet only. It was constructed in 1921.

All stations were inter-connected by telephone and certain stations were also connected by the railway telegraph system. This was in addition to the ordinary telegraph lines which were controlled by the Director of Posts and Telegraphs[8].

Roads

There was only one metalled road in the Sudan, the Khartoum-Sennar road. It ran along the west bank of the Blue Nile. All other roads had mud surfaces and had to be rebuilt after the rains every year. In dry weather, the going across the country was good, the only obstacle being the tall elephant grass.

ERITREA

Eritrea was the next region where Indian forces were engaged in fighting the Italians. This country is triangular in shape with

[8] *ibid.* p. 144.

a long projection in the south-east corner. The apex, at Ras Kasar, is a cape on the Red Sea coast, one hundred and ten miles to the south-east of Suakin. One side of the triangle is formed by the Red Sea coast and the other by the frontier with the Sudan which runs south-west from Ras Kasar to Om Ager. The third side of the triangle is formed by the frontier with Ethiopia and runs east from Om Ager. The projection in the south-east corner consisted of a stretch of the coastal plain, one hundred and fifty miles long and forty miles wide, which ran to the south-east as far as the boundary with French Somaliland.

The main region covered by this triangle is a plateau forming part of the Ethiopian table-land. It rises abruptly from the foot-hills bordering on the coastal plains in the east where its highest parts lie and where the general elevation is about six thousand feet and the highest hills above ten thousand feet. To the west and north-west, the plateau drops gradually, in a series of terraces until in the west, on the frontier with the Sudan, the general elevation goes down to about one thousand five hundred feet. The east coast consists of sandy country covered with bushes. It is frequently intercepted by water courses near which vegetation is somewhat richer.

CLIMATE

The country may be divided into three distinct climatic zones.

The Coastal Region (Upto 1,650 feet)

This region is very hot and humid during most of the year. June, September and October are the hottest months. Massawa in this region has an average temperature of 88°, but the maximum in summer is 120° in the shade. Most of the rainfall is during the summer monsoon season. There are occasional showers in winter also.

The Zone of Escarpments and Valleys

This zone has a temperate climate with a considerable variation of temperature between day and night. It gets summer monsoon rains only, except areas bordering on the coastal region, where there is some winter rain also. May is the hottest month.

The High Plateau

It is moderately cool. Heavy monsoon rains occur from June to September with slight showers during April and May. The dry season from November to April is the hottest. Climate above 8,500 feet is distinctly cold, sub-alpine.

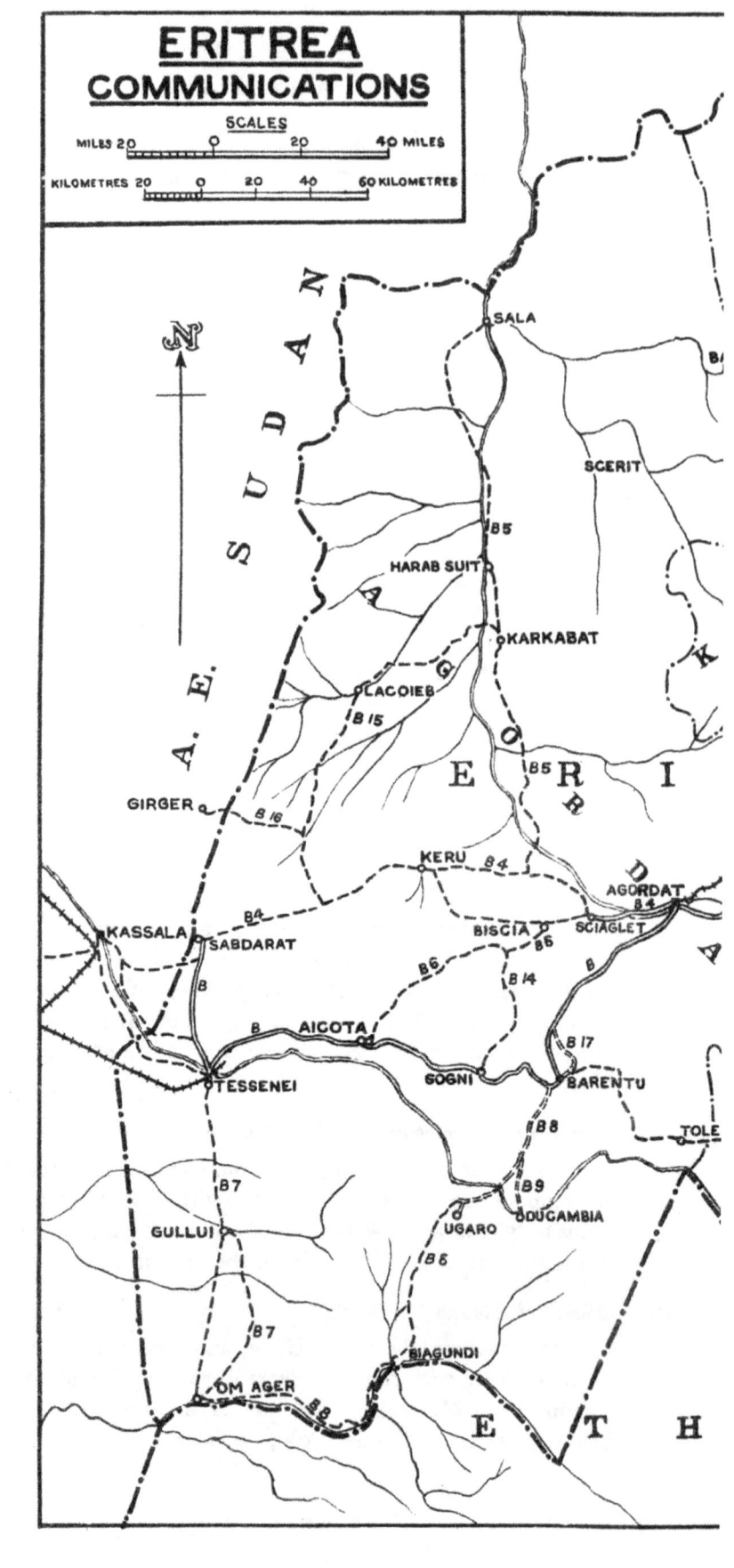

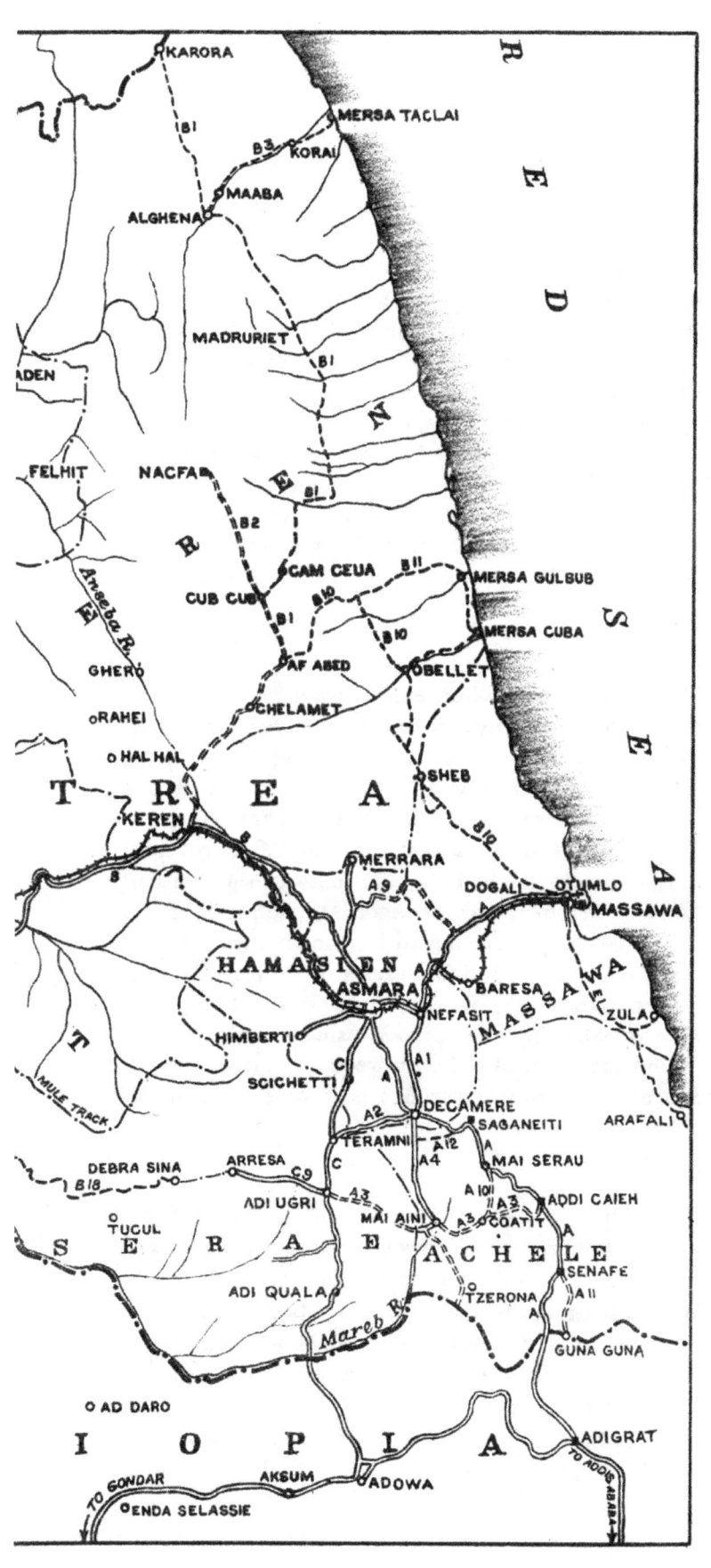

COMMUNICATIONS

Eritrea was accessible from the Red Sea which provided its most important means of communication with the outside world. However, Massawa was its only port of importance. It was laid out on two peninsulas and three islands which complicated the system of communications within the town. Ships of 10,000 tons could enter the various basins, where port facilities included large petrol storage tanks. The town and the port areas each had a telephone exchange accommodating a hundred subscribers. There was an emergency wireless set also. Water for Massawa was pumped from wells at Dogali, twelve miles away for there was no good local supply. Food and fuel also had to be imported. The town was not capable of withstanding a long siege without large stocks of water and provisions. The population of Massawa comprised 3,000 Italians and 12,000 local inhabitants.

Railways

On land, Eritrea had no navigable waterways and there was a single railway line from Massawa to Agordat via Asmara. This railway was a single track line of the unusual gauge of 95 centimetres or about 3 ft. 1$\frac{3}{8}$ in. and thus 4$\frac{5}{8}$ inches narrower than the Sudan Railway. The distance from Massawa to Asmara was seventy-three and a half miles, and the railway climbed 7,900 feet from the sea level at Massawa to the highest point only one and a half miles short of Asmara. From Asmara to Agordat, one hundred and nineteen miles, the line dropped again to just under two thousand feet. There were two hundred and four arches of bridges of a total length of 2,230 yards and 4,950 yards of tunnels. Culverts were generally small, especially in the Ghinda-Asmara section. The winding track round the spurs of hill with frequent narrow culverts liable to landslides and blocked culverts in heavy rains made movement difficult.

Roads

Asmara, the capital, was the centre of land communications in the country. In addition to the railway, all major roads passed through this place. In Eritrea there were a number of trunk roads. The first was Sabderat-Asmara road. It was laid through Tessenei, Aicota, Barentu, Agordat and Keren. This route was one of the oldest in Eritrea, dating back to the early days of Italian colonization. It was built upto its modern standard in 1937-38. It was a wide (6-8 metres), graded and banked, all-weather road the whole way, with some fine bridges; but out of the total length of two hundred and forty miles only the last eighty miles upto Asmara were tarred. The surface upto that point was, by contrast, definitely poor, consisting of small stones and earth, badly packed; and was very hard on tyres. But for its poor surface this section also had all the characteristics of a first-class road, including large kilometre posts and warning signs. It was the only all-weather road leading to the Sudan frontier which could carry heavy traffic.

Deployment off the road was usually possible, until just below Keren, but it was not easy, because all this region was badly eroded and the Khors were many and deep. The road provided poor facilities for cover. However, there were several sites on it which were suitable for effective demolition. The chief among them was the Dongolaas George below Keren. At several points the railway ran close alongside the road and both could be damaged by the same bomb or charge.

The next major road was that between Asmara and Massawa. This road was perhaps the most important road in Eritrea, as it carried by far the greater part of all the goods imported into the country. The road was an old one, but it was rebuilt and modernised in 1935. It was a first-class road, eight metres wide. Of the eight thousand-feet climb from the sea level, seven thousand feet were compressed into the last thirty-five miles, and this section formed one of the most striking hill roads in the world. Long sections were cut out of the steep face of the escarpment. During the winter the hill was shrouded in thick mist, often for days on end.

Asmara-Decamere-Adi-Caieh-Ethiopian Boundary road was the third important route in Eritrea, owing to its approach to the Ethiopian borders. This road was built long before 1935, but like other main roads in the country, it was straightened, widened and tarred between 1935 and 1938, when it became a first-class road in every way. The road ran first over the high plateau near the Red Sea, and no big streams were crossed until south of Saganeiti, thirty-eight miles from Asmara. From there to Adi Caieh it passed through much more difficult country and there were many vulnerable points. From Adi Caieh to the frontier it kept along a narrow strip of plateau. Cover was poor along almost the whole route.

The fourth was the Asmara-Adi Ugri-Adi Quala-Ponte Mareb road. It was intended to join Asmara with Addis Ababa via Gondar. The Asmara-Gondar section had been completed before the outbreak of the war.

The next important stretch of the road serving as a bypass round Asmara for traffic coming from Massawa, and destined for

Southern Eritrea or Ethiopia, was that of Nefasit-Decamere road. It was a first-class road with a tarmac surface. It left the Massawa-Asmara road at Nefasit just as it began the steep climb up the hill. This road traversed an escarpment and passed through a very difficult country. Deployment was seldom possible and the road was very much vulnerable to air attacks and blocks. It was also liable to blocking by the fall of rocks.

In addition to these roads there were a number of motorable tracks in Eritrea which provided movement during operations. One of these was the track Sabderat-Wakai-Keru-Mogareh-Sciaglet-Agordat. This was a dry weather motor track which was used a great deal before the reconstruction of the main road via Barentu in 1937-38. Cover on this route was good and deployment easy almost anywhere. The defile at Keru was the only good holding place for defence.

The next, Aicota-Biscia-Sciaglet, was a well-defined but difficult track, crossing a great many Khors deeply cut, and sandy in patches. It passed through the three-mile-long Adal Gorge, at 23-25 miles from Aicota, where no deployment was possible as, although the gorge was not very deep, it had steep and rocky sides. The track was fit only for strong vehicles, but desert tyres were not essential.

Barentu-Tole-Debra Sina-Arresa track was probably intended to be a second east-and-west line of communication across the whole country; but it never assumed that position because of the difficult stretch between Debra Sina and Arresa, where it climbed on to the plateau. The route was however never completed.

The next track was Karora-El Ghena-Cub Cub-Keren, the chief importance of which lay in the fact that it connected the Sudan with Eritrea. From Karora on the frontier to Cub Cub, the route was a well-defined track, capable of use by mechanised transport. It followed the edge of the coastal plain, to the east of the foot of the hills and required little maintenance. Except during the rains, it could be used by vehicles properly equipped for desert work. Water was scarce along this route, but generally enough for a brigade, even in the driest season. Generally available in shallow wells or water holes, water was dirty and sometimes brackish, but quite drinkable in case of necessity.

The section Cub Cub-Keren was along the third class dry-weather road from Nacfa to Keren. It passed through the hills and crossed many Khors and rivers. It was generally graded.

ETHIOPIA

Ethiopia was annexed by the Italians to their African dominions immediately before the war. Northern Ethiopia where Indian forces took part in fighting consists of a table land in the centre with an average height of six thousand feet, many of the mountain tops being even higher. On the east this table land drops abruptly to the Afar or Danakil plain. To the west and north-west the plateau falls in terraces to the plains of the eastern Sudan.

The climate of this region varies according to the situation of the area or its altitude. The eastern plain is hot and dry almost having semi-desert climatic conditions. On the table land it is temperate and healthy. The valley of the river Taccaze, lying north and south, about seventy miles to the east of Gondar, which debouches from the plateau, is tropical and malarial. The rains occur from June to September and average about thirty inches in the year.

Administration

In May 1936, subsequent to the Italian invasion and annexation of Ethiopia, the King of Italy was declared Emperor of Ethiopia, and the Italian colonies of Eritrea and Somalia together with Ethiopia were incorporated into a single state called Italian East Africa. The new state was subsequently divided into six provincial governments; Eritrea, Amhara, Socioa, Harar, Somalia and Galla Sidama. Every province was divided into districts, residencies and sub-residencies. In the six provinces there were in all 72 districts, 259 residencies and 65 sub-residencies.

COMMUNICATIONS

In most mountainous countries river valleys are lines of communication and mountain ranges are barriers. In Ethiopia the opposite is true; here watersheds are lines of communication and rivers are barriers. This is because most Ethiopian rivers have cut deep gorges across an upland plateau. There are hardly any navigable rivers; they are to be regarded primarily as obstacles to communication and often very formidable ones too. Ethiopia had no openings on the sea.

Railways

The Franco-Ethiopian Railway ran from Jibuti to Addis Ababa. It was a single line metre gauge track. The distance from Jibuti to Addis Ababa was 491 miles ; of this the first 61 miles were in French Somaliland. The railway was started from Jibuti in 1896,

railhead reached Dire Dawa in 1902 and Addis Ababa in 1917. The capacity of this railway at the time was about seven hundred tons daily, actually the maximum it had ever attained was four hundred tons daily in 1937. The most vulnerable point on this railway was the Awash River bridge at mile 339. If this were destroyed replacement would take a long time and would be very difficult. The next most vulnerable point was the tunnel at mile 114½. It was the only tunnel on the line but its destruction must cause considerable inconvenience.

Roads and Tracks

I. The Asmara-Addis Ababa road. It was laid through Asmara, Decamere, Adigrat, Quiha, Mai Mescic, Toselli Pass, Mai Ceu, Quoram, Dessie and Addis Ababa and was 758 miles long.

This was a continuation of the Eritrean route from Asmara to the Ethiopian boundary described above. The Eritrean part of the road was built before 1935. It was extended to Addis Ababa between 1935-38. The road traversed a most difficult country. Its lowest point was 3,500 feet and its highest 10,200 feet. On crossing the frontier into Ethiopia it continued to follow the crest of the watershed, between the Mareb (Gash) and the Danakil depression, as far as Adigrat. From Adigrat to Mai Ceu it ran west of the watershed between the Taccaze and the Danakil. At Mai Ceu it crossed over to the east and at Debra Sina it crossed the watershed again and kept on the west, bridging the headwaters of several of the tributaries of the Abbai (Blue Nile) as far as Addis Ababa. Since the road followed the watershed pretty closely it did not have to cross any large rivers, an advantage however offset by the terrific climbs the road had to make. It was a first class road, eight to nine metres wide, of which six to seven metres were asphalted. The surface was asphalted throughout except for two stretches from mile 311 to 490 and from mile 525½ to 678. Where the surface was not asphalted the road was covered with loose metal. At the outbreak of the war the road was in a very good condition. It was one of the most important trunk roads in Italian East Africa.

II. The Asmara-Gondar road, via Ponte Mareb, Adowa, Axum, Debarec.

The Italians considered this as one of the nine important main roads in Italian East Africa. It was a well-built road of the same standard as the Asmara-Addis Ababa road. The surface for the most part was macadam only, which was very loose in the hills. The road was a great engineering feat and was probably the most spectacular in the country. It had to climb the sheer face of the mountains, 7,700 feet high before coming out on to the immense plain which sloped gradually to Gondar.

III. The Metemma-Gondar Road.

This route was opened as a motorable track in 1937. Economy was an important factor in its making and no macadamising or asphalting or any major road works were undertaken west of Azazo. It was simply a cleared motor track which was impassable during the rains. The road was not used between early 1938 and 1939 owing to a landslide which blocked the road near Wahni. Early in 1940, it was reopened after considerable hard work in the Wahni area.

In addition to the above the Italians had made comprehensive plans for making roads and in northern Ethiopia had built a major road from Assab on the sea coast to Dessie. They had intended to continue this from Dessie to Gondar. Of this road only a portion had been built—out of a total distance of two hundred and forty-five miles, ninety-three miles had been built at the outbreak of the war.

CHAPTER III

The First Encounters

When Italy joined the war against the Allies in June 1940, British forces in the Sudan comprised three British infantry battalions[1] and the Sudan Defence Force, a total of about 9,000 men. Italian forces in East Africa were estimated to be over 100,000 men. Viewed in the context of the general situation in the Middle East this position was highly unsatisfactory. Egypt, the Sudan, Kenya and British Somaliland, all were liable to attack by the Italians as their extensive frontiers were guarded by inadequate forces. In Egypt a strength of 36,000 men was pitched against an Italian force of over 215,000 in Libya. In other countries also bordering on Italian East Africa, British garrisons were equally weak. Kenya had about 8,500 men and British Somaliland about 1,475. These figures included local frontier police forces also. The Italians had also considerable numerical advantage in the air, though this was balanced by the superior skill and training of British airmen[2].

On 17 June 1940 the French Government asked for armistice terms. It was at first hoped that the French colonies and oversea territories would continue the struggle even after the French capitulation. But French General Nogues in North Africa decided to obey orders to surrender and his example was followed by the French Commander in Syria. At Jibuti, General Legentilhomme held out for nearly a month longer. The French collapse in North Africa changed the strategical situation for the Axis powers. It removed a major threat to Libya. The Italian forces in North and East Africa had no longer to concern themselves with Tunisia and French Somaliland and could be used for large-scale offensive operations. Egypt was now certainly to be attacked. The defection of Syria meant that the French force of three divisions which could have been used for helping Turkey, Greece or Egypt, if necessary, could not be counted upon by the British. Egypt and the Sudan were now to feel the pinch of Italian forces on their borders more than ever before.

---

[1] The 2nd West Yorkshires, the 1st Worcestershires and the 1st Essex.
[2] Wavell's Despatch on Operations in the Middle East from August 1939 to November 1940.

Captain Premindra Singh Bhagat, V. C., Royal Bombay Sappers and Miners

Subedar Richpal Ram
V. C.
4/6 Rajputana Rifles.

Gen. Sir Archibald P. Wavell

Lt.-Gen. Sir William Platt

Maj.-Gen. A. G. O. Mayne

Maj.-Gens. L. M. Heath and N. M. de la P. Beresford-Peirse

Ethiopian Patriots on the march

Captured Italian war
material at Agordat

With inadequate forces it was hardly possible for the British to cover the long and vulnerable 1,200 miles of the frontier of the Sudan with Italian East Africa. Therefore, a policy of defending only important places on the frontier with small mobile forces was adopted. They were asked to hold on till attacked by superior Italian forces. General Wavell who laid down this policy knew that these small numbers could not resist an advance by Italian forces—greatly superior in numbers. But he thought it desirable that they should fight a delaying action against the Italians rather than surrender without any fighting at all.[3]

The first three weeks of war passed without definite signs of Italian intention to start a large-scale offensive, though operations in the form of skirmishes did take place. Air forces on both sides attacked each other's places. Kassala, Port Sudan, Atbara, Kurmuk and Gedaref were subjected to air attacks. These affected the civilian morale to some extent though no military damage of any importance was caused. British air force attacked Italian warships based on Massawa and bases and supply depots in Ethiopia and Eritrea. However, on land the Italians made no advance. The Sudan Defence Force, on the other hand, frequently engaged in offensive patrolling across the Sudan frontier opposite Kassala and Gallabat. They made several successful raids on the Italian frontier posts. Major-General W. Platt, the General Officer Commanding Troops in the Sudan at this time intended to hold three important places, Khartoum, Atbara and Port Sudan and to delay an Italian advance as long as he could in the hope of receiving reinforcements. Anything beyond the defence of the Sudan was hardly feasible.[4]

Early in July 1940 there was a change in Italian attitude and they attacked the frontier posts of Karora, Kassala, Gallabat and Kurmuk, and by the end of the first week they were in possession of all these places. The defending troops offered resistance and inflicted heavy losses on the Italians which perhaps prevented them from following up their successes in spite of their superiority in numbers. Nonetheless these successes secured some important advantages to the Italians. Apart from enhancing their prestige, the Italians had succeeded in obtaining an important entrance into the Sudan at Kassala. The capture of Gallabat further made it difficult for the British to establish connection with the Patriots in Gojjam.[5] The

---

[3] Ibid.
[4] Playfair, *op. cit.* pp. 169-170.
[5] Ibid. p. 171.

Italians were also successful in taking Moyale on the borders of Kenya and in overrunning British Somaliland in August.

The British forces even after these initial reverses continued to patrol the frontier offensively and to be prepared against deeper thrusts by the Italians. Platt by these offensive patrols along the frontier succeeded in making a good show of his strength. He bluffed the Italians into thinking that he had far greater strength than he actually commanded. This perhaps had its effect in preventing an Italian advance against Port Sudan, Atbara and Khartoum. It is curious that the Italians failed to exploit their early successes and to take advantage of their superiority in numbers, weapons and aircraft. They at the time were in control of the entrance of the Red Sea and could well have tried to sweep up through the Sudan. An Italian pincer movement held chances of success, the northern arm of which would be Marshal Graziani's army advancing from Libya and the southern arm, Italian forces from East Africa. By a resolute and well-planned effort they might have succeeded in closing the two arms of the pincer. For the British it would have resulted in the loss of the Sudan, who would then not have been in a position to send reinforcements up the Red Sea to the Middle East and would have lost their supply route across Africa and Takoradi to Khartoum. But the Italians attempted no such venture which later, with the arrival of British reinforcements, ceased to be a practical proposition. "Any Italian general," it has been said, "who looks back at that time must feel inclined to kick himself for the waste of those precious weeks when, if he had only known it, resolute and co-ordinated attacks might have closed the jaws altogether——The wave of Italian opportunity swelled, rose, hung, and sank back again with a whisper like 'Italy' instead of bursting with a roar like 'Rome'".[6]

In September strong British reinforcements arrived in the Sudan. B Squadron 6th Royal Tank Regiment (cruiser and light tanks) arrived in early September from Egypt and in the second half of that month, the 5th Indian Division[7] less one brigade arrived from India. Soon after Wavell instructed Platt to make plans for minor

---

[6] *The Abyssinian Campaigns, The Official Story of the Conquest of Italian East Africa*, p. 22.

[7] The Division was formed in India in 1939 under the command of Major-General L. M. Heath. It left for the Middle East in the summer of 1940 where one brigade joined the 4th Indian Division. It had as its sign a red circle shown against a black background which gradually came to symbolise a ball of fire,

offensive operations as soon as it might be practicable. The recapture of the frontier post of Gallabat was suggested as a suitable objective. No general offensive was contemplated at this stage. In Kenya, General Dickinson was to concentrate upon an active defence and to make plans for a future offensive.

With the arrival of reinforcements reorganisation was effected to make use of the available forces to the best advantage. A provisional plan was made on 26 September according to which the Headquarters 5th Indian Division was placed in command of all the troops in the area. They had under their command the 10th and 21st Indian Infantry Brigades, one Motor Machine Gun Group, Sudan Defence Force, 1st Essex and a mixed tank company. These troops were reorganised in 9th, 10th and 29th Indian Infantry Brigades, giving full complement to the division.[8] Reorganisation continued till about the middle of October when a mobile force was formed, known as Gazelle Force, to watch the frontier.[9]

A Division Operational Instruction, issued on 13 October 1940, provided for the defence of Khartoum as the main objective. The line of British defence extended from Port Sudan in the north to Roseires in the south. Kassala, an important communication centre, occupied the middle of this line. The defence force was so disposed as to prevent any incursion of hostile troops from the north or west of this line. Certain places were declared vital for the defence of Khartoum. These were Port Sudan, Haiya Junction and Atbara, in the north, and in the south these included Gedaref, Showak, Khashm el Girba and Sarsareib. The defence of Khartoum was assigned to the 5th Indian Division and it was disposed in the neighbourhood of Kassala. The 29th Indian Infantry Brigade under the direct command of Headquarters Troops was deployed on the coast. Gazelle Force was employed in the Gash Delta north of Kassala under the command of the 5th Indian Division.

Gazelle Force

On 25 October a patrol of 1 Motor Machine Gun Group sent by Gazelle Force cut over a thousand yards of telegraph line east of Kassala. Another patrol returned to the same area on 28

---

[8] Major-General L. M. Heath was the Division Commander. The brigades were commanded respectively by Brigadier A. G. O. Mayne, Brigadier W. J. Slim and Brigadier J. C. O. Marriott (See Appendix I).

[9] For composition of Gazelle Force see Appendix II.

October, removed the cable put down to repair the damage caused by previous patrol, and ambushed an Italian party, destroying three lorries and capturing six prisoners. The patrol returned without suffering any loss[10]. From 1 to 11 November Gazelle Force fought an action with an Italian force in the area of Yodrud, twenty-five miles to the north-east of Kassala. During the night of 31 October/1 November, an Italian force, estimated about six hundred strong, crossed the frontier and established itself in the area of the Tehamiyam Wells, to the south of Yodrud. It was watched by 6 Motor Machine Gun Company and information about it was passed to the Commander Gazelle Force, who ordered A Squadron 1 Horse to proceed to the area of the Tehamiyam Wells and with 6 Motor Machine Gun Company to surround the hostile force so as to capture or destroy it. The remainder of 1 Horse, due to move from Derudeb to Mekali Wells between 1 and 6 November, was ordered to move up as soon as possible.

The position by the evening of 1 November was that the hostile Italian force was being watched by a force consisting of A Troop 1/5 Field Battery RA, A Squadron 1 Horse, and 6 Motor Machine Gun Company, the last of which, with the field troop in support, was based on the area of Haldeid, five miles to the south-west of Tehamiyam Wells. A Squadron 1 Horse was to the south-east of the Italian position in the area of Tamanau.

On 2 November the Italians spent the day in improving their positions and working on their defences, while British artillery kept up a continuous harassing fire. B Squadron and Headquarters 1 Horse arrived at Mekali Wells in the evening and were ordered to move as early as possible on 3 November to the area of the battle and close the gap to the north and north-east of Tendelai. Meanwhile, at dawn on 3 November, another Italian party of three hundred men with some animals, was seen moving from east to west through the gap near Tendelai. It joind the other party at Tehamiyam

---

[10]The following extract, from the patrol report giving details of a talk with an Arab Sheikh, contacted east of Kassala throws an interesting sidelight on the effect of active patrolling on the British side.

"The Sheikh of the large Arab encampments north of the telegraph line Kassala-Sabderat, a Beni Amir, said that the line had been repaired by 1800 hours the previous day by a patrol which came out and made itself generally unpleasant to the locals from about 1500 hours. The main point of grievance was that the inhabitants had not warned the Italians of our patrol. He said that they were a lot less brave than before".

Wells. However, the gap was finally closed at midday by B Squadron 1 Horse. On the same evening one company 3 Royal Frontier Force Regiment, also arrived with four medium machine guns. The Commander Gazelle Force decided to take personal command of the operation and moved to Girger near Haldeid on the evening of 3 November.

At 0630 hours on 4 November, another party of the Italians, four hundred strong, was reported to be moving from the east towards the Tendelai Gap. It was engaged by A and B Squadrons 1 Horse and pinned to ground by a fire-fight which lasted the whole day. As the area was found clear the next day it was assumed that they had withdrawn towards Serobatib. In the evening, orders were issued for a company 3 Royal Frontier Force Regiment to advance, on 5 November, to Tehamiyam Wells through the Tamanau Gap. After leaving its camp (near the Advanced Headquarters of Gazelle Force in Girger) A Company 3 Royal Frontier Force Regiment moved on Tehamiyam Wells at 0300 hours on 5 November when it found that the real Italian position was not at Tehamiyam Wells, as marked on the map, but at a place two-and-a-half miles to the north in Yodrud. It was, therefore, withdrawn to its old camp, and forces were regrouped in the following manner:—

C Squadron 1 Horse was ordered up to join the regiment. A Southern group of A and C Squadrons was formed with the role of preventing the Italians from reinforcing from the south and breaking the cordon.

B Squardron 1 Horse and 6 Motor Machine Gun Company were to hold the close ring round the hostile force and prevent it from escaping.

At 2300 hours on 5 November, a party of the Italians, escorting animal transport carrying stores to the Yodrud area, ran into a small picquet of A Squadron 1 Horse on a small feature in the Tamanau Gap. The picquet was overrun. C Squadron was sent in to gain touch with A Squadron but had some difficulty in doing so at first. In the morning on 6 November, A and C Squadrons were in contact with the Italians on the foothills in the gap and were engaging them with fire form the west. At 1000 hours an attack was launched from the south by A Company 3 Royal Frontier Force Regiment and by 1300 hours the hill was captured, the Italians losing one hundred and fifty prisoners. The remainder of the hostile force retreated to the main hill, and was pursued. By 1630 hours ninety more soldiers were taken prisoners and a considerable quantity of arms and ammunition was captured. The hostile force was a party of *II Group Bande Polizia*, with detachments from *35th* and *101st Colonial Battalions*, escorting one hundred camels carrying stores and provisions for the Italian troops in the Yodrud area. On the British side three persons were killed and five wounded. The losses of the Italians amounted to one Italian officer and two hundred and forty-one other ranks captured and twelve killed.

The Italian air force had been active and, on 7 November, it carried out extensive raids in which the Advanced Headquarters Gazelle Force came in for a good share. The Headquarters lost four killed and four wounded in one of these raids. It was accordingly moved to Mekali Wells area the same evening. On the same day a further regrouping was ordered to take place on 8 November. A detachment from 2 Motor Machine Gun Company (four Bren vans, four armoured cars and one infantry platoon) was to move up and take the place of B Squadron with the task of keeping the inner ring tight round the hostile force. B Squadron was to revert to the command of 1 Horse, whose sector was extended to include the Tendelai Gap. Two companies of 3/2 Punjab (29th Indian Infantry Brigade) arrived at Mekali Wells during the night of 9/10 November in support of the forward troops. On the evening of 8 November, A Troop Sudan Regiment (four 3·7-inch howitzers) also joined Gazelle Force and was placed under the command of 1 Horse.

An operation was planned to take place on the morning of 11 November, in which 1 Horse and 1 Motor Machine Gun Company were to hold the possible exits for the Italians to the south while the infantry was to attack from the north. Starting at 0500 hours the infantry was to capture Big Hill, a large feature extending for one mile from north to south, and immediately to the north of the Italian position. It was then to exploit through the Italian positions to the south for a distance of one thousand yards. This plan was based on information obtained from intelligence to the effect that the strength of the hostile force was only four hundred and that their morale was so low that the majority would surrender at the first opportunity.[11] In actual fact this estimate proved to be wrong both regarding the strength and the morale of the force.

The Attack

At 0500 hours on 11 November, the advance started according to the plan. By 0700 hours the company on the east side of the hill

---

[11] Report on Gazelle Force Operations, 1 to 11 November 1940, p. 6. (Appended to Hq. Gazelle Force War Diary for November 1940).

could be seen half way along Big Hill. At this stage the advance was held up by fire from a ridge in the southern half of the feature. Further artillery support was arranged and the reserve company put in. Some more ground was gained but, owing to the steepness of the ground, accurate artillery support was difficult and in some cases the shells fell too near the troops and in one case behind them. This had an adverse effect on the momentum of the attack. The Italians fought stubbornly and no headway could be made against them. At 1200 hours, the commander of the infantry force was ordered to hold the ground gained, and told that the Commander Gazelle Force would visit him and see the situation for himself. The latter arrived forward at 1300 hours. By this time the Italians had started infiltrating single men round the flanks on to Big Hill, who began sniping the observation posts and the Headquarters. It was obvious to the Commander Gazelle Force that the attack had no chance of success. He, therefore, issued orders to the commander of the infantry force to start thinning out at 1500 hours and finally abandon his position at 1700 hours. The withdrawal was carried out without any incident and was completed by 0100 hours on 12 November. Gazelle Force then moved back to its normal dispositions in the Gash Delta.

It was a bitter blow to have to break off the engagement without having captured or destroyed the hostile force, after Gazelle Force had kept it encircled so tenaciously for eleven days. But the infantry had been loaned only for a short time and was required to return to its own formation. The Italians had been seen supplying the troops from the air, a factor over which Indian forces had no control at that time. The Indian and British troops had been continuously in action for eleven days without rest.

Gallabat (6-7 November 1940)

Another engagement was fought in the Gallabat-Metemma area which also failed in its object. As mentioned above, with the arrival of the 5th Indian Division in the Sudan some offensive action was considered desirable. At a conference held at Khartoum in October which was attended by Mr. Anthony Eden, then Secretary of State for War, and General J.C. Smuts, offensive plans and preparations were considered. Eden expressed the general feeling when he proposed that Gallabat should be attacked early in November and Kassala early in January.[12] On the instructions of Wavell a plan

---

[12] Playfair, *op. cit.* p. 392.

GALLABAT —

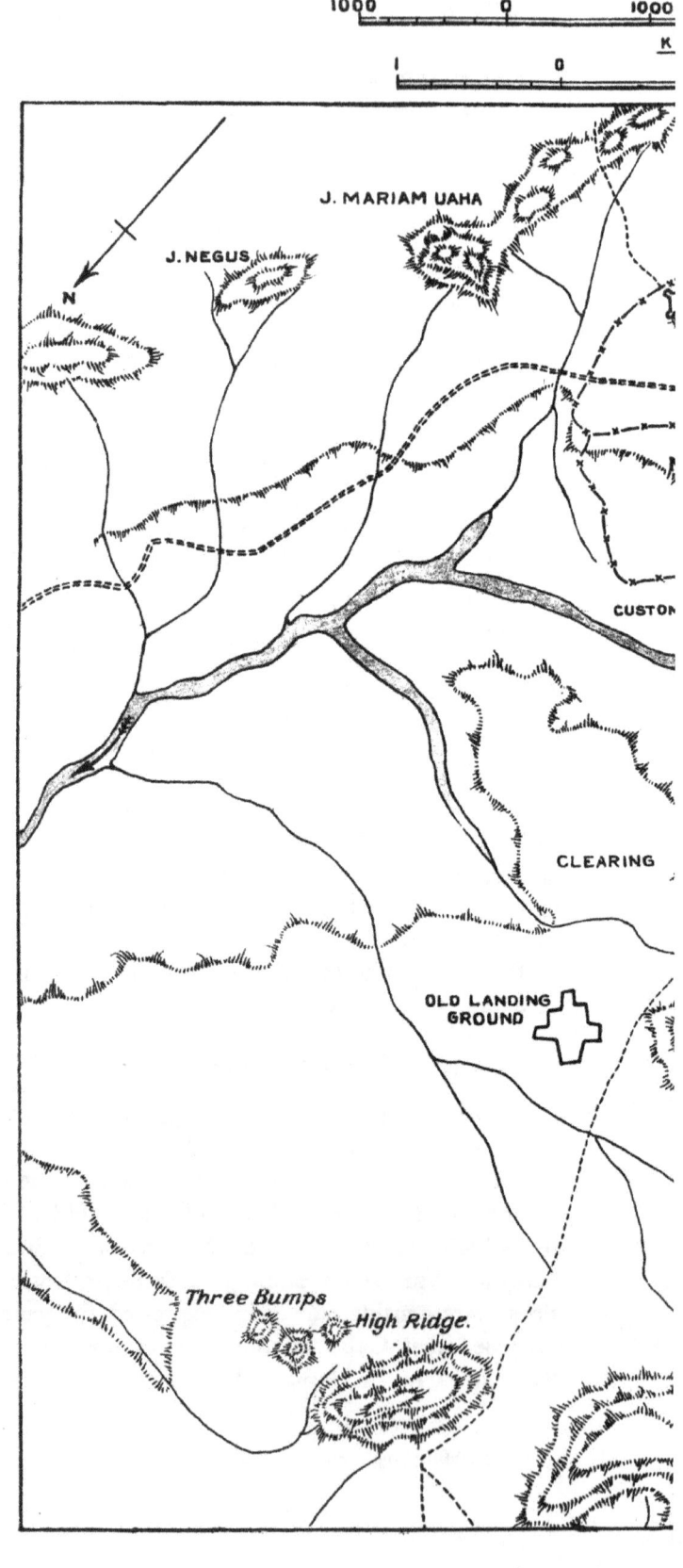

METEMMA AREA

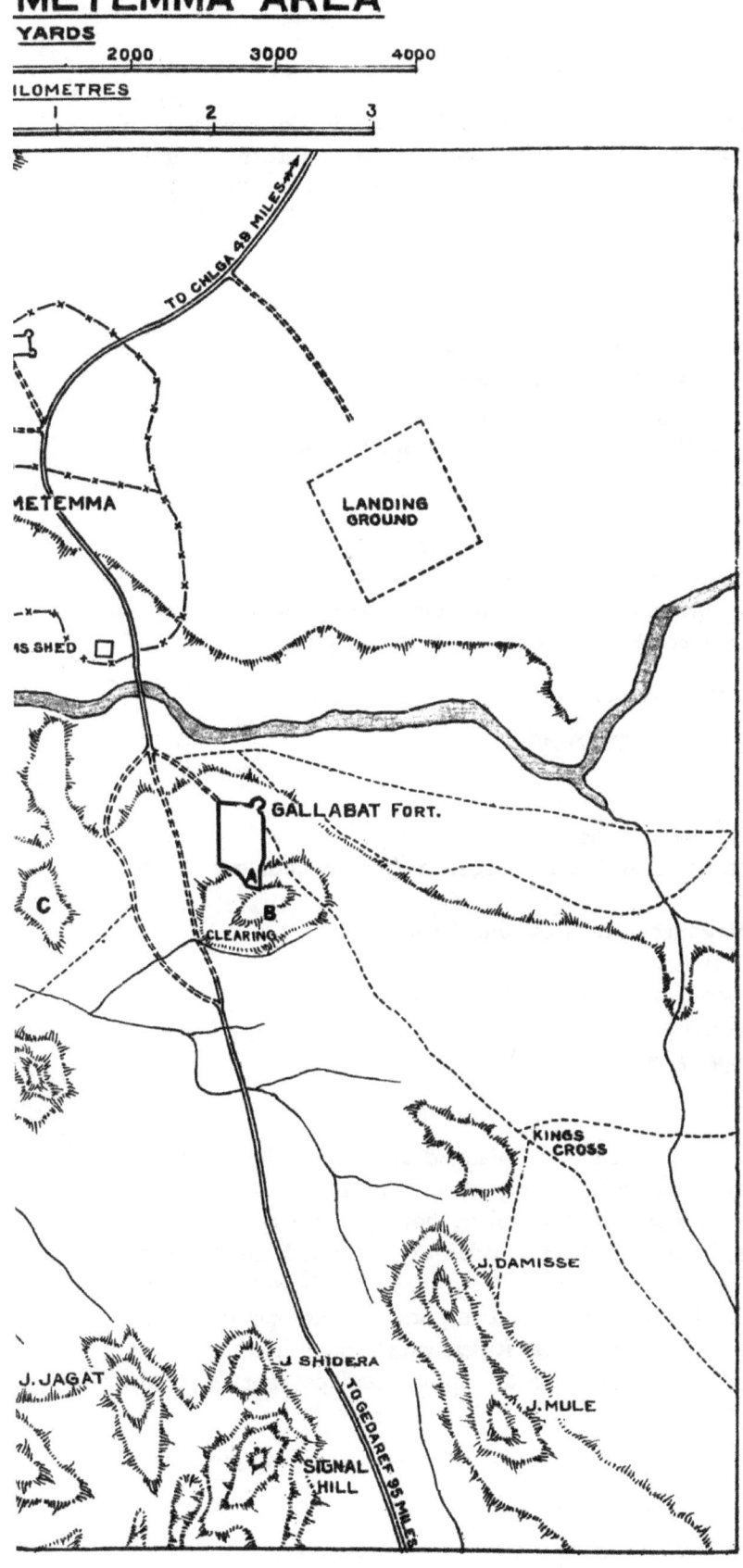

was prepared by Major-General L. M. Heath Commanding 5th Indian Division for an operation against the Italian troops in the Gallabat-Metemma area, to be carried out by the 10th Indian Infantry Brigade and a squadron of the 6th Royal Tank Regiment.[13]

Italian Forces

At this time the Italians were estimated to have the following forces in the Gallabat-Metemma area:—

27th Colonial Battalion in Gallabat
25th and *77th Colonial Battalions* camped outside the wire east of Metemma.
Bande in Metemma.
Some pack artillery (four to six guns).
Some anti-tank weapons (about one platoon)
A column reported on the road from Gondar, was believed to include one *Blackshirt* battalion and some anti-tank guns.

British Forces consisted of:—

10th Indian Infantry Brigade
1st Essex
4 Baluch
3 Royal Garhwal Rifles
B Squadron 6th Royal Tank Regiment (Six medium and six light tanks)
28 Field Regiment RA (less one battery)
7/66 Field Battery RA.
21 Field Company (Sappers and Miners)
20 Field Ambulance
No 3 Company AEC SDF

Plan

The operation was originally planned to start on 8 November, and concentration of troops was therefore arranged to take place by that date. At the end of October, however, reports of Italian reinforcements moving up from Gondar were received and the date of attack was advanced to 6 November in the hope of forestalling these reinforcements. There were to be two phases of the operation. In the first phase, 3 Royal Garhwal Rifles, with B Squadron 6th Royal Tank Regiment in support, was to capture Gallabat Fort and ad-

---

[13] Wavell's Despatch on Operations in the Middle East from August 1939 to November 1940.

vance up to the Boundary Khor and, if possible, establish a bridgehead there with a view to enable the tanks to cross the Khor in the later operations against Metemma. The attack was to be preceded by air and artillery bombardment. In the second phase, 1st Essex was to attack Metemma. 4 Baluch, which was holding the outpost line before the start of the operations, was to be in brigade reserve throughout.

Operations

On the evening of 5 November there was a heavy local shower of rain which rendered the advance landing ground, at Saraf Said, unserviceable until 0900 hours on 6 November. This affected the momentum of operations by the air force. However, air and artillery bombardment opened at 0530 hours on 6 November. The bombardment lasted upto 0615 hours and at that hour 3 Royal Garhwal Rifles, with the tanks leading, attacked the fort and the ground round it. The leading company of the battalion advanced through some scrub for two hundred yards, to reach the Right Golf Course, a clearing burnt by the Italians to obtain a field of fire and dominated by the Dog's Head portion of the Gallabat Fort. The shape of the ground in the Right Golf Course was slightly convex and, aided by this fact and the tanks, the company reached the wire. The tanks, however, failed to cut the wire or to break down the stockade of Dog's Head. Instead, they wheeled left and right of the fort and eventually effected an entry further down.

The company of 3 Royal Garhwal Rifles was faced with uncut wire and a strongly fortified stockade. The advance was held up and a close battle ensued in which grenades were freely exchanged. A second company of the battalion was brought up at 0700 hours and put in to attack Dog's Head from the north. Machine guns were brought into action within fifty yards of the stockade and silenced an Italian light automatic gun. Thereupon, two riflemen dashed forward and, with great gallantry, cut the wire and both the companies poured through the gap. The fort was soon overrun and occupied by 0730 hours, although isolated posts still hung on courageously and had to be mopped up later.

Tanks

The tanks had come to grief very early in the operation. Six cruisers and four light tanks had crossed the start line at 0615 hours and four cruisers had managed to effect an entry into the fort at 0640 hours. The remainder had broken down before then. Of these four, three broke down soon after entering the fort and could only give fire support. The fourth did manage to circle round inside the fort and neutralize some Italian machine gun posts.

Two companies of 3 Royal Garhwal Rifles had been directed to advance along the west of the road and to capture the Left Golf Course clearing and then advance as far as the Boundary Khor and establish a bridgehead across it where the road crossed the Khor. Two light tanks were in support of these companies. The company advancing on the Left Golf Course captured its objective and consolidated the ground gained. In this area it came under fire from the fort. This fire was returned and the attack on the fort supported. The other company had good cover and advanced to within five hundred yards of the Khor. Here the cover was thinner and the ground was generally flat, but shallow nullahs afforded good approaches to within two hundred yards of the Khor, where the plateau dropped steeply into the Khor itself. The advance was continued to the edge of the plateau without much difficulty but on reaching that line the company came under heavy fire from machine guns in the Khor itself and in the forward positions in Metemma.

The company in the Left Golf Course area, with its two light tanks, also started advancing towards the Khor and arrived on the left of the other company just as an Italian counter-attack was being made. At the same time the one surviving tank from the fort came to the Khor. The counter-attack was soon repulsed and heavy casualties were inflicted on the Italians. Meanwhile, the situation as regards tanks was serious. Only one cruiser tank, out of the six cruiser and four light tanks, which had taken part in the attack on the fort, was serviceable. In view of this and the strength of the wire round Metemma, the Commander of the 10th Indian Infantry Brigade decided not to go on with the attack on Metemma and ordered the ground gained to be consolidated. 1 Essex was brought up and with a detachment of 3 Royal Garhwal Rifles, less the detachment, was concentrated in the area just outside the fort and the two companies on the Khor were withdrawn as there was no point in holding the bridge-head.

Air

The air situation deteriorated after this and the Italians gained complete command of the air over the battle area. Starting from 0915 hours on 6 November they carried out four heavy raids, during the day, on the Gallabat Fort and the area round it. In the fort itself there was no cover from view, the existing slit trenches were inadequate and the digging of fresh ones was very difficult because of the hard ground. In the area round the fort there was cover from view but proper slit trenches were not completed until after the first raids. The air defence was negligible, there were no anti-aircraft guns except the unit light machine guns, and the casualties among the forward troops were heavy. In the afternoon, there was a certain amount of confusion and demoralization on account of this, and elements of battalions in the rear areas started a withdrawal without orders. Those in the front, however, did not take part in the withdrawal and the situation was soon brought under control.[14]

The night passed quietly; some Italian patrols crossed the Boundary Khor, moved up as far as the wire of Gallabat and then retired. There were no counter-attacks on the fort. On the morning of 7 November, the Italians continued their heavy air raids. There was no hope of improvement in the matter of tanks. The one workshop vehicle had been hit and there was no chance of a replacement. In view of this and the continued Italian air superiority, Brigadier Slim, the Commander of the 10th Indian Infantry Brigade, decided to evacuate Gallabat and withdraw to positions within artillery range of Metemma, and make it untenable for the Italians. Before the withdrawal a successful destructive shoot on Metemma stores dump was carried out without interference on the evening of 7 November, and was completed by 2000 hours. The Italian casualties were 189 killed, 231 wounded and 214 captured. On the British side 33 were killed and 154 wounded. The operation had failed to capture the objectives. Though losses were inflicted on the Italians and the Patriots got encouragement to defy their rulers the results were rather disappointing. The operation had failed mainly due to two reasons. The first was the breakdown of tanks from mechanical causes. The second was the Italian superiority in the air. There was a general shortage of anti-aircraft guns in the Middle East and none was available for the support of the 10th Indian Infantry Brigade. Hence when the British fighter aircraft had been shot down the Italian bombers had an easy time. The operation showed the necessity of protection against air attack for all forward troops.

Subdued Activity

The 5th Indian Division continued active patrolling during the rest of November and December, which enabled it to dominate the situation. Frequent ambushes were laid on the lines of com-

---

[14] War Diary, 5th Indian Division, From Hq. 5 Indian Division to Hq. Troops in the Sudan dated 17 November 1940.

munication and losses were inflicted on the Italians. This had a beneficial effect on the morale of the Indian troops and accounted, to some extent, for the dash with which the pursuit of the Italians was carried out later on. In addition the screen put up by these patrols was very effective and the Italian Intelligence was unable to assess correctly the strength of the British forces in the area which they were led to over-estimate.

Planning for further Offensive Action

Early in December 1940, planning for a bigger attack was started. In view of the limited resources, the object was to capture Kassala and the area east as far as Sabderat. This attack was to be carried out early in February 1941, provided the necessary reinforcements were available. In the south, the policy was to maintain pressure at Gallabat, but not to attempt any large-scale operations for the time being. The main idea behind these decisions was to foment the Patriot revolt in Ethiopia to the greatest possible extent and thus to render Italian position impossible. "I did not intend", General Wavell observed in his despatch, "at the time a large scale invasion either from Kassala towards Asmara and Massawa, or from Kismayu to the north. The two operations to Kassala, and Kismayu were designed to secure our flanks and I intended that our main effort should be devoted to furthering and supporting the rebellion by irregular action. I intended after the capture of Kassala and Kismayu to withdraw as many troops as possible from the Sudan and East Africa for the theatres further north."[15]

The Italian strategy of this time was supposed to be (1) to prevent help reaching the Patriots from outside and to suppress the revolt inside the country (2) to protect Asmara and Massawa and to be on the defensive in the Kassala and El Ghena areas. Though the main Italian strategy was defensive an attack to recapture Gallabat appeared likely. If this were successful it would prevent the British from sending men and material from the Sudan to Ethiopia to further the Patriot revolt there.[16] However, the success of British offensive in the Western Desert of Egypt in December 1940 enabled General Wavell to transfer the 4th Indian Division to the Sudan to enable the Kassala operation to be undertaken early in 1941. It was led by Major-General Sir Noel de la P. Beresford-Peirse. The

---

[15] Wavell's Despatch on Operations in East Africa, November 1940 to July 1941.

[16] Platt's Despatch on Operations in Eritrea and Abyssinia, dated 11 September 1941.

decision for this transfer was made at a very short notice while the battle in the Western Desert was being fought, because otherwise it was thought shipping would not be available. Part of the 4th Indian Division was actually moved from the battle of Sidi Barrani to ships which brought them to the Sudan. The 11th Indian Infantry Brigade led by Brigadier R. A. Savory arrived in the Sudan before the end of December, the division as a whole, however, could not be concentrated and be ready for action for some more time. The transfer of the division presented difficult administrative problems. It entailed moving the division partly by sea and partly by the rail-river route. The Sudan railways were single-track and very limited rolling-stock was available. The signal resources were also inadequate and the quick transmission of orders was very difficult. On account of the pressure for time, some units had to move to their concentration areas without their transport which followed later. However, this difficult task was creditably accomplished. The only mishap during the move occurred on 19 January when a train carrying 3/14 Punjab was bombed by the Italians and the battalion suffered some loss. The concentration of the 4th Indian Division was expected to be completed by 31 January.

Regrouping in the Sudan

With the arrival of the 4th Indian Division, a regrouping of forces was carried out on the frontier as below :—

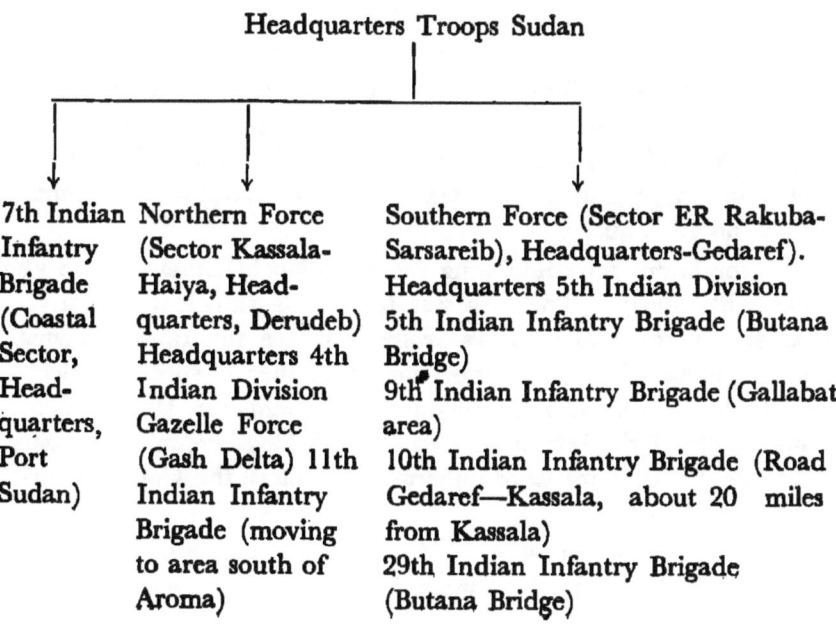

Headquarters Troops Sudan

7th Indian Infantry Brigade (Coastal Sector, Headquarters, Port Sudan)

Northern Force (Sector Kassala-Haiya, Headquarters, Derudeb) Headquarters 4th Indian Division Gazelle Force (Gash Delta) 11th Indian Infantry Brigade (moving to area south of Aroma)

Southern Force (Sector ER Rakuba-Sarsareib), Headquarters-Gedaref). Headquarters 5th Indian Division 5th Indian Infantry Brigade (Butana Bridge) 9th Indian Infantry Brigade (Gallabat area) 10th Indian Infantry Brigade (Road Gedaref—Kassala, about 20 miles from Kassala) 29th Indian Infantry Brigade (Butana Bridge)

Italian Forces

At this time, the Italians had the following forces in the frontier area :—

Kassala—two divisions in strong defensive positions.
Kassala—Tessenei—Sabderat area—one division.
Gallabat—Gondar area—about two divisions.

Possible offensive action by the Italian forces had to be kept in view during the planning for the attack and imposed a limit on the forces which might be spared for actual operation.

Deception

An elaborate deception plan was worked out by the 5th Indian Division to give the impression to the Italians that they were reinforcing Gallabat area thus inducing them to send troops to that part of the front. The deceptive measures included the building of dummy camps, landing grounds with dummy aircraft and bogus wireless traffic. Actual concentrations of troops were carefully concealed.

Withdrawal of Italian Forces

From early January there were indications of Italian intention to withdraw from the Kassala area. In the beginning it was difficult to ascertain whether they were regrouping their forces or preparing for a withdrawal. It was feared that a hurried attack, launched with insufficient force, would probably prove disastrous. However, as time passed the Italian intention to withdraw became clearer. An operation was, accordingly, planned to prevent the Kassala garrison from getting away and to destroy it. This operation was to take place on 19 January and troops of both the 4th and the 5th Indian Divisions were to participate. On 18 January, the Italians forestalled the attack by evacuating Kassala. Orders were issued for the pursuit to be taken up immediately. The pursuit started on 19 January.

Preparations for stimulating the rebellion in Ethiopia were also made with energy. The idea was to place a sufficient quantity of food and stores before the escarpment before the rains. A small force of one battalion of Sudanese and a number of specially selected British officers were also sent forward. The emperor, Haille Selassie, himself crossed the border and entered his kingdom on 20 January. Subsequent operations were undertaken to clear the Gojjam district of large Italian forces.

In organising this work two British officers took a leading part. They were Colonel D. A. Sandford, head of 101 Mission and Colonel O. C. Wingate.

The Italians had started withdrawing from the Sudan frontier. They had lost the initiative and the chance of a regular invasion of the Sudan which lay in their grasp after their initial successes. The danger to the Sudan was now over. After the disaster suffered by the Italians in Libya the only role left for Italian East Africa was protracted defence in order to prevent as long as possible the transfer of British reinforcements to Egypt. The initiative now came to rest with the British and once having seized it they were never to lose it. They could now well think of effecting a speedy conquest of Italian East Africa and of stepping up the Patriot revolt there which had received an impetus by the arrival of the Emperor in his country.

CHAPTER IV

Italians on the Retreat

Anticipating a British advance on Kassala the Italian force had withdrawn from it before the arrival of the British troops who took up the pursuit of the former. It was found that Kassala had suffered very little damage. Watertanks at the railway station had been destroyed and some rails removed from the sidings and trucks had been made into air-raid shelters. The Italians had left no stores but signal cable lines were still there without being damaged. The repair of the railway line was started immediately and Kassala started functioning as railhead on 25 January.

The country round Kassala was a desert plain with occasional rocky hills and knee-high scrub which was found almost everywhere. To the west of Kassala the hills were few and far between but eastwards they increased in size and numbers. North and south of Kassala lay hills of considerable tactical importance. Mechanical transport of all types could be used in the desert plain. Concentration of large forces in this area was rendered difficult by the non-availability of adequate cover for them and by the deficiency of water. In the north of Kassala the Gash Delta was thickly covered with bush and contained ample water. It afforded some cover for the concealment of forces.

To the east of Kassala lay Sabderat, a small post at the eastern end of a valley between high hills. There was a small dry riverbed at the bottom of the valley and the hills rose steeply from near the banks of the river. The valley was rocky and covered with scrub. It was not suitable for mechanical transport. The hills running from Sabderat and ending at Haurab were steep, rugged and bare. They were quite impassable by mechanical transport. To the north of Haurab were a number of hills and outcrops of rock. In between were Khors and in many cases mechanical transport could pass through the gaps. To the east of Serobatib the country was thickly covered with scrub and had many Khors. It was passable by mechanical transport though only with the greatest difficulty. South and east of Kaukawab the scrub was thinner. Between Pt. 649 and Wakai the scrub was thick on the west side and thin on the east bank of the Khor.

Throughout all this area the scrub was thickest on the banks of the Khors. There was ample cover but mechanical transport had to pick its way with care. The country between Sabderat and Keru varied considerably. It consisted of the following stretches :

  (i) Sabderat-Enkiabellit. It was undulating with thin scrub which was thicker at the Khors.
  (ii) Enkiabellit-Tegawa. It was open and mechanical transport was possible on a wide front.
  (iii) Tegawa-Dugurba. Thick scrub was found here and mechanical transport was possible off the road only with difficulty.
  (iv) Dugurba-Amien. The road passed through a gorge below Dugurba and then came out in the open country.
  (v) Amien-Keru. Movement off the road was not possible and at Keru the road passed only through a narrow defile.

Capture of Keru

The Italians were found to have evacuated Kassala when troops of the 4th Indian Division advanced on the morning of 19 January. It appeared at the time that they had intended to withdraw from Sabderat and Wakai also. The 4th Indian Division, in the north, was directed along the dry-weather track to Sabderat and Wakai and was later to exploit towards Keru up to the limit of administration. The 5th Indian Division was directed to Tessenei and thence along the motor road to Aicota. It was to be ready to exploit towards Barentu or Biscia afterwards.[1]

In the north, Gazelle Force led the advance followed by the 11th Indian Infantry Brigade and Divisional Headquarters. The 5th Indian Infantry Brigade was still moving towards Kassala and did not get there until 20 January when it reverted to the command of the 4th Indian Division. First contact was made by Gazelle Force with an Italian battalion holding Wakai at 1350 hours on 19 January. The troops closed up in the afternoon with the intention of attacking the next morning, but at 0830 hours on 20 January the Italians were reported to be evacuating their positions and by 0930 hours they had abandoned Wakai. The pursuit was resumed at 0945 hours. Although contact was made on one or two occasions with the retreating troops, no real resistance was met until 0430 hours on 21 January at Keru, forty miles east of Kassala.

---

[1] For a description of forces in the Sudan at this time see Appendix III.

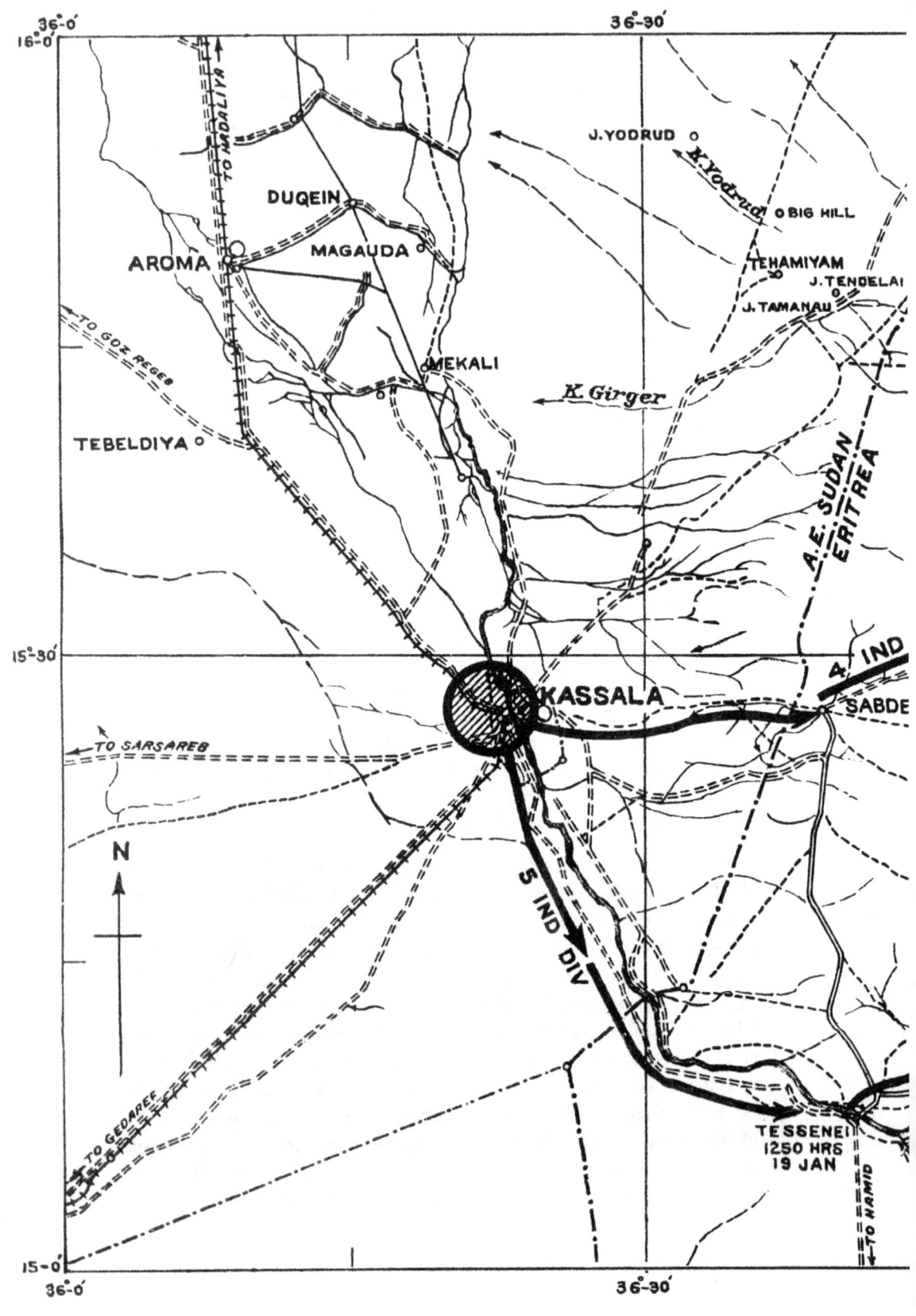

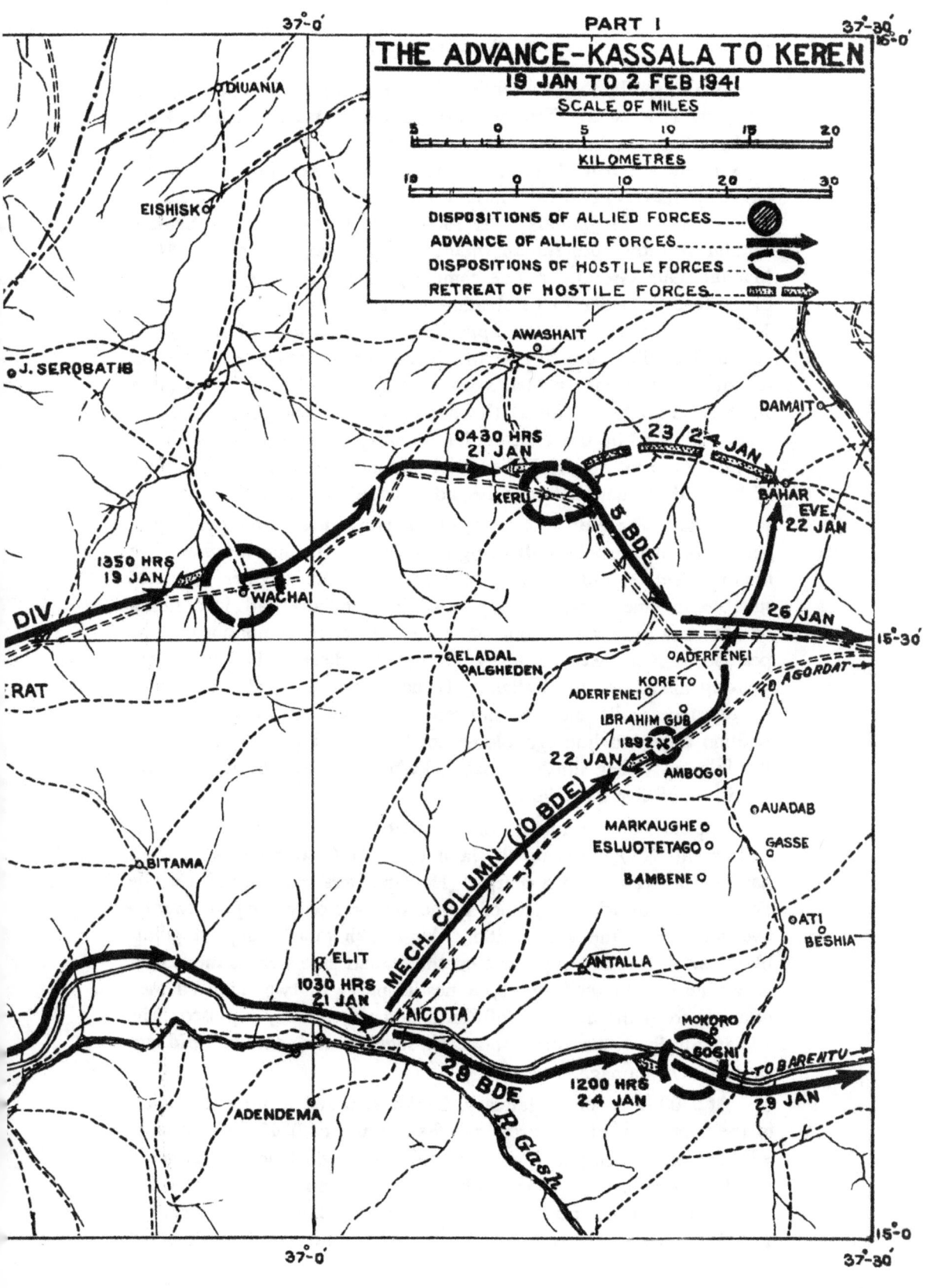

In the south, the 10th Indian Infantry Brigade was leading the 5th Indian Division. Tessenei was found evacuated and was occupied at 1250 hours on 19 January. Work was required on the Gash crossing and the brigade did not start moving across until 1415 hours on 20 January. The 5th Indian Division found Aicota clear at 1030 hours on 21 January. At 1500 hours that day, a mechanised column from the 10th Indian Infantry Brigade consisting of 2 Motor Machine Gun Group, less one company, was sent along the Aicota-Biscia road in order to get behind the Italian positions at Keru. This column met with some opposition in the area of Pt. 1892, twenty-five miles from Aicota, which held up its advance until it was reinforced by an infantry battalion on 22 January. The 29th Indian Infantry Brigade continued the advance along the Aicota-Barentu road. Thus while the 29th Indian Infantry Brigade made a thrust towards Barentu, the 4th Indian Division and the mechanised column of the 10th Indian Infantry Brigade pushed on Keru.

At Keru the road crossed a long narrow ridge through a deep gorge with steep rocky hills rising to a height of one thousand five hundred feet on either side. It was only a dry-weather road not suitable for mechanical transport. The Italians had laid mines on the way and carried out some very effective demolitions. The position of Keru was naturally strong. Its defence had also been well-organised by the Italians. It had been fortified with thorn fences, stone walls and trenches and small posts in the hills. The position appeared impregnable except by a turning movement over the hills on either side. It was held by the *41st Colonial Brigade* consisting of five battalions.

Gazelle Force made its first contact with the Italians in this position at 0430 hours on 21 January. At 0700 hours an Italian party of sixty cavalry men charged Headquarters and guns of Gazelle Force. This attack was pushed home and was only stopped, twenty-five yards from the gun positions, by British guns firing at point-blank range. Some 40 persons on the Italian side were either killed or wounded. At 0800 hours, a hostile party of two hundred men attacked from the direction of Keru, and were easily repulsed. The Italian air force remained active throughout the day but did not cause much damage.

At 0400 hours on 22 January, 4 Sikh attacked a hill to the south of the gorge. They captured the feature and at 0545 hours attacked the main Italian position but found it strongly held by a brigade. Hard fighting continued throughout the day and the Indian troops held their ground under heavy machine gun, mortar and artillery fire. Meanwhile, troops of the 11th Indian Infantry Brigade started arriving in the afternoon and at 1630 hours a company of 2 Camerons reinforced the Sikhs on the hill. Efforts were also made without success during the day to get round the flank.

By the evening of 22 January the mechanised column from the 10th Indian Infantry Brigade, advancing from Aicota, had cut off the Italian communications at Bahar, to the east of Keru. The Italians, therefore, abandoned their position that night. On 23 and 24 January, the Italian garrison while withdrawing from Keru, ran into the troops of the 10th Indian Infantry Brigade. Heavy casualties were inflicted on the Italian troops. Over seven hundred prisoners were taken, including the Commander *41st Colonial Brigade* and his staff.

Demolitions and mines held up the advance of the Indian troops. Though Keru was occupied by 1430 hours on 23 January, Gazelle Force did not get through the gorge until 0530 hours on 24 January. 1 Rajputana Rifles relieved 4 Sikh as the motorised battalion with Gazelle Force. 4 Sikh reverted to the command of the 11th Indian Infantry Brigade. The advance was continued and on 25 January forward elements of Gazelle Force were in contact with the Italians outside Agordat at 1010 hours, and the Barentu-Agordat road was cut at 1415 hours.

Capture of Agordat

On 26 January, the 5th Indian Infantry Brigade, less one battalion (4 Rajputana Rifles) and all its carriers, were concentrated at Sabderat. B Squadron 4th Royal Tank Regiment, which had been placed under the command of the 4th Indian Division, continued to move forward and, by the evening of 26 January, was at Biscia. The 11th Indian Infantry Brigade, which had been joined by 4 Sikh, relieved Gazelle Force in its positions to the west of Agordat. 1 Rajputana Rifles reverted to the command of the 11th Indian Infantry Brigade. On 26 and 27 January, Gazelle Force made reconnaissances with a view to get round Agordat in the south and in the north, but no routes worthy of taking mechanical transport were found owing to the difficult nature of the country. Units of the 11th Indian Infantry Brigade also made reconnaissances to the south-west of Agordat and towards Laquatat.

Agordat was the first town of any size to be captured in Eritrea. It commanded a strong defensive position. To the north and west of it was the Baraka Valley, and to the south a feature known as Laquatat, an isolated rocky feature, with concrete trenches, emplacements and observation posts. East of the Laquatat feature and extending for about two miles was an open plain, intersected by dry stream beds. It was defended by a series of field defences and anti-tank pits. This plain was bounded on the east by Mt. Cochen, a massive hill feature rising some two thousand feet above the plain with a crest nearly two miles long. It was very steep with a certain amount of scrub on it. At the foot of Mt. Cochen towards Laquatat was a low under-feature, a mere pile of rocks hundred feet high, forming a natural flank to the line of artificial defences across the plain. This feature was named "Gibraltar" by the 4th Indian Division. The motor road from Barentu approached Agordat from a direction slightly west of south, and on entering the town turned sharply east and ran through a narrow gorge, north of Mt. Cochen.

It was difficult at this time to know the strength of the Italian garrison at Agordat with accuracy. It was estimated to consist of the *2nd*, the *12th* and the *42nd Colonial Brigades*, three *Black-shirt Battalions*, two Field Artillery Groups, two Medium Artillery Batteries, one Company Medium tanks, one Company Light tanks, three Groups *Bande* troops, and also one German Company. Although the Indian troops had been in contact with the Italians opposite Agordat since 25 January, very little information about their dispositions was available. In the afternoon of 27 January, 4 Sikh was ordered to move forward towards Laquatat and make contact with the Italians. They started at 1600 hours and advanced to within two thousand yards of the feature.

On 28 January, the 5th Indian Infantry Brigade moved up into the front line, when the following dispositions were adopted. On the right was the 11th Indian Infantry Brigade and on the left the 5th Indian Infantry Brigade, with Agordat-Barentu road dividing them. On the left of the 5th Indian Infantry Brigade was Gazelle Force protecting the north flank. 4 Sikh came under the command of the 5th Indian Infantry Brigade. On the evening of 28 January, the 11th Indian Infantry Brigade moved up and at 1810 hours occupied the top of Mt. Cochen without opposition. At 0315 hours on 29 January, the 5th Indian Infantry Brigade probed further into Italian positions at Laquatat to ascertain their exact strength and locations and to take them, if possible. They were, however, found to be too strong to be captured and so the Indian troops withdrew to their original positions at first light. Later, on 29 January, a further regrouping was carried out and the 5th Indian Infantry Brigade moved east of the Barentu road to a position behind the 11th Indian Infantry Brigade. 2 Camerons and one troop "I" tanks came under the command of the 5th Indian Infantry Brigade. Gazelle Force took over all the area to the north-west of Barentu road and 4 Sikh, remaining in the area of Laquatat, came under the command of Gazelle Force. During the night of 29/30 January efforts were made to capture "Gibraltar" and were successful to the extent that the Indian troops were established on the feature though unable to drive the Italians from it.

During 29 January, the Italians had not reacted in any way to the occupation of the top of Mt. Cochen by the Indian troops. Thereupon, the 11th Indian Infantry Brigade was ordered to advance and to try to cut the Agordat-Keren road. It started at 0530 hours on 30 January and made some progress. It was found that the country around Mt. Cochen was larger than had been anticipated. Strong Italian opposition was met here. As everything had to be manhandled on Mt. Cochen only one company per battalion could be used for porterage. The weather also was hot and trying. In view of these difficulties and also of a threat to the security of forces on the top of Mt. Cochen, which developed later in the day, it was decided to abandon the attempt to cut the road and to consolidate British position on the top of Mt. Cochen and features just forward of it. The Italians continued pressing British forces on Mt. Cochen and hard fighting went on throughout the day. In the afternoon Italian pressure increased as they had managed to get some pack-guns into positions overlooking some of the Indian forward troops. This made those positions untenable and a reorganisation became necessary. As the Indian forces had grown tired on account of continuous fighting in the steep hills it was decided to hold only the top of Mt. Cochen and to withdraw troops forward of it under cover of darkness and let them rest for a little time. After a short rest these troops were to go up and reinforce positions on the top by dawn, and also hold the ground necessary for covering the approaches. This was carried out during the night of 30/31 January. Both 1 Rajputana Rifles and 3/14 Punjab were withdrawn, and the covering positions were held during the night by 4 Field Company and A Company 1 Rajputana Rifles, all under the control of the Commander 4 Field Company.

On 30 January, fighting on "Gibraltar" continued. Indian troops were shelled and sniped during the day. At 0520 hours on 31 January, the 5th Indian Infantry Brigade with "I" tanks in support carried out an attack on "Gibraltar" and the Italian positions on the plain between Cochen and Laquatat. The positions on the plain were captured except those on the left, where machine gun fire from Laquatat direction held up the advance of the Indian troops and those positions could not be occupied until 1200 hours.

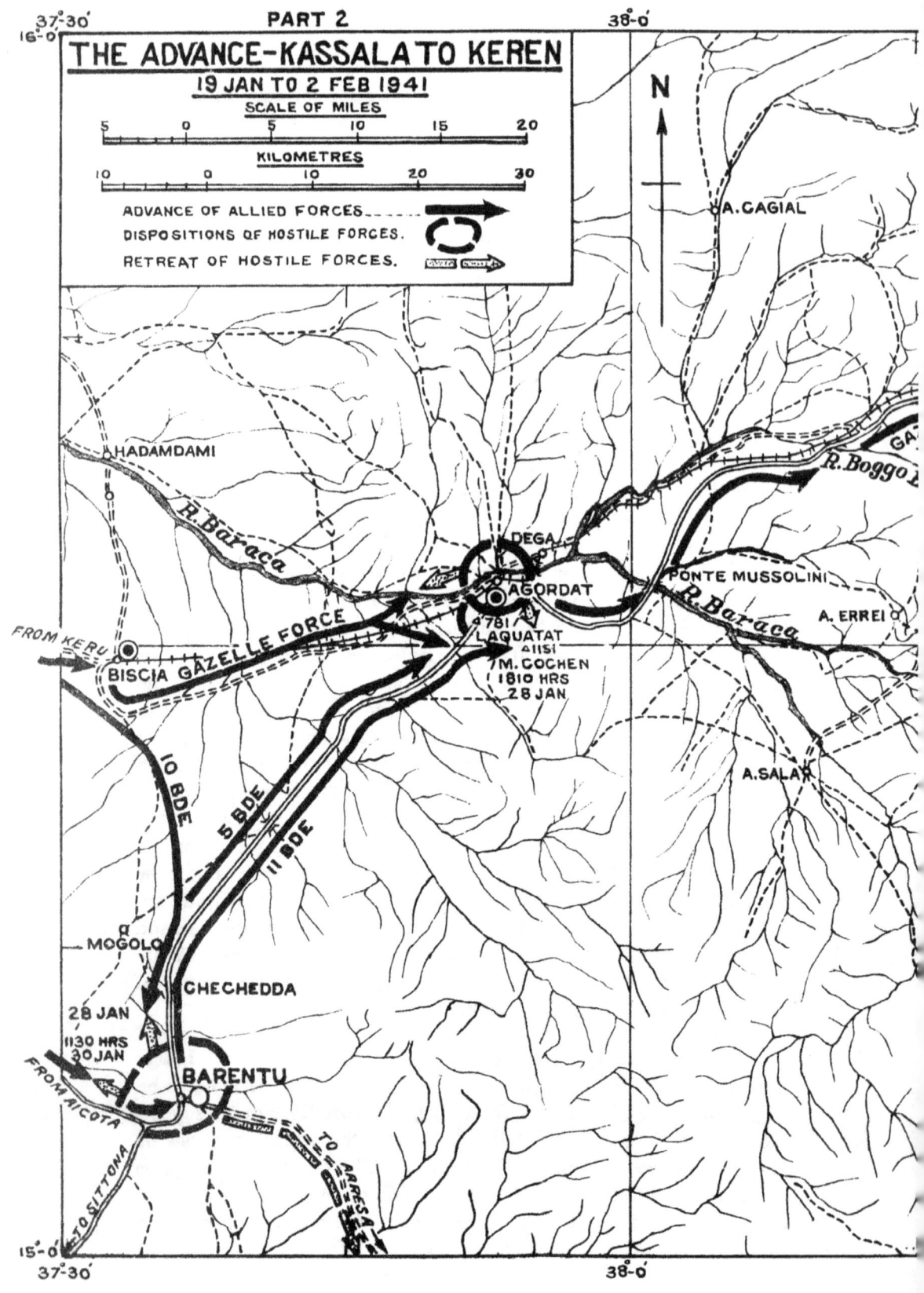

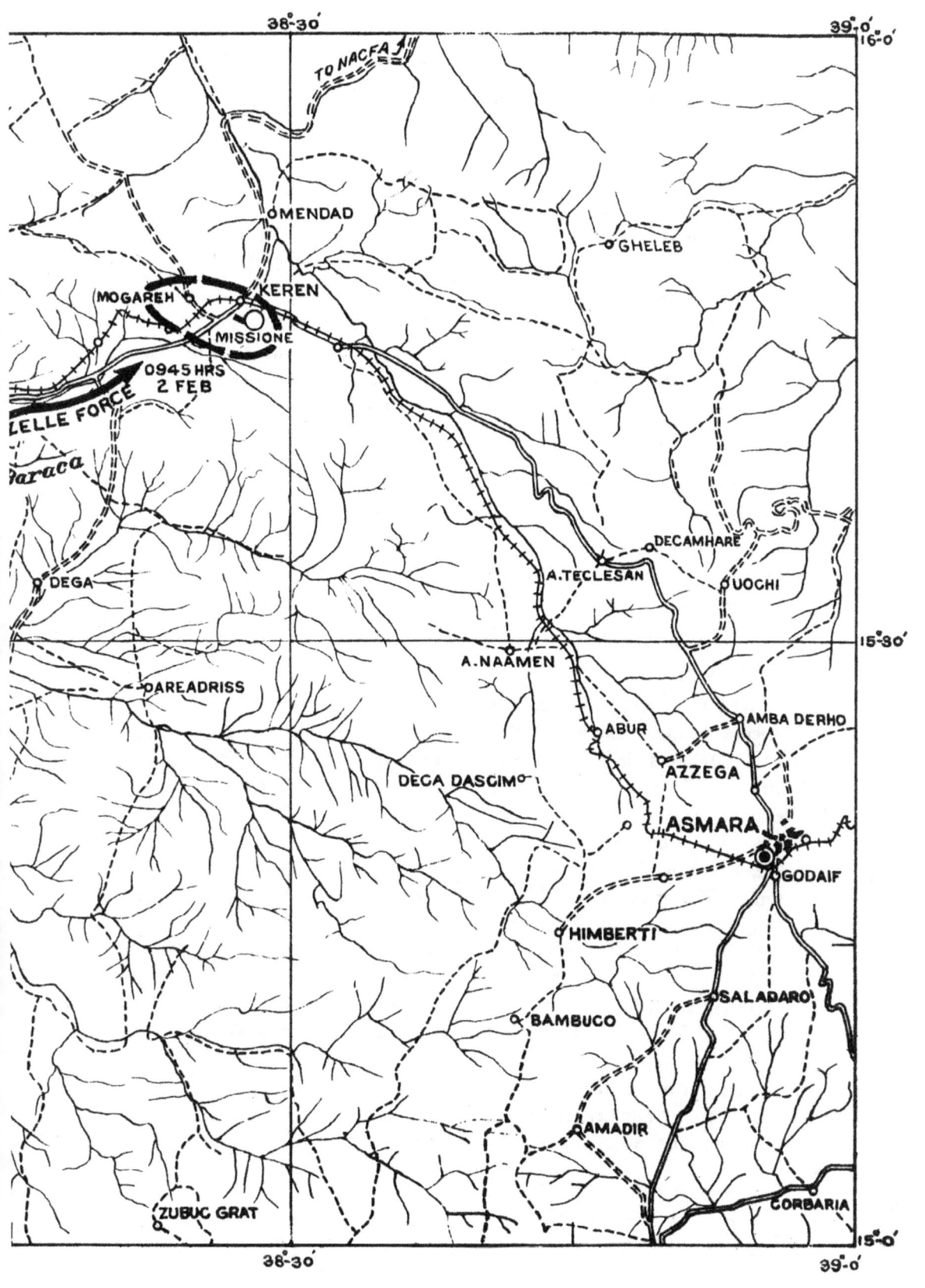

By this time reports were received that the Italian forces were moving eastwards along the Keren road. A column of three tanks and seven carriers was sent in to exploit on the road. In moving towards the road this force met hostile tanks which were probably concentrated for a counter-attack. However, they were engaged by "I" tanks and eleven of them were destroyed. The exploitation towards the road was carried out with great success.

After the capture of positions on the plain between Cochen and Laquatat, the 5th Indian Infantry Brigade advanced at 1245 hours and cut the Keren road to the east of Agordat. The Italian resistance was now crumbling and by 1630 hours another battalion had been put across the road. At 1630 hours the Italian forces hurriedly started evacuating the Laquatat position and retired through Agordat along the northern track following the railway line. On Mt. Cochen practically no Italian opposition was encountered on 31 January.

On 1 February at 0530 hours, Gazelle Force, which had been kept in readiness, took up the advance east of Agordat along the Keren road. Agordat was occupied without opposition at 0700 hours.

Aicota to Barentu

In the south, the 29th Indian Infantry Brigade, moving from Aicota towards Barentu, advanced against some opposition until, at 1200 hours on 24 January, it came up against the Italians in strong defensive positions in the area of Gogni, twenty-five miles east of Aicota. This position was held by three battalions (*16th Colonial Brigade*). On 26 January at 0510 hours the 29th Indian Infantry Brigade organised an attack on it, but with partial success only. The ground gained was, however, lost when the Italians counter-attacked at 0830 hours. Hard fighting continued during the day but, by the evening, Indian troops had captured most of their objectives. The hills overlooking Gogni from the west were occupied by 1030 hours on 27 January but fighting continued in the hills to the east. These were not occupied until 0800 hours on 29 January after the Italians had withdrawn during the night. The advance then continued, with some delays caused by demolitions and mines. Further contact was not made until 1130 hours the next day on the last ridge west of Barentu.

Capture of Barentu

Having been relieved on the north road in the area east of Keru by the 4th Indian Division troops, the 10th Indian Infantry

Brigade advanced south on Barentu. By midday on 27 January it had pushed the Italians to within seven miles of Barentu. Continuing the advance on 28 January it captured the hills overlooking Barentu from the north, on the west of the road. The Italians had carried out very effective demolitions on the road in the gorge immediately to the north of Barentu by blowing hundreds of tons of rock, and this held up the advance. Features to the east of the Agordat road were still strongly held by the Italians. Efforts were therefore, made to get round the eastern flank but the track was poor and mechanical transport could move with difficulty. In the evening of 29 January 2 Motor Machine Gun Group, after having managed to get through round the east flank, met with strong opposition from the Italians west of Barentu and had to withdraw northeast into the hills. On 29 January, the Italians counter-attacked the 10th Indian Infantry Brigade troops on the hills overlooking Barentu from the north on two occasions. Both attacks were however repulsed.

By the evening of 29 January the 29th Indian Infantry Brigade was advancing from the west towards the last ridges before Barentu. On 30 January at 1130 hours, Indian troops made contact with the Italians holding the last ridge west of Barentu, but the advance was held up for a time and the ridge was not occupied until the afternoon. At 1030 hours on 31 January, the Italians counter-attacked with tanks and infantry. Severe casualties were inflicted on their infantry and the tanks withdrew. By 1830 hours Indian troops had got astride Om Ager-Barentu road and also occupied the ridge running north-west from the road junction.

On 1 February, although the Italians appeared to be withdrawing along the Barentu-Tole-Arresa track, their rearguard in Barentu continued to fight stubbornly and all efforts to overcome them were unsuccessful. They finally evacuated Barentu on the night of 1/2 February and the 10th and the 29th Indian Infantry Brigades occupied the town early on the morning of 2 February. 2 Motor Machine Gun Group assisted by the Royal Air Force took up the pursuit of the Italians, and inflicted casualties on them all along the route.

Capture of Om Ager

British Intelligence had reported as early as 13 January that the Italians were thinning out in the area of Om Ager. Mobile columns to carry out the pursuit were formed and aggressive patrolling was carried out but the Italians held on until 25 January. On the night of 25/26 January the Italians broke contact and got away

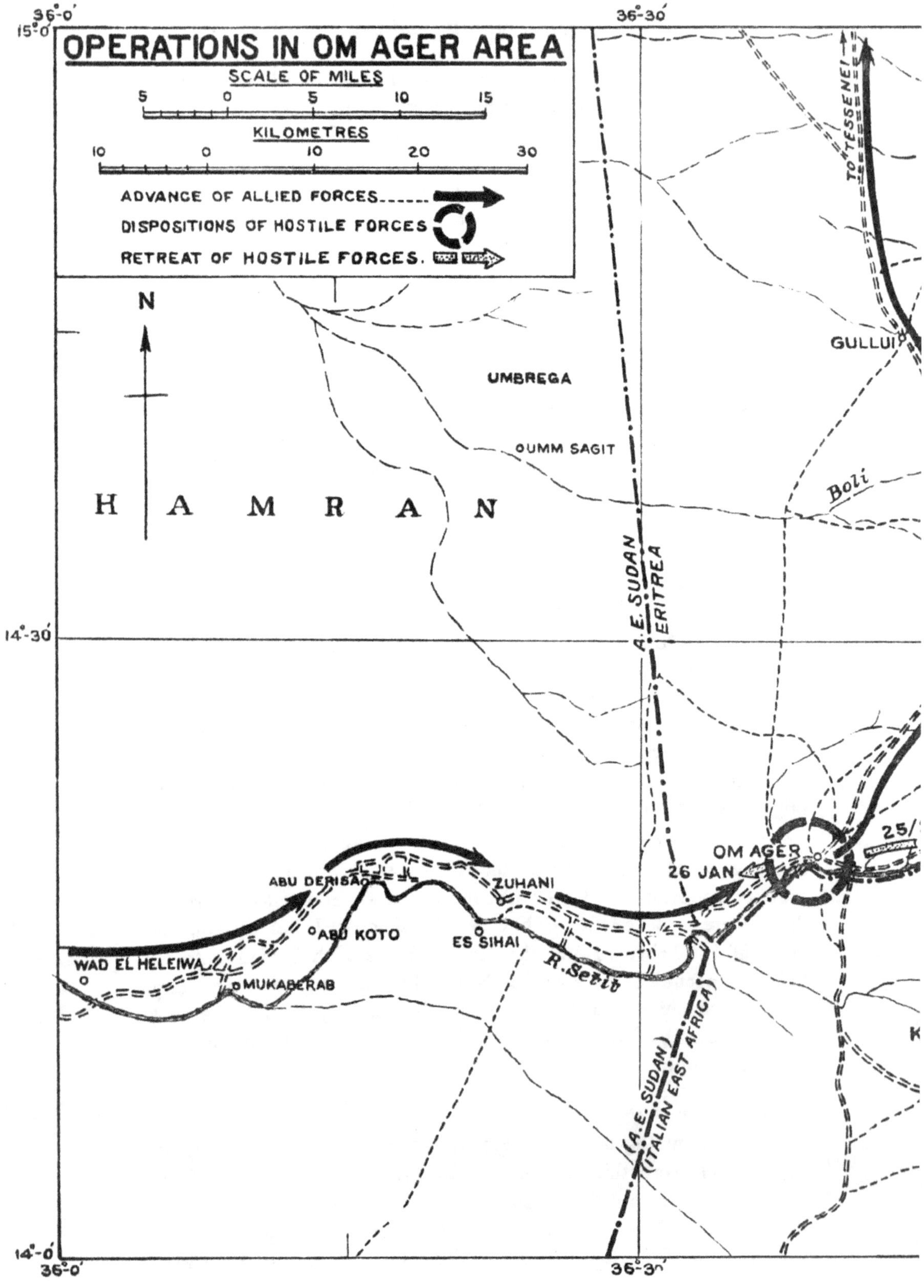

OPERATIONS IN OM AGER AREA
SCALE OF MILES
5 0 5 10 15
KILOMETRES
10 0 10 20 30
ADVANCE OF ALLIED FORCES
DISPOSITIONS OF HOSTILE FORCES
RETREAT OF HOSTILE FORCES.
N
HAMRAN
UMBREGA
OUMM SAGIT
A.E. SUDAN
ERITREA
TO TESSENEI
GULLUI
Boli
OM AGER
26 JAN
ABU DERIBA
ZUHANI
ABU KOTO
ES SIHAI
WAD EL HELEIWA
MUKABERAB
R. Setit
(A.E. SUDAN)
(ITALIAN EAST AFRICA)
36°0'
36°30'
15°0'
14°30'
14°0'

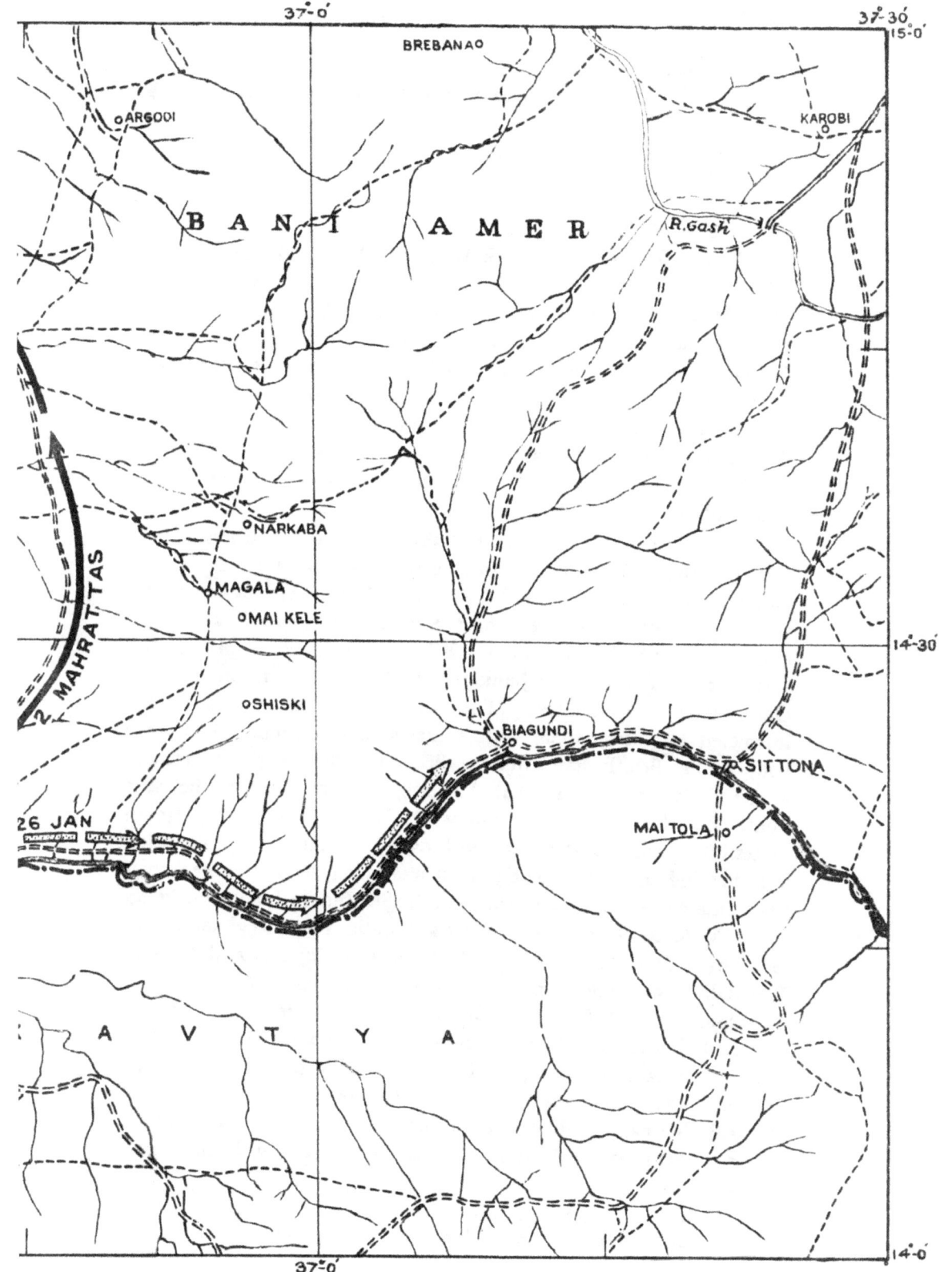

towards Biagundi. On 26 January Indian troops advanced and occupied Om Ager, but no contact was established with the Italian troops. After a few days 2 Mahratta moved to Tessenei from this sector, and was thence ordered to Aicota. It came under the command of the 4th Indian Division on 6 February.

Capture of Gallabat

At the frontier post of Gallabat the Italian forces were contained by the 9th Indian Infantry Brigade. In Eritrea the pursuit of the Italians had been so successful that it had been decided to make this the main thrust and to do no more than watch the Gedaref-Gallabat-Gondar route with a minimum force. Orders were, therefore, issued cancelling the work already done on the extension of the Sudan railway from Gedaref towards Gallabat. The railway from Kassala, on the other hand, was to be extended as quickly as possible as far as Tessenei. This work was given priority over all other railway work in the Sudan.

First indications that the Italians intended to withdraw from Gallabat came from British Intelligence sources early in January and it appeared that this withdrawal would be co-ordinated with the withdrawal from Om Ager and the Kassala-Sabderat-Tessenei triangle. The 9th Indian Infantry Brigade continued to patrol actively. It was not until 30 January that the Italian withdrawal from Gallabat became imminent. The 9th Indian Infantry Brigade was instructed to pursue them with a mechanised column. The main body of the 9th Indian Infantry Brigade was ordered to remain in the Metemma area so that they might be switched to the main front. On the night of 31 January/1 February the Italian troops successfully broke contact and got away without any molestation from the Indian forces. The pursuit was taken up by the mechanised column consisting of the carriers of the 9th Indian Infantry Brigade and a Motorised Company of 3 Royal Frontier Force Regiment, preceded by a detachment of 21 Field Company, Sappers and Miners. The Italian withdrawal on this front was much less hurried than on the 4th and the 5th Indian Divisional lines of advance as the Italians had made lavish use of mines on the road, and movement off the road was impossible owing to Khors and thick bushes. It was in clearing these mines that Second-Lieutenant P. Singh Bhagat of 21 Field Company, Sappers and Miners, earned his Victoria Cross for his courage and gallantry[2]. Contact was made with an Italian

---

[2] Lt. Bhagat and his men were given the difficult task of clearing the road full of minefields and booby traps. He worked forty-eight hours non-stop and exposed

(Contd. on Page 49)

force at Wahni, forty-eight miles east of Gallabat, on 6 February, but it withdrew towards Chelga. The advance was now merely a matter of clearing mines. By 10 February contact was made with the Ethiopian Patriots in Wahni. The 9th Indian Infantry Brigade, less one battalion (3/12 Frontier Force Regiment) and one section Field Company, concentrated at Gedaref on 11 February and then moved to Sabderat concentrating there in the first week of March.

Thus Keru, Agordat, Barentu, Om Ager and Gallabat were occupied by Indian troops. In a short time the Indian divisions had wrested the initiative from the Italians who were now retreating towards Keren and Gondar. This encouraged the Middle East command to assume an aggressive attitude. From a defensive role the British now turned to an offensive one. General Wavell who had at first thought of going no further than Kassala and occupying a small part of Eritrea now reviewed British strategy in a broader perspective. He favoured a large-scale operation into Eritrea with the object of capturing Asmara. This, he knew, would prevent him from sending reinforcements from the Sudan to Egypt. But operations were going on well in the Western Desert (Egypt) and he anticipated no immediate need of additional forces in Egypt. He therefore instructed General Platt "to continue his pursuit and to press on towards Asmara". He also approved of General Platt's proposal to use some Free French troops who were then arriving at Port Sudan together with the British and the Indian troops already there to advance along the Red Sea coast and into the hills towards Asmara.[3] So on to Keren and Asmara the Indian forces went.

(*From Page 48*)

himself to great danger. "Twice his carrier was blown up and many of his men killed. Despite this he carried on, finally collapsing from exhaustion and shock and with both eardrums damaged by explosions. He had cleared 15 minefields and 55 miles of road". *The Victoria Cross, India's V. C.s in two World Wars*, p. 2.

[3]Wavell's Despatch on Operations in East Africa, November 1940 to July 1941, para. 12.

CHAPTER V

The First Assault on Keren

Agordat was occupied without opposition by the 5th Indian Infantry Brigade at 0700 hours on 1 February. All Italian troops had been withdrawn from the town and about 50 lorries were captured intact. About 300 prisoners were taken during the day and more were coming in. The day was spent mostly in reorganisation. Advanced Brigade Headquarters moved up to the main Agordat-Keren road, approximately 3 miles from the town, during the morning. The 5th Indian Infantry Brigade moved into Agordat and cleared up the area north and north-east of the town. The 11th Indian Infantry Brigade reorganised in the area of "Gibraltar", a prominent sub-feature of Cochen.

Immediately after the battle of Agordat, Gazelle Force was directed to follow up the Italians retreating towards Keren. But owing to the demolition of Ponte Mussolini, it was held up until 1700 hours. The main girders of the bridge at Ponte Mussolini had been blown and it was impossible to get mechanical transport over it. The Baraka at this point was 150 yards wide, and at that time was merely a strip of soft deep sand over which vehicles could not pass without some form of temporary track. But construction of such a track was made difficult by the large number of mines which the Italians had laid around all the approaches to the bridge, and along the only alternative route. The Italians had also covered this demolition and minefield by a pack-gun and a few machine guns. However accurate shooting by a section of field artillery succeeded in knocking these out quickly, and by the evening of 2 February, Gazelle Force with "I" tanks and the 11th Indian Infantry Brigade were only five miles from Keren. Here their advance was held up by a strong Italian position with a road block in the gorge.

Topography

The town of Keren stood over 4,300 feet above the sea level and all approaches to it from the north, west and south lay through the surrounding mountainous country. The road from Agordat which was being used by the Indian forces for the pursuit, gradually rose in north-easterly direction up the narrow Ascidira valley towards a formidable range of hills which guarded the plateau on which the town of Keren was situated. This range extended in an arc to the south-east and north-west. As the main road reached the lower features, it swung to the east into the more open Bogu valley and for six kilometres ran across the front of the range. The road then turned north and entered a narrow cleft known as the Dongolaas Gorge, which was nowhere more than 300 yards wide. Along the east wall of this gorge the road climbed up to the Keren plateau. The railway left the road soon after passing the Agat station, swung north-east up the Aroba valley, then turned south-east and followed the 1,200 metre contour of the main range before entering the Dongolaas Gorge, along the west wall of which it went up to the Keren plateau.

To the east of the gorge rose Mt. Dologorodoc with its fort, 800 yards from the bottom, at the summit. The road clung to the lower slopes of this hill, and it was here that it had been blocked by blowing the hill on to it for over two hundred yards. Beyond Dologorodoc rose the two massifs of Falestoh and Zeban, 2,000 yards to the east and north-east. Further to the east was the sharp peak of Zelale, another 3,000 yards from Falestoh, known as Sphinx. Between Falestoh and Sphinx was a low neck of ground by which a subsidiary track crossed the hills to reach Keren via Catholic Mission. This lower feature, known as Acqua Gap, was to be the scene of considerable fighting. It was approached by a series of jumbled ridges, and the final ascent, though not long, was exceedingly steep. Beyond Zelale, to the east, the Bogu valley closed again and disappeared into the impassable mountainous country.

To the west of the gorge the country was even more formidable. Rising from the gorge, 930 feet higher than Fort Dologorodoc to the east, was the vast bulk of Mt. Sanchil with Pt. 1616 (Cameron Ridge) as its offshoot to the south. From Sanchil the range extended north-west to Mt. Samanna and thence to Beit Gabru. Mt. Amba covering the Mogareh valley lay north-east of the main range. Although Mt. Samanna lay on the line of the main range, it actually formed an entirely separate feature completely cut off from the other hills round it by deep ravines. Between Sanchil and Samanna along the ridge was a series of features which were all to receive local names: Brig's Peak, Saddle, Hog's Back, Flat Top, Mole Hill. Most famous was Brig's Peak, for whose capture a number of attempts had to be made.

Italian Forces

The strategic importance of the Keren position for the defence of Asmara and the Eritrean highlands had been appreciated by

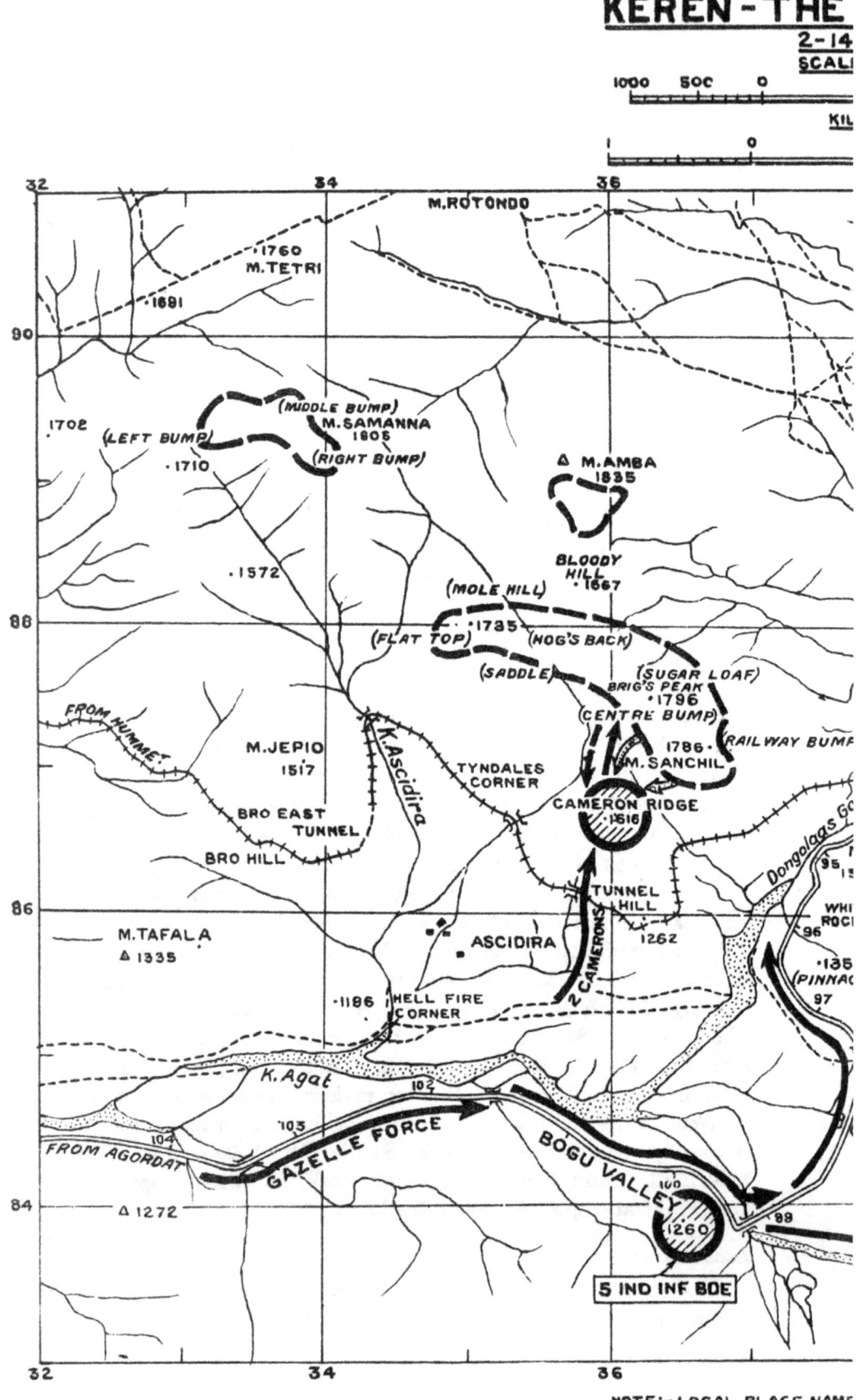

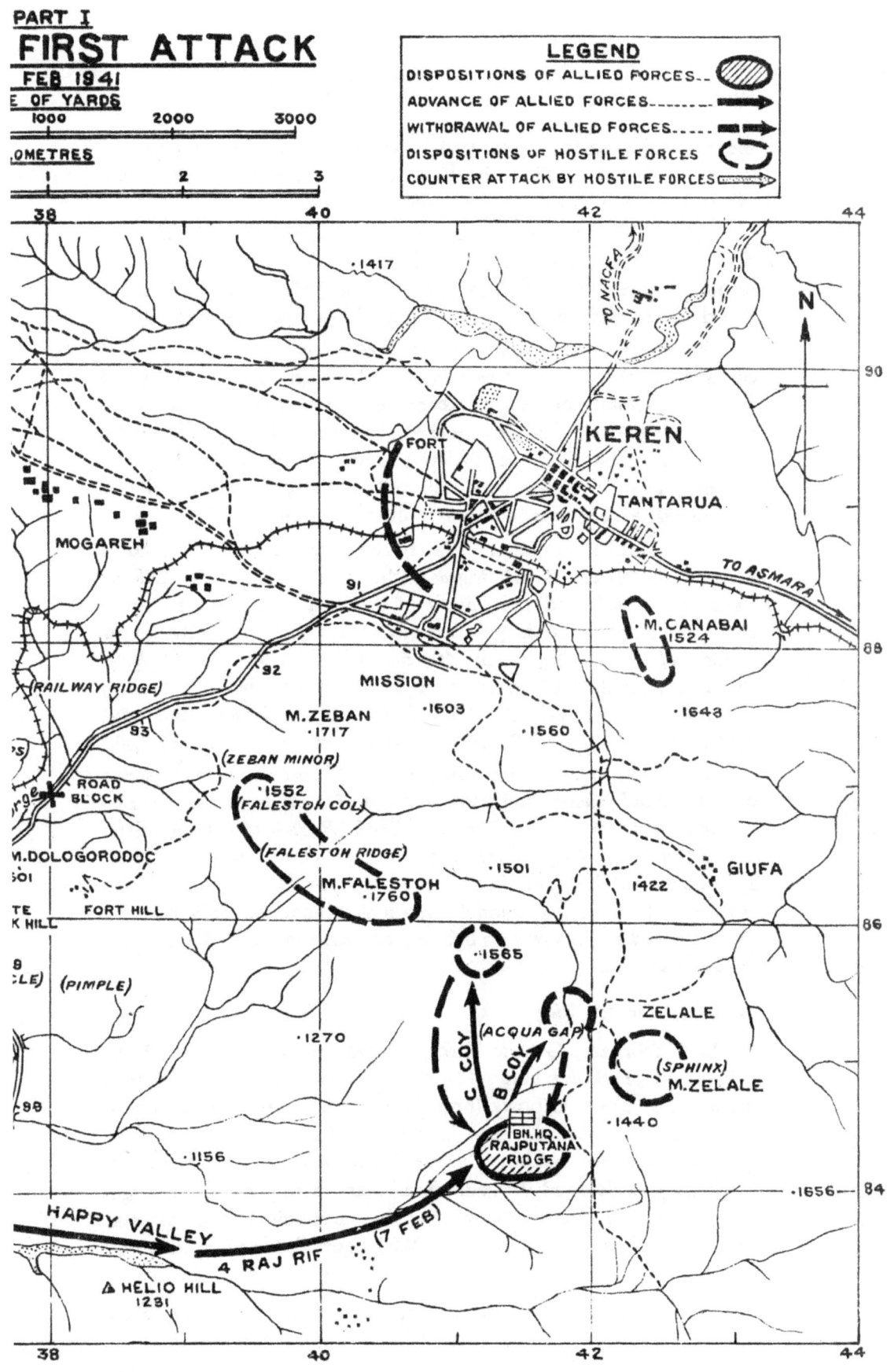

the Italians for many years, and it was here that General Frusci[1] had decided to make his main stand and to concentrate the bulk of his forces, which at this time were as follows:—

The *11th Colonial Brigade* consisting of the *5th, 52nd, 56th* and *63rd Colonial Battalions* fresh from Addis Ababa, had reached Keren on foot towards the end of January together with some artillery, believed to be chiefly 65-mm and 77-mm with a few 105-mm guns.

The whole of the *11th Grenadier Regiment* of the *Savoy Division* consisting of the *1st* and *2nd Grenadier Battalions* and the *Bersaglieri Battalion*, actually arrived in Keren on 1 February having been rushed up in three days in mechanical transport from Addis Ababa and one other battalion was believed to have accompanied it. The regiment was, according to a captured officer, complete except for the anti-tank section which was still at Metemma.

Of the Italian formations which had been present at Agordat, most of the *42nd Colonial Brigade* (the *35th, 101st, 111th Colonial Battalions*), which had been north of the Baraka and had not been involved in the fighting, got through to Keren intact. Remnants of the *2nd Colonial Brigade* (the *4th, 5th, 9th, 10th* and *151st Colonial Battalions*), much depleted in strength except for the *4th Colonial Battalion*, also got through. The *12th Colonial Brigade* (the *36th, 43rd* and *100th Colonial Battalion*) moved back to Asmara to refit.

In addition to the above forces, General Frusci had arranged for the *1st Colonial Division* from the Red Sea Coastal Sector to be concentrated south of Nacfa. The *5th Colonial Brigade* consisting of the *97th, 106th* and *Tipo Battalions* was also now converging on Keren. This made a total of three Italian and four *Colonial* battalions which were entirely fresh, six *Colonial* battalions which had only been slightly involved in the previous fighting, and the remnants of four other *Colonial* battalions.

Capture of Cameron Ridge

On 2 February, Gazelle Force, advancing in pursuit of the Italian forces, had been held up by the road block south-west of Keren, and all its attempts to break through this block with tanks and anti-tank artillery had failed. The 11th Indian Infantry Brigade moved up from Agordat behind Gazelle Force and, at 1000 hours on 2 February, Advanced Brigade Headquarters arrived in the Agat station area. 2 Camerons moving in mechanical transport also reached the Agat village at about 1200 hours followed by the 31st

---

[1] The Italian Commander responsible for opposing British advance into Eritrea.

Field Regiment, which arrived at 1800 hours, and the 4 Field Company shortly after. The mechanical transport used by 2 Camerons was sent back to lift 1 Rajputana Rifles which arrived later in the evening. 3/14 Punjab marched up from Agordat, spent the night on the way and reached the area west of Keren the next day, relieving 1 Horse in the plain. Thus was the 11th Indian Infantry Brigade concentrated in the Agat station area by 3 February.

After reconnaissance the Commander of the 11th Indian Infantry Brigade made a plan for an attack on Cameron Ridge.[2] 2 Camerons was to attack at 1400 hours on 3 February and capture the tunnel shoulder - a spur running from the railway tunnel near Pt. 1262 towards Pt. 1616. 1 Rajputana Rifles was to secure the gap south of Mt. Scialaco and reconnoitre with a view to finding a route round the southern flank of the Italian position. The 31 Field Regiment with a detachment of 4 Field Company RIE was placed under its command and the battalion was told to continue the operations the next day. Two "I" tanks from B Squadron 4th Royal Tank Regiment were ordered to try a break-through the road block.

Starting their attack at 1400 hours on 3 February, supported by 233 Medium Battery (6-inch howitzers), 390 Field Battery (25-pounders) and A Troop Sudan Regiment (3·7- inch howitzers), 2 Camerons reached the railway without opposition by 1500 hours. The ground was very bad and progress was slow but by 1650 hours the top of the shoulder had been captured.

1 Rajputana Rifles reported at midday on 4 February that the track round the south of Mt. Scialaco had been found impassable. The battalion was accordingly ordered to withdraw. It concentrated in the area of the road at kilometres 109-110 in the evening.

In view of the failure of the attempt to outflank the Italian positions from the south the Commander of the 11th Indian Infantry Brigade decided to capture Brig's Peak and Mt. Sanchil, the hills above the features held by 2 Camerons (Cameron Ridge) and overlooking Keren. 3/14 Punjab was detailed for this, and reconnaissances for the attack were made at 1200 hours on 4 February. 2 Camerons continued extending and consolidating its position and by 1430 hours on 4 February had captured Pt. 1616, the top of the Cameron Ridge.

[2]Brigadier R.A. Savory DSO, MC was the Commander of this brigade from March 1940 to September 1941.

Failure of the Attack on Brig's Peak

The attack by 3/14 Punjab on Brig's Peak and Sanchil was to be supported by the 31 Field Regiment. As the battalion, like all the other troops, was organised on a mechanical transport basis and the attack had to go up steep hills, one company of the battalion was employed entirely for porterage. The attack was to be carried out by B Company on Brig's Peak and, later by D Company on Sanchil. C Company was detailed for porterage and A Company, in reserve, was to move up as far as the railway line.

Cameron Ridge was completely dominated by Brig's Peak and 2 Camerons had asked permission to occupy the latter. At 1530 hours on 4 February, some *Colonial* troops were seen debussing near the road beyond the gorge. One platoon 2 Camerons was therefore sent forward at once to occupy Brig's Peak. No resistance was met until the platoon got to within 300 yards of the top, when the *Colonial* troops were seen to arrive on the far side. It was now getting dark. A scuffle ensued and the platoon, faced by superior numbers, was forced to withdraw to its starting point.

3/14 Punjab started moving at 1930 hours on 4 February and by 2115 hours had reached the forward positions of 2 Camerons. From there B Company began the advance on Brig's Peak at 2300 hours and the hill was secured by 0345 hours on 5 February. One platoon from A Company was sent forward to reinforce B Company on Brig's Peak. Advanced Battalion Headquarters and D Company also moved forward to the area of Brig's Peak, where they arrived at 0515 hours.

Brig's Peak consisted of three peaks. The right-hand peak was a pinnacle of rock on which it was possible to find room for one section only. The central peak, divided from the right peak by a col about 30 yards wide, was about 100 yards long and 50 yards wide. The third peak was almost the same, dropping down steeply at its northern end. There was room for only four platoons on the whole feature. The position appeared very strong and the commander of B Company was confident of being able to hold it against any Italian counter-attack.

The distance from Cameron Ridge to Brig's Peak was about a thousand yards as the crow flies. Brigade Signals and the artillery Forward Observation Officer did not have enough cable to establish line communication forward of Cameron Ridge. In any case the Forward Observation Officer, on Cameron Ridge, was not through to the guns. In the early hours of the morning 3/14 Punjab passed their messages by visual signal to the Forward Observation Officer on Cameron Ridge. He then passed his fire orders over the brigade lines to the guns.

After the reconnaissance in daylight, the attack from Brig's Peak on Mt. Sanchil by D Company was planned and artillery support arranged. The attack, excellently supported by the artillery, started at 0700 hours on 5 February. By 0830 hours a part of Mt. Sanchil was secured but the Indian troops could not clear the feature completely. The Officer Commanding 3/14 Punjab ordered A Company (less one platoon) to move from Cameron Ridge to Mt. Sanchil at once. By this time, the Italians had started shelling and mortaring the forward troops on Brig's Peak, Sanchil and Cameron Ridge. Their machine guns fired accurately on these features as well as on the ground between Cameron Ridge and Brig's Peak and Sanchil. A Company therefore could not get across from Cameron Ridge to reinforce Sanchil. At 0845 hours, the Forward Observation Officer and his party were either killed or wounded in the shelling on Cameron Ridge. No artillery support for 3/14 Punjab was therefore forthcoming. The Brigade Signal Officer and 3/14 Punjab Signal Officer were both wounded and communications broke down completely.

By 1030 hours, D Company on Sanchil had suffered heavy casualties and was running short of ammunition. Battalion Headquarters was no longer in communication with Cameron Ridge. No movement forward of Cameron Ridge was possible. Efforts to get in touch by a runner and liaison officer were unsuccessful. Thus cut off, the Officer Commanding 3/14 Punjab collected what small arms and ammunition he could, to be sent up to D Company. However, D Company had, in the meantime, been forced off Sanchil. Only one platoon from D Company had managed to join B Company on Brig's Peak. The other two platoons, being prevented by machine-gun fire from moving towards Brig's Peak, had been forced down another nullah and moved to the bottom of the hill.

At 1000 hours 1 Rajputana Rifles was ordered to move up the hill in support of 3/14 Punjab. 2 Camerons was also told to give such support to 3/14 Punjab as it could.

At 1045 hours, the Brigade Headquarters received a message from 2 Camerons to the effect that 3/14 Punjab had been seen withdrawing from Brig's Peak. At 1100 hours, some men of 3/14 Punjab were reported to be already at the bottom of the hill. 1 Rajputana Rifles also reported that two platoons of 3/14 Punjab had reached the plain already. The orders for 1 Rajputana Rifles were therefore changed. It was told to hold the high ground on the left of 2 Camerons. At that time the Brigade Headquarters was not in communication with 3/14 Punjab.

At 1100 hours, on 5 February, Brig's Peak was still being held by the four platoons of 3/14 Punjab, who had suffered heavy casualties during the morning. Communications with Cameron Ridge had been cut off and the Brig's Peak garrison was isolated. In spite of these difficulties, the Commander felt that there was no need to abandon the position before the arrival of relief. At about 1230 hours, the Italians attacked Brig's Peak supported by accurate mortar and machine-gun fire. At 1345 hours, they actually reached the top of the hill and had to be driven off by a bayonet charge. As there was little hope of relief, 3/14 Punjab withdrew from Brig's Peak at 1400 hours. It had suffered heavy casualties and was disorganised. It was ordered to collect and reorganise at the bottom of the hill where it had once again assembled by the evening. Its total casualties were 116—11 killed, 96 wounded and 9 missing.[3]

By 1500 hours, 1 Rajputana Rifles was in position to the west of the Camerons. The Commander of the 11th Indian Infantry Brigade had asked for another battalion to be placed under command. 3/1 Punjab was accordingly moved from Agordat and arrived in the area of kilometres 109-110 by 1715 hours. The situation at nightfall on 5 February was that 2 Camerons and 1 Rajputana Rifles were in position on Cameron Ridge, 3/14 Punjab was collected at the bottom of the hill and 3/1 Punjab was concentrated in the area of kilometres 109-110.

Italian Counter-attacks

6 February was a day of counter-attacks by the Italians. They carried out no less than five separate counter-attacks on the two forward battalions. The first of these took place between 0900 hours and 1000 hours on both 2 Camerons and 1 Rajputana Rifles. It was easily repulsed. There were reports of the *Colonial* troops trying to outflank 1 Rajputana Rifles from the west. Gazelle Force was, therefore, ordered to occupy Mt. Tafala and Mt. Jepio.

At 1200 hours the Italians counter-attacked 1 Rajputana Rifles again. This attack was repulsed, heavy casualties being inflicted. The Italians kept up continuous artillery and machine-gun fire, and C Company 1 Rajputana Rifles, which was in an exposed position to the west of Cameron Ridge, suffered many casualties; the strength of the Company falling to almost half by the evening.

---

[3] War Diary 3/14 Punjab.

One of the fine thoroughfares in Asmara

Lt.-Gen. Sir William Platt inspects guard of honour
at the Governor's Palace at Asmara

Sappers and Miners of the Indian Army clearing
a road block between Asmara and Massawa

The signpost showing Massawa

Men of the 4/10 Baluch march into Asmara

Indian troops manning an A.A. post at Tessenei

A view of the deserted Laquatat Fortress near Agordat

Captured Italian war material at Agordat

3/1 Punjab was therefore moved forward to the railway line below 1 Rajputana Rifles, reaching there at 1300 hours.

The next counter-attack started at 1530 hours, again on 1 Rajputana Rifles. It was repulsed and was over by 1730 hours. At 1630 hours 3/1 Punjab moved up in support of 1 Rajputana Rifles for repulsing the attack. D Company moved into line while the other companies were in reserve. At 1930 hours the Italians counter-attacked C Company 1 Rajputana Rifles again. Although the company's strength had been greatly reduced it beat off the attack with great gallantry. It was in this engagement that Lance Naik Bhaira Ram of the Rajputana Rifles distinguished himself. He was in command of a platoon reduced in strength to seven men. When the Italians launched a fierce counter-attack its brunt was borne by his two small platoon posts. A platoon of D Company 3/1 Punjab located in his immediate vicinity was forced to withdraw. Not daunted by this, Bhaira Ram continued to defend his post with the utmost vigour, knowing full well that if the Italians penetrated his position, the safety of the entire battalion would be endangered. Not only did he repulse this attack, but with his remaining two men he also chased the retiring Italians with the bayonet. When all was over 11 Italian soldiers lay dead just outside his post and many more on the hillside.

The last Italian counter-attack came at 2330 hours and was mainly directed against D Company 3/1 Punjab. C Company 3/1 Punjab had to be sent up in support of D Company before it was finally repelled.

Thus the Italians had opposed the advance of the Indian forces stoutly. Indian troops had reached Sanchil and Brig's Peak but lost them. They still held Cameron Ridge and some other features. Keren, however, stood defiant and impregnable, presenting a challenge to British strength and strategy.

The Decision to Fight at Keren

The storming of the Keren position was no light task. Its natural strength, the difficulties of maintenance and climatic conditions were powerful deterrents. Every day the temperature was rising. The Italians were numerically superior and had chosen Keren for a trial of strength. The battle here could well be a decisive one. They had every advantage of observation and possessed a strong and active air force. There was little chance of gaining a surprise here. The forcing of Keren was bound to mean hard fighting and losses were difficult to replace. Under these circumstances the desirability of finding a way round was obvious. From almost the day of the first contact at Keren continuous and wide reconnaissances were made to the north-west, south and south-east, to find alternative routes through the escarpment wall. Central India Horse searched south for sixty miles until it made contact with 2 Motor Machine Gun Group which was facing Arresa. At Arresa there was a possible gap, but the route had proved so difficult that the retreating Italians from Barentu had been forced to abandon all their vehicles. No road, capable of maintaining a force strong enough to fight its way through, existed east of Barentu. The time it would have taken to build one would have allowed the Italians to make the Arresa position as formidable as the one at Keren. Rain would have brought mechanical transport, moving between Barentu and Arresa, to a stand still. No way was found to the north either. Therefore, it was clear that Keren was the only practicable approach to the higher levels of the escarpment for a force of any size.

The Regrouping of Forces

The 5th Indian Infantry Brigade, less 4 Sikh, moved from Agordat on 6 February and was concentrated in the area of kilometres 109-110. Plans had been made by the Commander of the 11th Indian Infantry Brigade for another attack to capture Brig's Peak during the day but it was felt that it would be necessary to use 3/1 Punjab also for this operation. Divisional orders had been that 3/1 Punjab was only to be used defensively and only in the event of an emergency. Permission to use 3/1 Punjab in the attack was asked for by the Commander of the 11th Indian Infantry Brigade but was refused. At 1745 hours the Divisional Commander with the Commander of the 5th Indian Infantry Brigade arrived at the headquarters of the 11th Indian Infantry Brigade, and it was decided to place 3/14 Punjab under the command of the 5th Indian Infantry Brigade. The question of 3/1 Punjab being taken out and being reverted to the command of the 5th Indian Infantry Brigade was also considered. In view of the strong Italian pressure the Officer Commanding 1 Rajputana Rifles could not guarantee to hold his position without the help of 3/1 Punjab. The latter was therefore left under the command of the 11th Indian Infantry Brigade. Later, the same evening, it was decided to move 3/14 Punjab to Agordat in view of the losses it had suffered and to replace it by 4 Sikh, which was moved up during the night of 6/7 February and arrived at 0800 hours on 7 February, when it came under the command of the 5th Indian Infantry Brigade.

The First Attack on Acqua Gap

All efforts to break through the Italian lines or even to capture the heights overlooking Keren north of the road had failed so far. Efforts to discover possible routes of advance round the flanks had also been unsuccessful. The main road was very effectively blocked. There was still a possibility of getting into Keren without having to break through the main Italian defences. Between Mounts Falestoh and Zelale was a col named Acqua Gap, over which a secondary track ran from the south-east to Keren. The approaches to Acqua Gap were over very rocky and broken ground. Mounts Falestoh and Zelale overlooked the whole area on both sides. In fact, it was a very strong defensive position. But, as far as was known at the time, Italian forces holding Acqua Gap consisted of two *Colonial* battalions, whose morale was considered to be very low on account of many desertions from them. It was therefore planned to secure Acqua Gap by a surprise attack and then break through and capture Keren. The 5th Indian Infantry Brigade was detailed for this task.

The plan of the 4th Indian Division was to capture the Acqua Gap on the night of 7/8 February. The decision whether to advance on Keren or to cut the Keren-Asmara road after the Acqua Gap had been taken, was left to the discretion of the Commander of the 5th Indian Infantry Brigade. In the event of Acqua Gap not being captured on the night of 7/8 February, the 5th Indian Infantry Brigade, was ordered to withdraw on the night of 8/9 February to divisional reserve and not to persist in the attack. The hope of gaining a surprise was very strong and the low morale of the Italian forces was expected to be of considerable help. The 11th Indian Infantry Brigade was ordered to aid the operation of the 5th Indian Infantry Brigade. On the night of 7/8 February it was asked to harass the Italians with artillery fire. At 0530 hours on the morning of 8 February it was to demonstrate on its own front in order to distract Italian attention from the 5th Indian Infantry Brigade attack. It was also to take advantage of any success gained by the 5th Indian Infantry Brigade. If the Italians withdrew from its front it was to exploit vigorously towards Keren without getting heavily engaged and incurring casualties. It was to be prepared to maintain one battalion there (Keren) and concentrate the rest of its strength as ordered by the 4th Indian Division.

The 5th Indian Infantry Brigade had under its command for this operation 4 Sikh (in place of 3/1 Punjab), one troop B Squadron 4th Royal Tank Regiment, one battery 3·7-inch Howitzers Sudan Regiment, one troop anti-aircraft battery and the 12 Field Company RIE. The operation was to be carried out in three phases[4]:—

In the first phase, the Brigade Group was to start concentrating in the area of Pt. 1260 at 1200 hours on 7 February. In the second phase, 4 Rajputana Rifles was to capture the Acqua Gap. Other units were to move up behind 4 Rajputana Rifles and keep clear of the battle. In the third phase, after the Acqua Gap had been taken, 12 Field Company was to build a road from the foot of the Acqua Gap to over and beyond it. 4 Sikh was to secure the next bound—the high ground about Pt. 1560. After the completion of the third phase, 1st Royal Fusiliers was to advance on the orders of Brigade Headquarters.

Carrying Parties

A porter corps of one company per battalion was formed. It was to carry forward one day's hard ration and 80 water containers per battalion and dump them in an area about one mile south-west of Acqua Gap. It was also to carry wireless sets and other equipment for the use of forces and was to protect the rear areas.

Artillery Group

1 Field Regiment R. A., and one battery 3·7-inch Howitzers Sudan Regiment were to be prepared to support the advance from first light. One Forward Observation Officer was detailed with each infantry battalion. A medium battery was also available if required.

Great care was taken to conceal the move forward. The first phase was completed by 1700 hours on 7 February. No transport had been allowed. All arms, ammunition and equipment had to be manhandled. The weather was hot and the march very exhausting. 4 Rajputana Rifles which was to lead the attack was to capture the Acqua Gap from excluding Mt. Zemale, *i.e.*, Pt. 1704 (Sphinx) on the right to excluding Mt. Falestoh (Pt. 1760) on the left. Pt. 1565 (Sangar), about 800 yards from Mt. Falestoh, was the highest point of the objective. The plan was for D Company, leading the attack, to capture an intermediate objective—a ridge south of, and below, Sangar and north of, and above, the southernmost feature (Rajputana Ridge). The line of advance was via Rajputana Ridge. D Company was to be followed by C Company which was to secure Sangar and the outlying features—the line of advance stretching from the mouth of the gorge to Sangar. B Company was to follow initially the advance of C Company and on the

---

[4]5th Indian Infantry Brigade Operation Order No. 1 dated 7 February 1941.

capture of that Company's objective was to exploit eastwards along the Acqua Gap to the right. Battalion Headquarters was to move in the rear of B Company and to open near the track just below B Company's Headquarters, which was to open on the Acqua Gap itself. A Company following the Battalion Headquarters was to be in reserve.

The advance from the area of Pt. 1260 started at 1800 hours on 7 February. The order of march was according to the successive objectives to be captured, D Company, C Company, B Company, Battalion Headquarters, A Company, followed by 12 Field Company, Sappers and Miners, whose task was to prepare a track over the Acqua Gap as soon as it was captured. By 1930 hours, 4 Rajputana Rifles was at its forming-up place at the foot of the gorge. D Company went straight on to its objective and captured it without opposition. At 2000 hours, C Company advanced towards Pt. 1565 followed by B Company and the rest of the battalion. As these companies were moving from the bottom of the gorge the Italians opened heavy mortar, grenade and machine-gun fire. This caused considerable confusion. Battalion Headquarters opened on a ledge about 400 yards to the right of D Company at about 2200 hours but even then by 0030 hours (8 February) only 3 officers and 16 other ranks of A Company had been rallied, the rest having been dispersed by the heavy mortar, grenade and machine gun fire. The position was not reassuring particularly as D Company was under very heavy machine-gun and mortar fire in an exposed position. The Commanding Officer of 4/6 Rajputana Rifles therefore ordered D Company to move to Battalion Headquarters, whence they could support the forward companies by first light. D. Company got split into two parts en route and therefore did not complete its move until approximately 0530 hours.

Meanwhile C and B Companies too encountered stiff opposition. C Company came under heavy fire when it was about half way to its objective. Subedar Richpal Ram showed exemplary courage in leading the attack. With two platoons he pushed on through heavy mortar, grenade and machine-gun fire and captured Pt. 1565 about midnight at the point of the bayonet. B Company captured its objective at 0430 hours in the teeth of stiff opposition. Both the companies on Acqua Gap and Pt. 1565 had suffered very heavy losses in the fighting. Finally, after stoutly resisting Italian counter-attacks and running short of ammunition, C Company on Pt. 1565, fought its way out of the Italian encirclement. B Company was also driven off the Acqua Gap. The situation at daybreak was that A and D Companies were holding Rajputana Ridge with

Battalion Headquarters in the centre. The remnants of B and C Companies were collected by 1300 hours and placed in reserve.[5]

In conjunction with the 5th Indian Infantry Brigade the 11th Indian Infantry Brigade had planned an attack by one company 3/1 Punjab on Brig's Peak at 0600 hours on 8 February. Its object was to prevent the Italians from withdrawing troops from that front in order to reinforce those opposite the 5th Indian Infantry Brigade. At 0445 hours on 8 February, Headquarters 4th Indian Division informed the 11th Indian Infantry Brigade of the failure of the 5th Indian Infantry Brigade attack to secure Acqua Gap and said that the Divisional Commander did not wish to risk heavy casualties or involve the reserve. In view of this, the Commander of the 11th Indian Infantry Brigade was asked to consider if the attack by the company of 3/1 Punjab on Brig's Peak should be proceeded with. The Brigade Commander, thereupon, decided to cancel the attack.

On the 5th Indian Infantry Brigade front 4 Rajputana Rifles was ordered to hold the positions on Rajputana Ridge and the rest of the brigade was told to defend its areas in the bottom of the valley. Artillery maintained a steady fire throughout the day to neutralise any Italian activity. The 5th Indian Infantry Brigade found itself in a very precarious position in the valley. The whole area and the lines of communication were commanded by Italian positions all around. Although the Italians could not get vehicles through on account of their own road block, if they had shown a little enterprise, even a slight threat to the Indian lines of communication would have proved very embarrassing indeed. Actually, apart from artillery fire and air action, no threat materialised at all.

The surprise attack on Acqua Gap had failed. The Commander of the 5th Indian Infantry Brigade was of the opinion that a frontal attack with the resources available was not feasible. One battalion had already lost heavily. A frontal attack would have involved heavy losses to another battalion. There would not therefore, be two battalions left to exploit. He also thought that it was too late in the day to stage a deliberate attack with any chance of successful exploitation. Therefore he recommended a night withdrawal to the original positions on 8 February. Accordingly the Commander of the 4th Indian Division ordered Gazelle Force to relieve the 5th Indian Infantry Brigade in the Acqua Gap area by 2000 hours on 9 February. The relief was completed within

[5]War Diary 4/6 Rajputana Rifles.

Captured Italian war material at Agordat

Punjabi soldiers in position on a hill-top between Tessenei and Barentu

A Bren-gun Carrier section of the Garhwalis about to move off on reconnaissance somewhere in Eritrea

A panorama of the mountains around Keren

Supplies for troops by mules in the Keren Hills

Supplies for troops in Keren—unloading provisions and stores at the dumps

In the 'dug-out' office of the G. O. C. of an Indian Division at the foot of the Keren Hills

A view of Keren

two hours and the 5th Indian Infantry Brigade moved into the rest area behind Gazelle Force.

The Divisional Plan to break through the Acqua Gap

The Commander of the 4th Indian Division then planned a co-ordinated divisional operation for the capture of Keren. It was to take place in four phases :—

Phase I—It consisted of the capture of Brig's Peak. The 11th Indian Infantry Brigade was to carry out this operation, starting at 1500 hours on 10 February.

Phase II—This was aimed at the capture of the Acqua Gap. Gazelle Force with 4/6 Rajputana Rifles and 4 Sikh under command was to accomplish this object on 11 February. The following artillery was to support Gazelle Force :—

> 1 Field Regiment,
> One Battery 25 Field Regiment,
> One Troop Medium Artillery (eight 6-inch howitzers),
> One Troop Sudan Regiment (four 3·7-inch howitzers).

Phase III—In this phase the 5th Indian Infantry Brigade was to exploit towards Keren. 4 Sikh and 4 Rajputana Rifles were to be released after the capture of the Acqua Gap in Phase II. They were to revert to the command of the 5th Indian Infantry Brigade for exploitation towards Keren.

2 Mahratta[6] was ordered to come under the command of the 5th Indian Infantry Brigade as divisional reserve. It was only to be used for exploitation.

Phase IV—In this phase all available forces were to be used in pursuit to cut roads leading eastwards from Keren.

Italian Dispositions

In the earlier operations the Italian Colonial troops were known to have suffered very severely, and three battalions had been withdrawn owing to heavy casualties and desertions. By 9 February some

---

[6] 2 Mahratta joined the 4th Indian Division on 9 February 1941 from Om Ager.

700 deserters[7] had already come in (mainly from the *11th Colonial Brigade*), and on that day several Eritrean deserters surrendered for the first time. This was considered to be a good sign, as the Eritreans had always been considered as the best of the Italian Colonial troops.

At the time of the attack on Brig's Peak by 3/1 Punjab (11th Indian Infantry Brigade) the Italian dispositions were as follows:—

(a) *West of the Gorge*

    (i) Sanchil and slopes.
        The *11th Colonial Brigade* held this area with the *51st Battalion* and remnants of the *56th* and *63rd Battalions*. The *52nd Battalion*, which was much disorganised and had suffered many desertions, had been withdrawn.

    (ii) Brig's Peak—Flat Top
        The *5th Colonial Brigade* held this area with the *97th* and *106th Battalions*. *Tipo Battalion* had been withdrawn due to heavy losses in the attack on 4 February. Two companies *Bersaglieri* strengthened this brigade.

    (iii) Amba-Samanna Area
        The *2nd Colonial Brigade* held this area with the *151st* and *10th Battalions*. The third battalion was to the south of Amba. *1/11th Grenadier Regiment* and one company *Bersaglieri* were in reserve.

(b) *East of the Gorge*

    (i) Sphinx-Acqua Gap Area—Two battalions of the *2nd Colonial Brigade* (*9th* and *4th Battalions*), with 44 Pack Group Artillery and one company 81-mm mortar held this area. (The *9th Battalion* had resisted the attack of 4/6 Rajputana Rifles during the night of 7/8 February).

    (ii) Falestoh—*2/11th Grenadier Regiment* held this area.

(c) *Keren Area*

    This area held by the remnants of the *3rd Battalion* (*11th Colonial Brigade*), *2nd* and *3rd Groups Cavalry Squadrons* and *2nd Pack Group Artillery*. The *44th Colonial Brigade* (*105th*, *107th* and *112th Battalions*) was on its way to

---

[7] The deserters up to this date had been mainly Ethiopians.

Keren from the north. The *105th Battalion* arrived on 9 February and moved upto the Sanchil-Amba area during the night of 10/11 February.

A defensive position was being constructed across the plain just west of Keren, covering the rail and road approaches. It was well dug and manned by the *35th* and *101st Battalions* of the *42nd Colonial Brigade*, which had been at Agordat, together with eight pack-guns. The road was heavily mined. The *111th Battalion*, the remaining battalion, was further east on Mt. Canabai.

The Attack on Brig's Peak

According to the divisional plan the 11th Indian Infantry Brigade was to launch an attack on Brig's Peak at 1500 hours on 10 February 1941. The 31 Field Regiment, 25 Field Regiment and 233 Medium Battery were to support the attack with a concentration on the Italian positions from zero to zero plus 10 minutes, and thereafter by observation. 3/1 Punjab advanced from Cameron Ridge on a four company front-B Company to Hog's Back, A Company to Saddle, C Company to the centre of Brig's Peak and D Company to the right feature of Brig's Peak. The Punjabis captured the ridge from Brig's Peak to Hog's Back by 1615 hours in spite of strong opposition and heavy shelling by the Italian pack artillery. Consolidation was immediately taken in hand. Help was asked for. B Company 1/6 Rajputana Rifles was ordered forward and started moving at 1710 hours to occupy Hog's Back and thus enable B Company 3/1 Punjab to be concentrated at the left feature of Brig's Peak where the Battalion Headquarters had been opened. Four signal lines were carried forward during the attack but only one reached the objective. Even this was cut by shell fire and communications were broken for an hour from 1630 to 1730 hours.

At 1715 hours on 10 February, the Italians launched a counter-attack on the right feature of Brig's Peak. D Company offered resistance but ran out of ammunition and was forced to retire to the centre of Brig's Peak. Some of the *Colonial* troops who pursued D Company were scattered by mortar fire. At the close of the day the situation was that, with the exception of the right feature of Brig's Peak, the Punjabis had been able to consolidate their position on the ridge from the centre of Brig's Peak to Hog's Back.

At 0530 hours on 11 February, B Company 3/1 Punjab reinforced by a platoon launched a counter-attack and recaptured the right feature of Brig's Peak without much opposition. Two officers and twenty other ranks (including *Bersaglieri*) were captured. 3/1 Punjab and B Company 1/6 Rajputana Rifles held their positions under almost continuous shell and mortar fire throughout the day. Direct hits were scored on the Battalion Headquarters which knocked out one gunner observation post and wounded a British officer. B Company 1/6 Rajputana Rifles was counter-attacked at 0100 and 0530 hours on 11 February and frequently during the day. Defensive fire was brought down and all attacks were successfully repulsed. Although the counter-attacks were repulsed the position was not satisfactory for there was a gap of a thousand yards between the left of 3/1 Punjab (*i.e.*, A Company on Saddle) and the right flank of B Company 1/6 Rajputana Rifles on Hog's Back. Arrangements were therefore made to reinforce 3/1 Punjab and the following were ordered up :—

    Carrier platoon 2 Camerons (in infantry role),
    One platoon 2 Camerons,
    Brigade Anti-tank Company (in infantry role).

The Officer Commanding 1/6 Rajputana Rifles also used his own carrier platoon for this purpose. The 4 Field Company was kept in the area as a reserve, only to be used in an emergency. 3/1 Punjab had by this time been reduced to less than two hundred men.[8]

At 2300 hours on 11 February the Italians launched a heavy counter-attack through the gap between the positions, mentioned above, towards Saddle. All communications to the rear had broken down, including the wireless set which had been hit by Italian shells. Artillery support was, therefore, not possible. By 0200 hours on 12 February, A Company 3/1 Punjab was forced to withdraw to Battalion Headquarters. About 400 Italians infiltrated right into the Battalion Headquarters area. They continued to press the attack and by 0230 hours, 3/1 Punjab was driven off Brig's Peak. B Company 1/6 Rajputana Rifles, still on Hog's Back, was ordered to hold on. 1/6 Rajputana Rifles was told to be prepared to counter-attack. The casualties of 3/1 Punjab were 11 killed and 40 wounded.

This situation was reported at 0300 hours on 12 February to the Commander of the 4th Indian Division who cancelled the counter-attack. He issued orders for the original line to be held at all costs and for B Company 1/6 Rajputana Rifles to be withdrawn

---

[8] Actual Company strengths of 3/1 Punjab were A-51, B-30-40, C-27, D-10 Headquarters-65.

from Hog's Back. The 11th Indian Infantry Brigade had great difficulty in passing these orders to 1/6 Rajputana Rifles as communications had, in the meantime, broken down. However, a patrol was sent to B Company 1/6 Rajputana Rifles with orders for it to withdraw at first light. It was told to pass the message to the 4 Field Company and detachment 2 Camerons which was reported to be in touch with B Company 1/6 Rajputana Rifles. This patrol got through and all were back in 1/6 Rajputana Rifles area by 0625 hours on 12 February. The Officer Commanding 1/6 Rajputana Rifles was ordered to take command of the position. All personnel of 2 Camerons and 3/1 Punjab came under his command. The defensive position was organised and strengthened by 0645 hours on 12 February.

Plan for the Second Attack on Acqua Gap

South and east of the road, Gazelle Force had planned an attack for the capture of Acqua Gap on 11 February. The operation was to take place in two phases. In the first phase, 4/6 Rajputana Rifles was to advance from Rajputana Ridge at 0530 hours and attack Pt. 1565. In the second phase, 4 Sikh was to advance at 0700 hours from the foot of Rajputana Ridge by the track and capture Acqua Gap.[9] At 2200 hours on 10 January, the Commander of the 4th Indian Division informed Gazelle Force and the 5th Indian Infantry Brigade of the partial success of the 11th Indian Infantry Brigade's attack on Brig's Peak and of the further attacks being planned to complete its capture. He added that, until the situation north of the road was cleared up, 2 Mahratta could not be released for operations in the Acqua Gap area. In view of this the attack on Acqua Gap was postponed to 12 February. At 1230 hours on 11 February a conference was held at Headquarters 4th Indian Division where the Commander of the 5th Indian Division and Brigadier General Staff Headquarters and the Troops Sudan were also present. The following changes were made in the plan :—

(i) The 5th Indian Infantry Brigade was to take command of operations for the capture of Acqua Gap and to secure up to the general line Pt. 1422 - Pt. 1501 on 12 February.

(ii) The 29th Indian Infantry Brigade (5th Indian Division) was to move to the Acqua Gap area on 12 February into the rear positions evacuated by the 5th Indian Infantry Brigade. After capture of the objectives by the 5th In

---

[9] Gazelle Operation Order No. 17 dated 10 February 1941.

dian Infantry Brigade, the 29th Indian Infantry Brigade was to pass through and capture Keren.

The 5th Indian Infantry Brigade made slight alterations in Gazelle Force plans for the capture of Acqua Gap. 4/6 Rajputana Rifles was still to open the attack from Rajputana Ridge at 0530 hours and capture Pt. 1565, but 4 Sikh was now to be concentrated at the foot of Rajputana Ridge by 0645 hours and to attack Acqua Gap and the lower slopes of Mount Zemale on the receipt of orders from Brigade Headquarters. The attack by 4 Sikh was to be launched irrespective of the success or failure of 4/6 Rajputana Rifles. Both the battalions consisted of three companies each.

During the night of 11/12 February the 11th Indian Infantry Brigade was counter-attacked on Brig's Peak and forced to withdraw to its original line. The Commander of the 4th Indian Division informed the 5th Indian Infantry Brigade of the situation and ordered the attack on Acqua Gap to proceed according to plan. It was told that 2 Mahratta would not be available to it as it was being kept in the 11th Indian Infantry Brigade area as divisional reserve.

Attack on Sangar

The Commander of 4/6 Rajputana Rifles planned to secure the ridge from including Tree Hill on the right and including Pimple on the left. A Company on the right was to secure objective from including Tree Hill to excluding Sangar. In the centre B/C Company less one platoon was to secure Sangar (Pt. 1565). On the left, D Company was to secure objective from excluding Sangar to including Pimple. The attack was to be supported by 1 Field Regiment (sixteen 25-pounders), 25 Field Regiment (sixteen 25-pounders), 390 Battery (twelve 25-pounders), 7 Medium Battery (eight 6-inch howitzers) and one Troop (four 3·7-inch howitzers). Skinner's Horse was to support the attack by fire from Rajputana Ridge. One platoon B/C Company in reserve was to move forward with the Advanced Battalion Headquarters in the rear of B/C Company, to be ready to exploit success in any direction.

The battalion marched to its forming-up place on Rajputana Ridge at 0300 hours on 12 February and was in position ready to advance by 0515 hours. At 0530 hours the artillery bombardment began, and the forward companies crossed the start line followed by the Advanced Battalion Headquarters and the reserve platoon. The artillery barrage was greeted by a hail of machine-gun bullets and mortar bombs all along the front. The battalion fought gallantly, pushing home the attack with great determination, but it suffered heavy casualties and was only partially successful. On the right, A Company secured about two-thirds of its objective and beat off several counter-attacks. Naik Maula Baksh played a notable part in this attack. He was in command of a section. He advanced with a light machine-gun and took two Italian posts in the enfilade. He then attacked a third post and when the *Colonial* troops retired to dead ground he stood up and continued to fire on them until he was killed. Meanwhile B/C Companies were held up by terrific mortar fire just below Sangar. They had put out the T Panel and this area became a target for every Italian mortar within range. It was here that Subedar Richpal Ram (of 4/6 Rajputana Rifles) fought gallantly, leading the forward platoon through intense fire with determination and complete disregard for personal safety until his right foot was blown off by a mortar bomb. He was mortally wounded before he could be evacuated. For his conspicuous bravery and devotion to duty on this occasion and during the night attack on 7/8 February he was awarded Victoria Cross posthumously. At 0730 hours B/C Companies asked for artillery support for a final assault on Sangar. Not much progress was however made and at 0815 hours B/C Companies reported that they were being heavily bombed.

Meanwhile D Company had also encountered stiff opposition. It came under heavy machine-gun and mortar fire from the exposed left flank as soon as its men crossed the start line. They pushed on with determination despite heavy casualties. Havildar Sheodan Singh, Second-in-Command No. 16 Platoon, distinguished himself for his conspicuous courage. He continued to advance although he was wounded on two separate occasions. He along with five men reached the objective—Flat Hill. Supporting himself on the Boab Tree he hurled grenades at the Italians just over the crest, until he was hit again for the third time and fell down the hill. The small party was pushed back by heavy Italian counter-attacks. Finally the Company held on to a position just below the Boab Tree.

At 0845 hours, the Commanding Officer 4/6 Rajputana Rifles asked for a fresh battalion or at least a company to push home the attack to the full. This could not be provided. It was, however, arranged for all the artillery to fire concentrations on 4/6 Rajputana Rifles' objectives from 0920 to 0930 hours. The reserve platoon reinforced D Company for an attack at 0930 hours and B/C Companies were also ordered to attack at the same time. Only a few rounds fell on the target. The attack failed. The single artillery line from the observation post on Rajputana Ridge was cut at 0910 hours and was not repaired until 1010 hours. Efforts were made

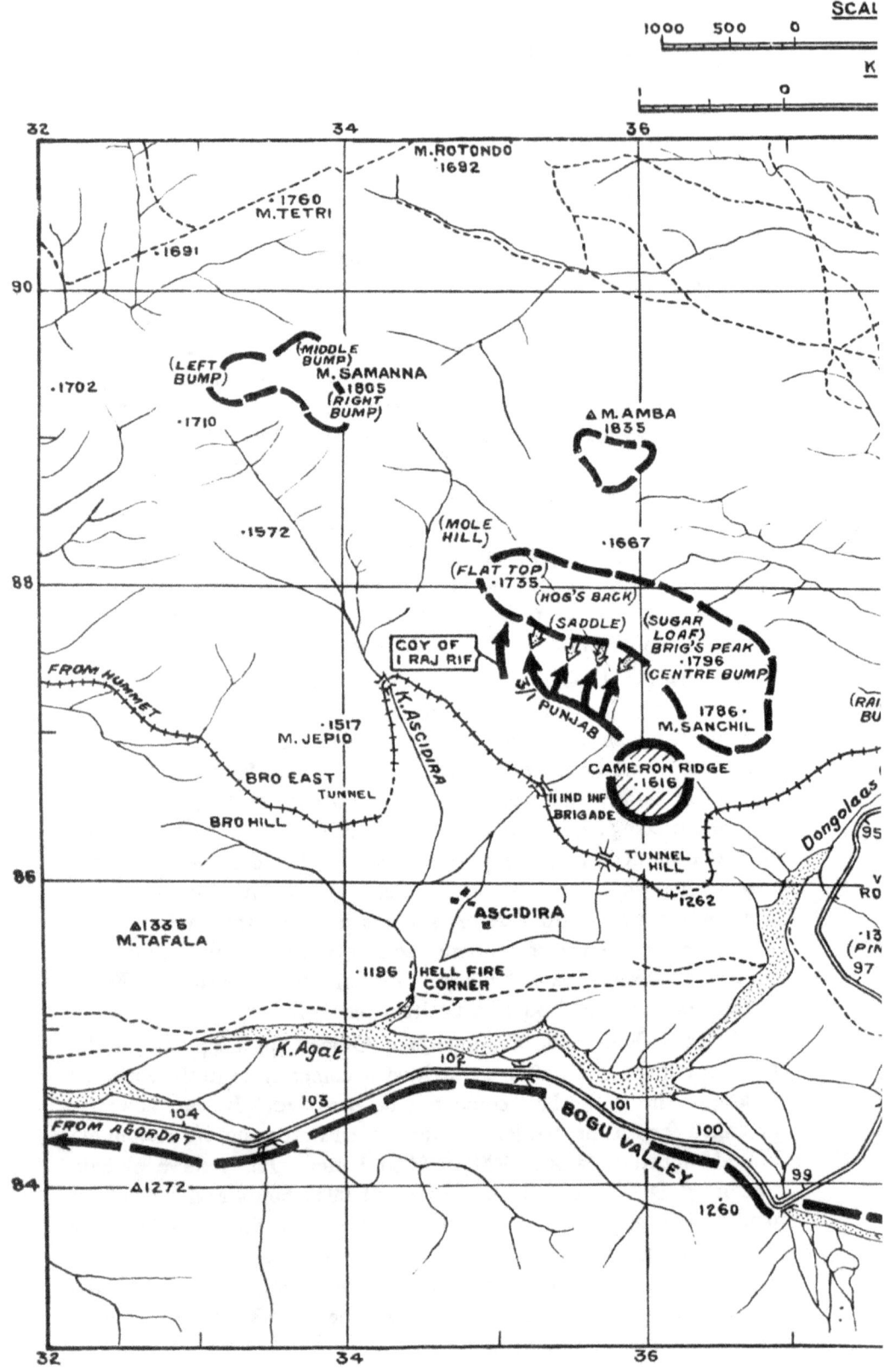

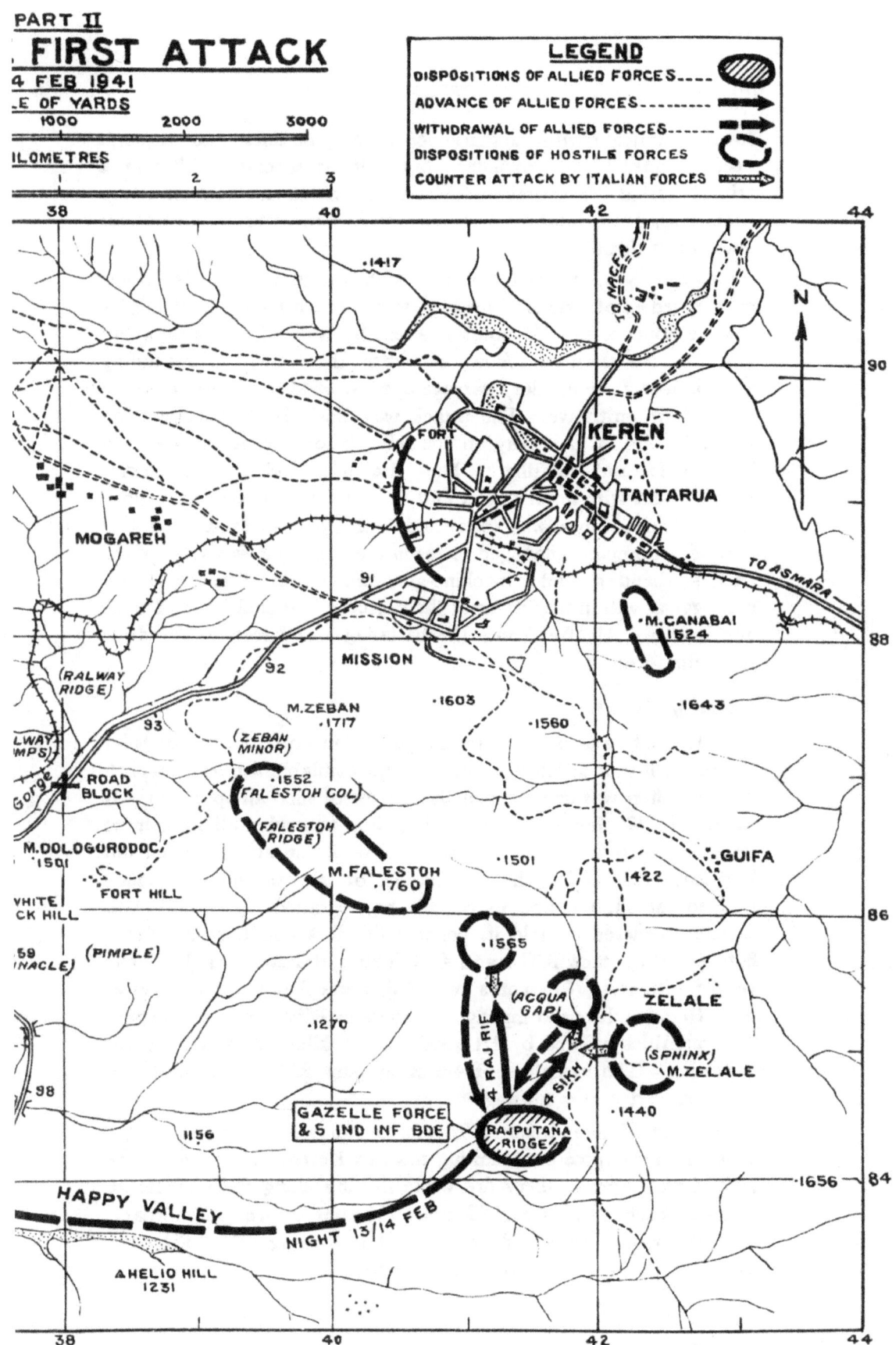

to communicate with the guns over the brigade lines and through headquarters Royal Artillery but without success. This was a critical period. The Italians were seen massing for counter-attack behind Pt. 1565. But no more than some mortar fire could be put down upon them.

To the right, the attack of 4/11 Sikh was to start at 0645 hours on the orders of Brigade Headquarters. The brigade signal to 4/11 Sikh to advance at 0645 hours was sent by two different means, but failed to get through. However, when the Officer Commanding 4/11 Sikh saw the artillery barrage open at 0645 hours, he advanced on his own initiative. The attack was made by C Company on the right and A Company on the left. Strong resistance was met in hand-to-hand fighting. The Italians had emplacements, trenches and wire on the crest and machine guns in defiladed positions. The advance was conducted with great determination and part of C Company managed to reach the crest, but was soon driven back by hand grenade, machine-gun and mortar fire. A Company got to within fifty yards of the objective but could not advance any further. At 1000 hours the battalion was forced to withdraw some distance.

Failure of the Attack

4/11 Sikh was ordered by Brigade Headquarters to consider the possibility of another attack with all available artillery support. The battalion was confident of the success of such an operation. It suggested 1400 hours as the starting time to enable all its men to be collected and organised. But in view of the attack having not been successful so far, the Commander of the 4th Indian Division decided, at 1120 hours, to cancel the operation. 4/11 Sikh was therefore ordered to hold its position till dark and then withdraw. Both 4/6 Rajputana Rifles and 4/11 Sikh withdrew from their forward positions at 1815 hours and Rajputana Ridge was taken over by 1 Horse with one company 1 Rajputana Rifles under command. The casualties suffered by 4/11 Sikh were 9 killed, 84 wounded and 9 missing. The casualties of 4/6 Rajputana Rifles were 37 killed, 176 wounded and 4 missing.

The 29th Indian Infantry Brigade had moved to the Acqua Gap area for the purpose of exploiting towards Keren. It suffered some losses from heavy artillery fire while moving along the main road. It moved back to the area of kilometre 110 after dark on 12 February, spent the night there and early on the morning of 13 February left in mechanical transport for Barentu.

It was decided to withdraw Gazelle Force and the 5th Indian Infantry Brigade during the night of 13/14 February from the Acqua Gap area. 13 February was a quiet day. At 1900 hours the Italians opened heavy artillery fire and it was thought that they were probably going to launch a counter-attack. But no counter-attack materialised and the fire died down an hour later. The withdrawal of the 5th Indian Infantry Brigade and Gazelle Force was completed by 0100 hours on 14 February without any loss. Both concentrated in the area of kilometre 110.

All efforts to break through to Keren had thus been unsuccessful. The Italians had fought stubbornly and aided by the natural strength of their positions, had held out. The British still held Cameron Ridge though they had lost Brig's Peak and other features to Italian counter-attacks. After the failure of these efforts it was clear that any further assault on Keren would be a major operation. So preparations for the next attack were planned and undertaken.

While these preparations were afoot the 7th Indian Infantry Brigade group had been advancing towards Keren down the Red Sea coast. As early as 21 January, the Commander of the 7th Indian Infantry Brigade had reported that the Italians were withdrawing from the Karora area and asked permission to start a minor operation against the Italian garrison there. This permission was given. The idea of a thrust down the Red Sea coast had been previously considered and at first it had been used to divert attention from Kassala. After consultation with the Royal Navy, it was considered feasible to direct a force of approximately one brigade group from Port Sudan via Suakin-Karora-Nacfa-Cub Cub and on to Keren from the north. We shall narrate the story of this advance in the next chapter.

CHAPTER VI

The Advance down the Red Sea Coast

The 7th Indian Infantry Brigade (4th Indian Division) arrived at Port Sudan from the Western Desert on 1 January 1941[1]. From there it proceeded to concentrate in the Gebeit area. The Brigade Headquarters was situated in the unoccupied railway quarters and the brigade signal section took over communication. The Brigade had as its role the line of communication duties and the defence of Port Sudan and the Red Sea Coast while the main British forces operated in the Kassala area early in February. The order of battle of the 7th Indian Infantry Brigade Group was as follows :—

    Headquarters
    Brigade Signal Section
    1st Royal Sussex
    4/11 Sikh[2]
    Brigade Anti-Tank Company
    Brigade Section of Divisional Mechanical Transport
    Meadowforce[3]

At that time the Italian forces on the northern frontier of Eritrea were holding El Ghena, Karora, Khor Falkat, Nacfa and Cub Cub. *Tipo Battalion* and Headquarters *5th Colonial Brigade* were at El Ghena, the *97th Colonial Battalion* at Karora, the *106th Colonial Battalion* at Khor Falkat (between El Ghena and Mersa Taclai), the *105th Colonial Battalion.* the *112th Colonial Battalion* and the *6th Cavalry Group* at Nacfa and one *Colonial* battalion at Cub Cub.

On 4 January, the 7th Indian Infantry Brigade was ordered to stimulate activity and display force to distract Italian attention from the Kassala area, where offensive action was being planned. Towards the end of January, as time for the attack on Kassala drew near, it was to intensify its activity. Accordingly, dummy dumps

---

[1] It was commanded by Brigadier H. R. Briggs.
[2] 4/11 Sikh left the 7th Indian Infantry Brigade on 12 January and joined Gazelle Force.
[3] Meadowforce was a small scout force of three officers and 90 Sudanese other ranks.

were made, camps erected, dummy airfields built, piers at Aqiq[4] improved, road and dhow convoys organised, and intensive patrolling started in the Karora area. 1st Royal Sussex (less one company) was moved up and by 22 January was widely dispersed between Aqiq and Karora. All this activity successfully misled the Italians, who reported the presence of nine thousand troops on the Red Sea littoral. Their air force carried out almost daily bombing attacks on the Indian and British forward troops and convoys.

The line of communication was now beginning to get extended. The distance between Port Sudan and Karora was one hundred and eighty miles, and the road was so bad that vehicles could seldom exceed a speed of 8 miles per hour. The going across the country was also poor and petrol consumption very high. During the subsequent operations, the petrol requirements of mobile columns were constantly underestimated. This led to serious delays in operations at a later date. Dumps had to be established before troops could be brought up. Petrol formed the most bulky load and the leakage from unprotected tins was considerable.

Aggressive Patrolling

Reports from forward troops of the Italians thinning out on the frontier were confirmed by statements made by agents and air reconnaissance. On 22 January, Brigadier Briggs, the Commander of the 7th Indian Infantry Brigade, asked permission to surround Karora, which was granted. At that time only one Coast-Guard battalion was guarding Karora and Mersa Taclai. An operation to surround Karora was carried out by the 1st Royal Sussex with Meadowforce under command on 23/24 January. As the area beyond the frontier had not been reconnoitred before, and in that portion the going was found to be very bad, the vehicles of the battalion could not get nearer than ten miles from the objective by 1700 hours. This influenced the Commander of 1st Royal Sussex to cancel the attack. The Carrier Platoon which had made good progress was recalled. But the orders were issued late and the platoon was caught the next morning by the Italian aircraft in an exposed position. Meadowforce which had not received the order cancelling the operation, continued the advance and was nearly surrounded by the Italians. However, it extricated itself with difficulty on 24 January after hard fighting. The failure of this operation was unfortunate as the element of surprise was lost. The Italian garrison

---

[4] Forty miles north of Karora, on the coast.

was reinforced and occupied prepared positions in the more difficult hilly country.[5]

Planning for an Advance down the Coast

The idea of a thrust down the Red Sea Coast had been previously considered although operations so far had only been intended to divert attention from Kassala. After consultation with the Navy, it was considered feasible to direct a force of approximately one brigade from Port Sudan via Suakin, Karora, Nacfa, Cub Cub and on to Keren from the north. On 5 February the following orders were issued :—

(i) The 7th Indian Infantry Brigade Group was to assist the 4th Indian Division by an advance on Keren along the coast as soon as possible.

(ii) After the capture of Karora, El Ghena, and Mersa Taclai, a new base was to be established at the last place where a small harbour was available. The capture of Mersa Taclai was considered necessary as it was intended to be developed and used as a base for supply and other administrative requirements.

(iii) Sea transport was to be organised to avoid the long road line of communication between Port Sudan and El Ghena.

The following were placed under command of the 7th Indian Infantry Brigade :—

4/16 Punjab
One Battery 25 Field Regiment
12 Field Company RIE
170 Light Field Ambulance
14 Battalion Foreign Legion
3rd Battalion Chad Regiment (Free French Forces)
4 Motor Machine Gun Group Sudan Defence Force
32 Construction Company (for repairing telephone lines Mersa Taclai-Keren)
55 Supply Depot Section
One Anti-aircraft Troop (for defence of Mersa Taclai).

In these operations sea transport was to be used to the full, to overcome administrative difficulties of an advance down the coast. The plan was to use barges, dhows, and small ships to move both troops and stores by sea first to Aqiq and later when open to Mersa

---

[5] Briggs, H. R., Account of the 7th Indian Infantry Brigade Operations on the Red Sea Littoral, Feb-Apr. 1941.

Taclai. If later it was decided to threaten Massawa, Mersa Cuba, thirty-five miles to the north, was to be opened.

The Brigade Plan

The Italian garrison of Karora was believed at this time to be about four hundred and fifty men with sixteen light machine guns and no artillery. Mersa Taclai was reported to be unoccupied except for a few coast guards. At El Ghena it was considered possible that there were two companies of the *47th Colonial Battalion.* All information indicated that these troops were nervous and their morale was low.

The Commander of the 7th Indian Infantry Brigade gave orders on 6 February 1941 for the capture of Karora and Mersa Taclai. It was to be followed by a rapid advance on El Ghena and exploitation towards Nacfa after the occupation of El Ghena. The force detailed consisted of 1st Royal Sussex, with the 7th Brigade Anti-Tank Company and Meadowforce under command. The Commander of 1st Royal Sussex was ordered to send a column of one company (embussed), carrier platoon less one section and one platoon Anti-Tank Company to capture Mersa Taclai on 9 February and then to advance towards El Ghena with the object of capturing that place and exploiting towards Nacfa. The remainder of the force was to capture Karora and press towards El Ghena. Bold action was stressed to force the Italians from their positions.[6]

Capture of Karora, Mersa Taclai and El Ghena

At this time the 4th Indian Division was heavily engaged with superior Italian forces in the Keren area and speedy operations by the 7th Indian Infantry Brigade for bringing pressure from the north against Italian forces in the Keren area were considered necessary to assist the 4th Indian Division.

On 9 February 1941, Karora was captured with very little opposition by a Royal Sussex column. The other column detailed for the capture of Mersa Taclai moved off on 8 February and advanced to within two miles of that place. Here the Commander decided to proceed to Skenat with the main portion of the column, so as to be in a better position to capture the wells at Kerai two miles to the south-west. These were believed to be strongly held by the Italians. A force of one platoon was detached to occupy Mersa Tac-

---

[6] War Diary, 7th Indian Infantry Brigade, Instruction No. 1, dated 6 February 1941.

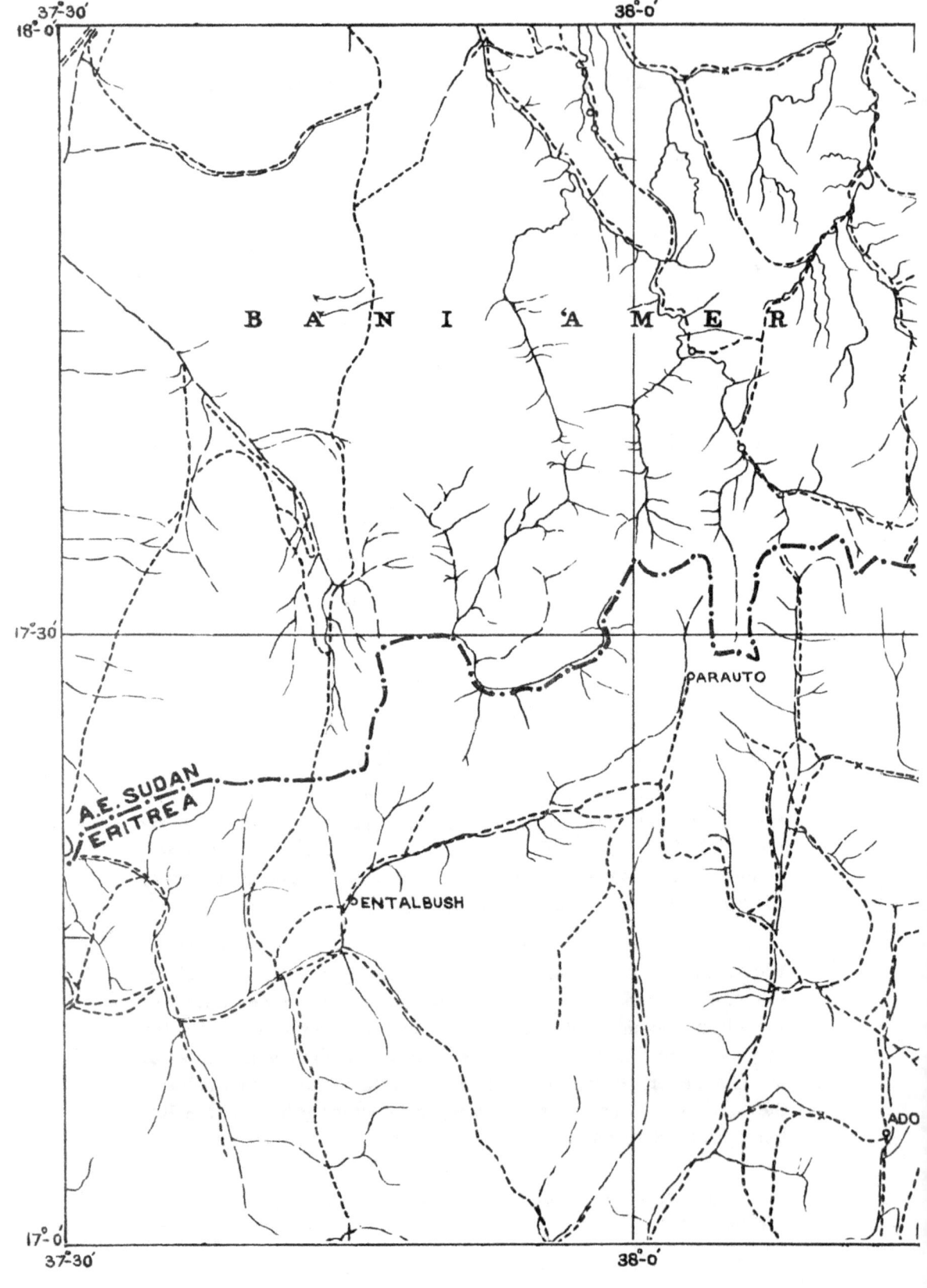

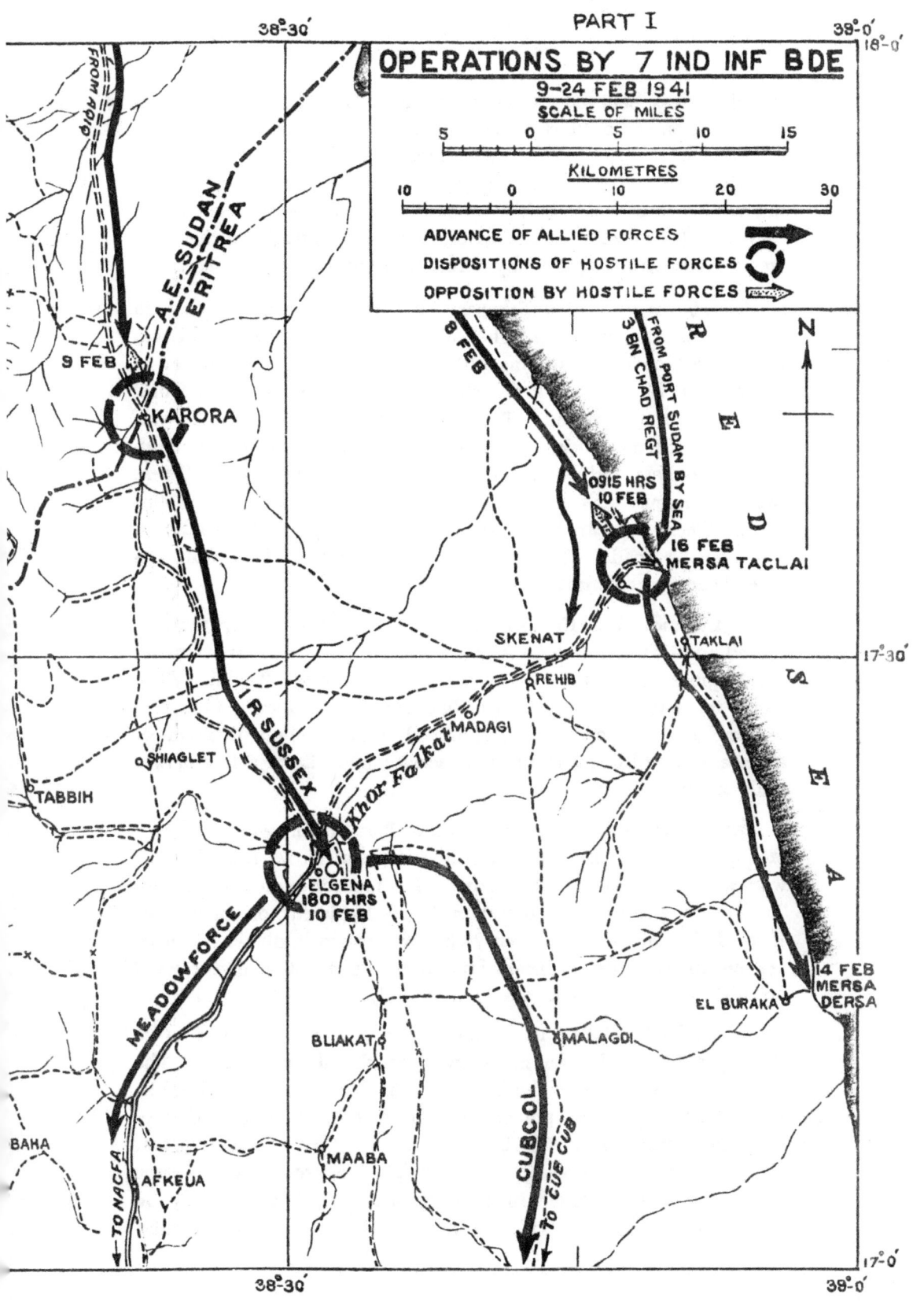

lai which was believed to be unoccupied. This platoon met with opposition on the outskirts of Mersa Taclai and the rest of the force from Skenat had to be called in. Mersa Taclai was finally captured at 0915 hours on 10 February and a sea base was now sought to be improvised there as it held possibilities for supply by dhows and coasters. It proved to be a valuable acquisition because of the large amount of petrol required by forces operating over soft sands.

At 1800 hours on 10 February, 1st Royal Sussex occupied El Ghena without opposition. The column from Mersa Taclai was immobilised owing to shortage of petrol, and could not move to Nacfa. On 14 January, a detachment, sent down the coast, found Mersa Dersa unoccupied. The main road (El Ghena-Nacfa) was unsuitable for mechanical transport. The lower road ran through Asmat Awi Pass and was suitable for mechanical transport. There were numerous tank pits covered with brush wood along this route. There appeared to be no through way into the hills at Nacfa on this road. The road from Cam Ceua to Cub Cub was suitable for mechanical transport.

In the meantime the Brigade Headquarters was busy tackling the administrative problems in Port Sudan. On 11 February naval and engineer officers were sent by air to Mersa Taclai. They found the jetty broken and the harbour very shallow. One tug, a barge and a dhow were despatched immediately with engineer stores and patrol to make the jetty serviceable. Later a lighter was sunk to form an extra pier.

Every dhow in the neighbourhood of Port Sudan was commandered and loaded with petrol and the services of H. M. I. S. *Ratnagiri* were secured for transporting troops. The first convoy to reach Mersa Taclai brought the 3rd Battalion Chad Regiment on board the H. M. I. S. *Ratnagiri*, and twenty-one days' ration in dhows. It arrived on 16 February. Uncertainty as to the direction of the wind delayed the dhow convoys considerably.

Mersa Taclai itself had no water, and a water point had to be developed at Rehib, ten miles away on the El Ghena road. The first twenty-five miles of the El Ghena road were almost impassable. All available men were put on to improving this road and developing the water point. On 25 February a grader and one section 12 Field Company became available for this area. By this time Mersa Taclai had started functioning as a base, though mainly by improvisation. It was also being used as a forward landing ground by the Royal Air Force.

Capture of Cub Cub

On 12 February, one company with two sections carrier platoon 1st Royal Sussex and one platoon Brigade Anti-Tank Company were despatched to Nacfa. This force was all lorried and was later called Cubcol. As reports indicated that Nacfa was unoccupied, the force was redirected to Cam Ceua. Meadowforce was ordered up the Nacfa road, on camels. At 1500 hours on 14 February Cubcol made contact with the Italians two miles north of Cam Ceua. The road was heavily mined and Cubcol was held up. It was relieved on 17 February by the 3rd Battalion Chad Regiment, and moved back to a distance of about fifteen miles. On the same day a message was received from the 4th Indian Division to the effect that early pressure on Keren from the north was essential. On 20 February in a preliminary operation, the 3rd Chad Battalion captured the ridge covering the entrance into the Cub Cub valley.

The Commander of the 7th Indian Infantry Brigade reconnoitred the Italian positions, which contained the *112th Colonial Battalion* with four guns. The Italians appeared to be holding the lower hills in the valley only and it seemed possible to surround them on the hill tops, which the Italians were known to dislike. Having no artillery, he decided to manoeuvre the Italians from their positions. He ordered Cubcol to move via Wadi Athara to the south of the Cub Cub positions and cut their lines of communication. Two companies from Chad Battalion were to get behind the Italians' right flank. The remainder of that battalion was to attack frontally; all objectives were to be reached by 1000 hours on 21 February. The attack of the Chad Battalion was fiercely pressed home, but the Italian resistance proved too strong. Cubcol lost its way, going too far east and south, and then ran out of petrol.

On 22 February the Commander of the 7th Indian Infantry Brigade was able to put into battle the battery from the 25 Field Regiment and the carriers and Anti-Tank Platoon of 4/16 Punjab which had unexpectedly reached El Ghena the previous night. These were rushed up. The determined attack of the Chad Battalion, thus reinforced, and finally the belated arrival of Cubcol at Cub Cub from the south-west on 22 February, broke the Italian resistance and Cub Cub was captured on 23 February with four hundred and thirty-six prisoners, four guns and a large dump of stores.

Cubcol was immediately ordered to advance southwards, as fast as possible. During the night of 23/24 February, Chelamet (twenty-five miles south of Cub Cub) was reached before the Italians had time to destroy the Pass. A small column moving from Cub

Cub occupied Nacfa without opposition, although Meadowforce, which had reached Madruiet on 17 February was still held up by the Italians at Debelai Pass.

Mescelit Pass

4 Motor Machine Gun Company (Sudan Defence Force), which had arrived from Khartoum on 22 February, with one platoon of the Brigade Anti-Tank Company under command, was ordered to pass through Cubcol and take up the pursuit as far as the main Italian positions covering Keren on the north-east. Cubcol was to move in the rear and in support of the 4 Motor Machine Gun Company until relieved by 4/16 Punjab. In addition to the above, 4 Motor Machine Gun Company was to reconnoitre possible routes leading from the Chelamet-Keren road, which could be used for attacks on Keren from the north, north-east, east, or south-east. The 7th Indian Infantry Brigade was to concentrate in the Cub Cub area as soon as transport resources permitted.

On 24 February, 4 Motor Machine Gun Company passed through Cubcol. Armoured car patrols moved ahead of the column and reported a road block at the entrance to the Mescelit Pass. The column continued the advance on 25 February until the leading elements came under pack artillery fire when approaching the pass. On 25 February 1941, the advanced Battalion Headquarters and two companies 4/16 Punjab reached the area behind the Motor Machine Gun Company in the evening. C Company 1st Royal Sussex (Cubcol) moved back for the defence of Chelamet. The remaining two companies of 4/16 Punjab were still at Mersa Taclai and on the line of communication. One section was detailed for work on the road and pier at Mersa Taclai. The last unit to arrive was the 14th Battalion Foreign Legion, which disembarked at Mersa Taclai on 27 February. This completed the 7th Indian Infantry Brigade Group which now consisted of :—

    Headquarters
    Brigade Signal Section
    7th Brigade Anti-Tank Company
    1st Royal Sussex
    4/16 Punjab
    3rd Chad Battalion
    14th Battalion Foreign Legion
    12/25 Field Battery RA
    12 Field Company RIE
    4 Motor Machine Gun Company, Sudan Defence Force
    170 Field Ambulance

1st Service Company Sudan Defence Force
55th Supply Depot Section

The Italians appeared to be holding Mescelit Pass in some strength and efforts were made to discover the exact strength and extent of their positions. Fighting patrols were sent out on 26 and 27 February, as a result of which the position was believed to be held by one company *107th Colonial Battalion* with six mortars, four to eight machine guns and possibly some guns. An operation to outflank the Italian position was planned. 4/16 Punjab less two companies, with two companies 1st Royal Sussex under command and A Troop 12/25th Field Battery in support, was detailed to carry out the operation. On the evening of 28 February one company made a frontal demonstration while the other moved off round the left flank, spent the night of 28 February/1 March in a deep nullah and by 0600 hours was established on the left of the Italian positions. By 0830 hours, the pass was captured without loss, the negligible opposition having been neutralised by the guns.

The administrative situation had again become difficult. Mersa Taclai was already one hundred and fifty miles behind. Before troops could be brought up, a forward dump of supplies had to be formed. Cub Cub was selected for this purpose. It entailed a three day round trip for the mechanical transport, without allowing time for maintenance. The round trip by dhow from Suakin took at least a week, while the tug and barges took four days. H. M. I. S. *Ratnagiri* was being used for bringing up troops and taking back casualties. The supply problem was complicated by the fact that separate scales and types of rations were required for the British, Indian, French, French Colonial and Sudanese troops. The varying speeds of the shipping used made the question of priority of arrival at Mersa Taclai very difficult. Shortage of transport, forward of Mersa Taclai, further complicated the question of priorities between the various types of rations and the other necessaries like ammunition and petrol. Communications were only possible by wireless and each message had to be ciphered and deciphered. The wireless sets available thus became overloaded. Also the sets were transmitting over distances well beyond their normal capacity and the reception varied considerably. To these was added the difficulty of finding adequate supplies of water. Except at Cub Cub, water was difficult to find anywhere. Issues, therefore, varied from one gallon to half a gallon per man throughout these operations.

Extensive demolitions on the road had been carried out in the pass and it was estimated that it would take two days to get vehicles through. 1st Royal Sussex took over the pass from 4/16 Punjab on

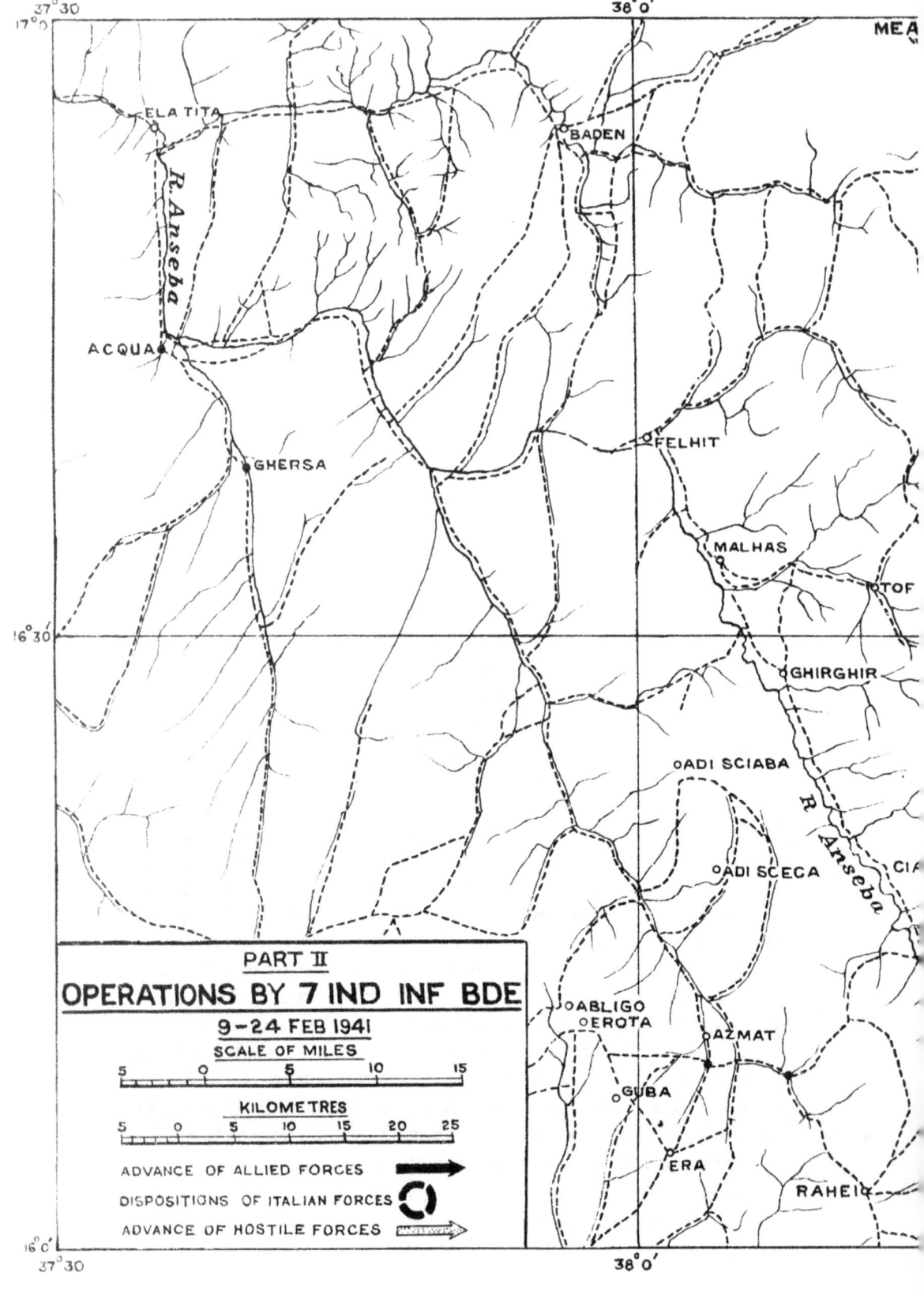

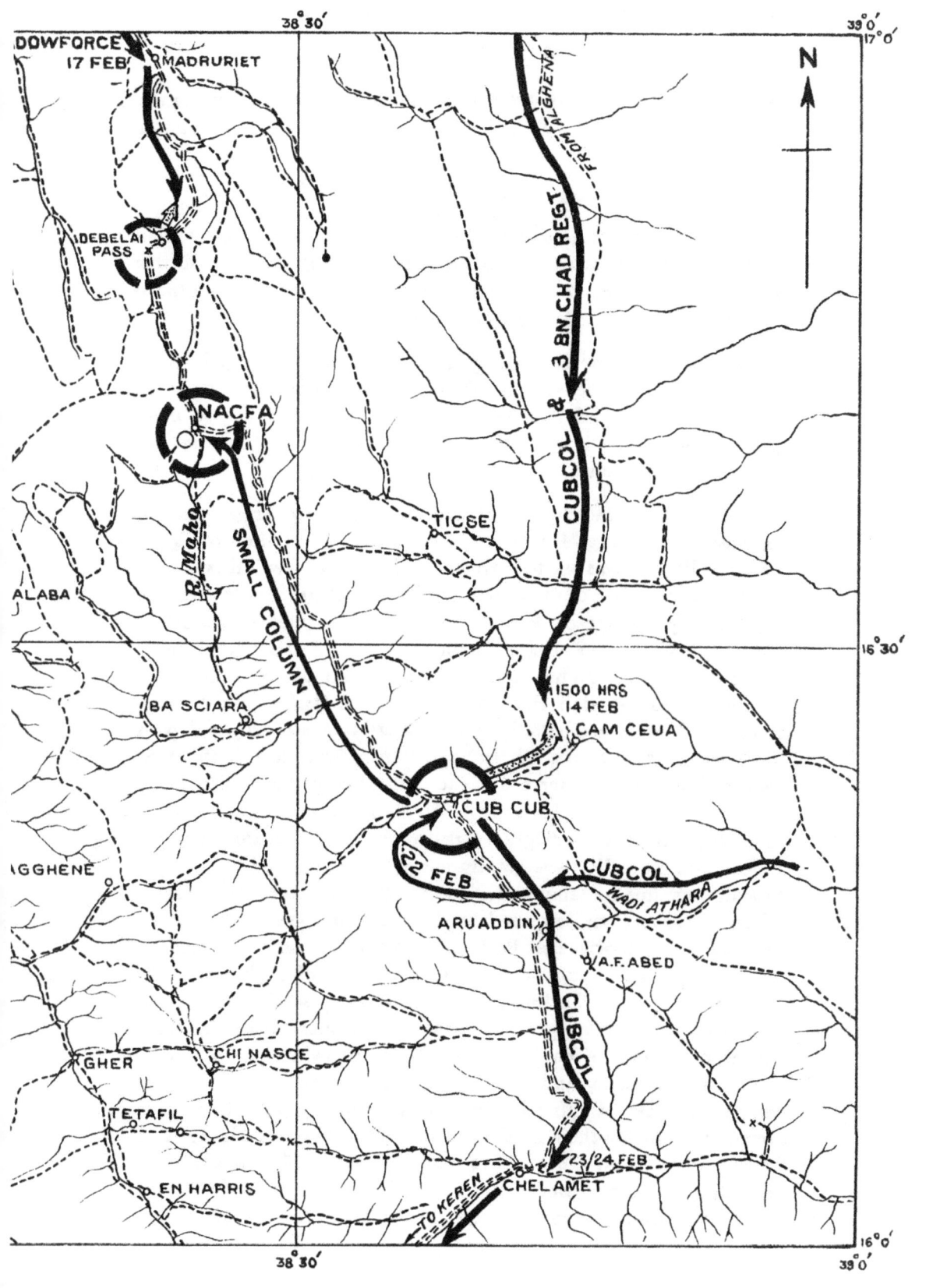

2 March. Patrols were then sent forward to discover Italian dispositions and movements. Brigade d' Orient was concentrated in Chelamet area.

Contact with the Italian Forces at Keren

On 3 March, 1st Royal Sussex moved forward of the Mescelit Pass and advanced as far as the Anseba road crossing. Patrols further moved beyond the cross roads and reached the northern outskirts of Mendad the next day without opposition.

4 Motor Machine Gun Company and one platoon Brigade Anti-Tank Company, were sent to Obellet, on the coast route to Massawa to protect the left flank of the line of communication. A company of the Italians in the area was driven back by this force in the direction of Massawa.

On 4 March, Headquarters 7th Indian Infantry Brigade moved forward to the Cogai Pass area. Reconnaissance of the area south of Mescelit Pass was started. Keren was only a few miles to the south and the sound of the guns could be heard, but between the two positions lay a range of formidable hills covering the pass south of Mendad. The main Italian position extended from the upper slopes of Mt. Ab Aaures on the east through Mt. Cubub, across the Anseba to Mt. Bab Harmas and Mt. Laal Amba. In the beginning of March, six battalions, with possibly a seventh, had been identified in front of the 7th Indian Infantry Brigade. It appeared that the Italians were nervous of the infiltration of the Indian forces through the mountain passes of the Ab Aaures range and had made their dispositions accordingly. Artillery had been located near the Anseba and the valley was heavily mined. The 7th Indian Infantry Brigade was thus containing considerable Italian forces which would, otherwise, have been employed to the south of Keren. It had by this time, since its arrival at Port Sudan, advanced some two hundred miles in Italian territory against a series of Italian defences. In addition to men on the front, the administrative services had done their work commendably in this phase of the operations. On them fell the heavy task of ensuring supplies, of transporting men, equipment and provisions, and maintaining communications, which they executed in spite of difficulties which were courageously faced and overcome. But for their good work the rapid advance of the Allied forces on this front would have been delayed. This would have prevented the accomplishment of the desired object, namely, bringing pressure from the north upon the Italian forces in the Keren area.

CHAPTER VII

Plan for the Final Attack on Keren

After the second unsuccessful attack on the Acqua Gap on 12 February, General Platt decided that in view of the natural strength of the position and strength and determination of the Italians, the assault on Keren woud have to be undertaken by both the 4th and 5th Indian Divisions.

The relief of the 4th Indian Division in the forward areas by 5th Indian Division was considered very desirable. But before an operation involving the use of both the divisions could be undertaken, dumps of ammunition, petrol and rations had to be built up forward. Shortage of transport did not allow of carrying out the relief of 4th Indian Division and the continuation of the dumping programme simultaneously. Therefore, it was decided to have the 4th Indian Division to hold the heights already secured opposite Keren.

In order to avoid the strain on transport required to maintain troops on the road line of communication, it was decided to have the 29th Indian Infantry Brigade in Barentu and to withdraw the rest of the 5th Indian Division to the area Sabderat and Tessenei, where it could maintain itself with its own first line transport from the railhead at Kassala. This plan was modified later and Headquarters 5th Indian Division and one battalion (6 Royal Frontier Force Rifles) only were left at Barentu. While in the area of Sabderat and Tessenei, the 5th Indian Division carried out intensive training in mountain warfare.

Disbandment of Gazelle Force

It had been decided early in February to disband Gazelle Force. Created originally for the task of harassing the Italians north of Kassala and at the same time acting as a flank guard to the east of river Atbara, it had, in January 1941, changed its role and acted as an advanced guard mobile troops to the 4th Indian Division in its rapid advance from Kassala to Agordat, and then further up to the gates of Keren. Now there was no room for further manoeuvre and no routes over which its armoured vehicles could be employed; the units could only be employed as infantry as was recently shown by the employment of 1 Horse on Rajputana Ridge.[1] It was decided to form a new force by name of Kestrel in place of Gazelle Force with effect from 27 February. This was to be cammanded by Lieutenant-Colonel P. S. Myburgh DSO, MC, 25 Field Regiment and was to consist of Headquarters 25 Field Regiment, (Central India Horse) 1st (Independent) Anti-Tank Troop R. A., A Troop Sudan Regiment and 1 Motor Machine Gun Group less two companies.

Flank Protection

The 5th Indian Infantry Brigade relieved the 11th Indian Infantry Brigade in the forward line during 15/16 February. 3/1 Punjab,4 Sikh and 2 Mahratta were under command the 5th Indian Infantry Brigade. 4/6 Rajputana Rifles remained in the rest area coming under the command of the 11th Indian Infantry Brigade. Italian movements at this period were aimed at infiltration round the north flank. *2nd* and *3rd Groups Cavalry Squadrons* based in the Mogareh area, were sending out patrols as far north as Izel and to the west in the hills to the east of Mt. Beit Gabru. One patrol was reported as far west as Mt. Siuma on 17 February. As there appeared to be genuine threat to the left flank of the Indian forces it was decided, on 23 February, that 4/6 Rajputana Rifles would occupy a position to the west of 1/6 Rajputana Rifles on the general line (Pt. 1572- Pt. 1710- Pt. 1702) to provide flank protection. During the night of 24/25 February, two companies of 4/6 Rajputana Rifles took over this position without opposition. At about 1830 hours on 25 February, there were sounds of very heavy firing in the area of Pt. 1710, and defensive fire was called for. It was reported that the Italians had gained a footing on the northerly slopes of Pt. 1710 under cover of very heavy mortar fire. The eight men comprising the post had all been wounded. At 1945 hours, 4/6 Rajputana Rifles was ordered to move up the remainder of the battalion, actually due to move later, and arrived during the night of 25/26 February. By this time, however, the situation had improved and the Italians had withdrawn.

---

[1]As a result of the decision to disband Gazelle Force, the following moves were ordered. 1 Horse and 390 Field Battery to Barentu on 15 February, the former rejoining the 5th Indian Division as divisional cavalry regiment; the latter rejoining 144 Field Regiment ; 4 Motor Machine Gun Company was to proceed to Khartoum and thence to join the 7th Indian Infantry Brigade on the coast; 170 Field Ambulance to Kassala, also to join the 7th Indian Infantry Brigade. On 15 February, Colonel F. W. Messervy, Commander Gazelle Force, left to take over the command of 9 the Indian Infantry Brigade and Lt-Col J. G. Pocock CIH assumed command. Thus the force functioned for a few days more.

The 51 Commando, of the strength of three hundred men and six vehicles, moved up to Keren on 23 February and came under command of the 4th Indian Division. On 25 February, this force was sent to Mansciua area to deal with any Italian cavalry it might find in the area, and also to see how far it could get round the north-west flank. Between 25/27 February, the 5th Indian Brigade was relieved by the 11th Indian Infantry Brigade. It was then decided to strengthen 4/6 Rajputana Rifles on the left by relieving it of the responsibility of holding Pt. 1572, and arrangements were made for one squadron Central Indian Horse, reinforced by a detachment of Sudan Defence Force, to take over this point. Central India Horse was no longer responsible for Mt. Tafala.

On 2/3 March, two Italian observation posts were located on Pt. 1968 (Mt. Beit Gabru) and Pt. 1451. They had the whole of the British and Indian gun area under observation. A carrier from the 11th Indian Infantry Brigade patrolled the railway line south of Pt. 1451 during daylight on 3 March. During the night of 3/4 March, 2 Mahratta patrolled the area. An attack was put in on the morning of 4 March by a troop from 51 Commando and both the observation posts were dislodged.

During the night of 4/5 March, another troop of 51 Commando fought a very successful engagement while patrolling to the north-west of Pt. 1702 and Pt. 1710. It ran into an Italian post, protected by a single apron barbed wire fence, charged it in the face of heavy fire and captured it without loss. One Italian Officer and five other ranks were killed. The patrol, forty-four strong, held the post until morning, when it was counter-attacked by a force of one hundred and thirty men with heavy mortar and machine-gun fire support. As it was running out of ammunition, the patrol withdrew, after inflicting about forty casualties on the Italians. The 11th Indian Infantry Brigade remained in the line for about ten days. Between 5 and 8 March, the 5th Indian Infantry Brigade relieved the 11th Indian Infantry Brigade in preparation for the final assault on Keren on 15 March 1941.

ITALIAN DISPOSITIONS

The Italian forces were also being reorganised to meet the attack by the British and Indian forces. On 12 March they were reported to be thus deployed for the defence of Keren:—

East of the Gorge

The *11th Colonial Brigade* was holding the Acqua Gap sector with the *63rd Colonial Battalion* at Sphinx, the *52nd Colonial Battalion* at Acqua Gap, the *56th Colonial Battalion* at Pt. 1565 and the *51st Colonial Battalion* in the area of Pt. 1643. The *Bersaglieri Battalion* of the *Grenadier Division* was in the Fort Hill area. One *Blackshirt Battalion* was at Mt. Falestoh.

West of the Gorge

Part of the *Grenadier Division*, the *5th Colonial Brigade* and the *2nd Colonial Brigade* were deployed in the sector west of the Dongolaas Gorge. Area Sanchil—Brig's Peak—Flat Top was held by the *97th Colonial Battalion (5th Colonial Brigade)*, *Carabinieri* and possibly one battalion *10th Grenadier Regiment (Grenadier Division)*. Mt. Amba and Bloody Hill were held by the *4th Colonial Battalion (2nd Colonial Brigade)*, one battalion of the *10th Grenadier Regiment* and one battalion of the *11th Grenadier Regiment (Grenadier Division)*. Samanna was held by the *Alpini Battalion* less two companies *(Grenadier Division)*. Pts. 1691, 1680 and 1789 were held by the two companies of *Alpini Battalion (Grenadier Division)* and the *106th Colonial Battalion (5th Colonial Brigade)*. The Dongolaas Gorge was held by the *24th Colonial Battalion (6th Colonial Brigade)*.

North-west Sector

The *36th Colonial Battalion (12th Colonial Brigade)* was in Aful area; the *5th Colonial Battalion (2nd Colonial Brigade)* at Mt. Tetri; the *3rd Battalion (11th CCNN Legion)* and *15th Group Cavalry Squadrons* in area Pt. 1767—Mt. Modacca—Mt. Dobac—Mt. Rocciosa; and the *103th Colonial Battalion (12th Colonial Brigade)* in the Laal Amba area.

Nacfa Road Front

The following units were supposed to be deployed in this sector:—
2nd Battalion (11th CCNN Legion)
9th Colonial Battalion
10th Colonial Battalion (2nd Colonial Brigade)
105th Colonial Battalion (44th Colonial Brigade)
107th Colonial Battalion (44th Colonial Brigade)
112th Colonial Battalion
151th Colonial Battalion (2nd Colonial Brigade)[2]

The number of guns on all the Keren fronts amounted to 126. Of these 30 were Medium, 42 Field, 48 Pack and 6 Anti-Aircraft.

---

[2] 4th Indian Division Intelligence Summary No. 122 dated 5 March and No. 128 dated 12 March 1941.

Signalmen operate the field telephone at Battalion Hq. on top of one of the Keren Hills

Men of the Central India Horse in action in the front line in the Keren Hills

Bren-gun Carriers of 4/11 Sikh coming into action around Keren

Keren at last

These Punjabis in Eritrea with an anti-tank gun are ready for all comers

Men of 4/16 Punjab in action with their 3″ mortars in Eritrean highlands

Indian troops constructing a road in Eritrea

Some of the Bren-gun Carriers of a famous Indian Cavalry Regiment in the mountains of Ethiopia

The Italians appeared to have planned the defence on a semi-circle starting from the south-west of Keren, passing through Laal Amba and settled on both sides of the Keren-Nacfa road. They were aware of the importance of retaining their hold on Keren and had brought up their best available troops there. Both native and white troops, *Bersaglieri*, *Alpini* and *Blackshirts* had been assembled. Italian deserters warned the British authorities of the danger of indiscriminate entering of any defended localities or villages by mechanical transport as the Italians had dug a number of long-deep holes covered with brush, hessian and sand, so as to be invisible to the moving transport.

The Italians thus had troops facing all the three possible approaches to Keren. They had also constructed a strong lay-back position in the Habi Mantel area. The extension of their positions to the north-west was designed to cover their observation posts and new gun positions from where they could shell the British gun areas and the line of communication. It was not considered likely that the Italians would start an offensive, although their *Cavalry Group Squadrons* (the *15th Group* had relieved the *2nd* and *3rd Groups*) had begun to be active in patrolling, going as far north as Al Al. The strength of the Italian forces in the Keren area at the beginning of March was approximately 350 Cavalry, 14,350 Infantry and 2,200 artillery—about 17,000—which with engineer and administrative services gave a total strength of approximately 30,000. It was clear by about 9 March that the Italians had mostly white troops in the front line between Sanchil and Samanna, and there was wire over most of the front, possibly to discourage desertions.

Attempts to outflank Keren

While preparations were made for a large-scale frontal attack on the Keren positions, attempts to outflank the Italian positions were not abandoned. Beginning with the first attempt by 1/6 Rajputana Rifles to find a way round Mt. Scialaco on 3 and 4 February, in all seven separate attempts were made. Of these, four were directed at getting round the south and south-east on to the Keren-Asmara road and three round the north and north-west.

The very day 1/6 Rajputana Rifles returned from its first attempt on 4 February, a patrol from Gazelle Force went along the River Baraka in an effort to get through to Asmara. It reached Mai Aghif, twenty-five miles north-west of Asmara, where the track became unsuitable for mechanical transport. Another patrol striking further south reached Pt. 900 near Mai Beicui on 8 February, after which it could not make further progress. On 15 February, two patrols were sent out from Central India Horse. The one to the north had orders to reconnoitre a route to Keren round the north flank via Mamud. On 16 February, it came to a halt at Mansciua, unable to go any further. The second going to the south reached Mai Aghif on 17 February, but like the Gazelle Force patrol it could not get any further. On 22 February, an Intelligence Officer went on a four-day reconnaissance of the Amer and Haris areas in an endeavour to locate Italian positions and to find a possible route to the Keren - Asmara railway. He could not proceed beyond Pt. 2182. The farthest point in the south was reached on 24 February when the Central Indian Horse patrol in Mai Beicui area reached Mai Aragghez, another five miles south-east of Mai Beicui. The patrol was recalled 'the next day as it could not make further progress.

On 5 March, another patrol consisting of an officer from the Headquarters 4th Indian Division and Sapper and Royal Tank Regiment representatives went on a reconnaissance to the north-east of Mt. Beit Gabru to find a possible route for mechanical transport and tanks round the north flank. But it could not find any practicable route. Again on 8 March, a patrol from the 51 Commando was sent to the Mansciua area with similar orders but without success.

Outline Plan for the Attack

On 1 March 1941, an outline plan for a fresh attack on Keren was formulated. Both the 4th and 5th Indian Divisions were to carry it out together. The 4th Indian Division was to operate on the north and west of the road and its objectives included Mt. Sanchil, Brig's Peak, Hog's Back, Saddle, Flat Top Hill, Mole Hill and Samanna. After the left flank had thus been secured, the 5th Indian Division was to attack east of the road. The exact objectives for this division were not defined at this stage. In the north, the 7th Indian Infantry Brigade was ordered to launch an attack towards Keren from near the Anseba and Mescelit Junction. It was also directed to exert pressure by operating towards Keren-Habi Mantel road. The date for the attack was fixed as 15 March.

In order to obtain the maximum artillery support, the attack of the 5th Indian Division was planned to take place after that of the 4th Indian Division. Sufficient time was allowed between the two attacks to enable defensive fire on the 4th Indian Division front and concentrations in support of the 5th Indian Division to be arranged.³

After further reconnaissance, the 5th Indian Division was directed to capture Mt. Dologorodoc and Mt. Zeban. This objective, though very formidable, had certain advantages. The reverse slopes of the hills were comparatively gentle and it was possible for the artillery to hit targets on the other side of the crest. This fact was expected to be of great value in breaking up counter-attacks. Being near the 4th Indian Division, close co-operation between the two divisions might be ensured and each could help the other effectively. The problem of the artillery switching from the support of the 4th Indian Division to the support of the 5th Indian Division was comparatively simple. The objectives were within range of almost all the guns of both the divisions, and it was not necessary to move the guns. The time lag between the two attacks was thus reduced to a minimum. This automatically relieved the strain on the 4th Indian Division, which was bound to be counter-attacked strongly, soon after reaching its objective.

The alternative course was once again to force Acqua Gap. Success in this area offered the chance of cutting off the greater part of the garrison of Keren. Its disadvantages were that the two divisions could not effectively support each other, the 5th Indian Division not having the benefit of all the 4th Indian Division guns. Against numerically superior Italian forces, there was a danger of both the attacks failing for want of weight. The maintenance of the 5th Indian Division through the bottleneck between Fort Dologorodoc and the bridge would be liable to interference by the Italians. Also, there was no chance of getting the tanks and carriers up Acqua Gap. Thus, although a drive through the Dongolaas Gorge would not succeed in cutting off so many Italian forces, it offered a better chance of opening the road to Asmara.

The 5th Indian Division was not to move forward until the last possible moment. This was both to keep the Italians in the dark about the date of the intended attack and to allow the forward dumping programme to continue unhindered.⁴

The 4th Indian Division Plan

In the battle of Keren the role of the 4th Indian Division was threefold:—

---

³Platt's Despatch on Operations in Eritrea and Abyssinia, dated 11 September.

⁴Ibid.

(i) to secure the general line Sanchil-Brig's Peak-Hog's Back-Flat Top-Samanna,
(ii) to co-operate with the 5th Indian Division by giving it artillery support, and
(iii) to be prepared to exploit forward to Mt. Amba and Mogareh.

The Commander of the 4th Indian Division planned the attack on a two brigade front. The objectives of the 11th Indian Infantry Brigade were Mt. Sanchil, Brig's Peak, Hog's Back and Flat Top. The 5th Indian Infantry Brigade on the left was detailed to capture Mt. Samanna. The 51 Commando was to operate under Divisional orders from the area of Cle Aful to the south-east towards Mogareh. The zero hour for the attack to start was fixed at 0700 hours on 15 March 1941.[5]

Brigade Plans

At the time of this operation the 11th Indian Infantry Brigade consisted of 2 Camerons, 1 Rajputana Rifles and 2 Mahratta and had under command the 1st Royal Fusiliers, 4 Rajputana Rifles and the 4 Field Company Sappers and Miners. The objectives allotted to the battalions were as follows :—[6]

2 Camerons — Mt. Sanchil and Brig's Peak.
1 Rajputana Rifles — From Brig's Peak exclusive to Hog's Back inclusive.
2 Mahratta — From exclusive Hog's Back to inclusive Flat Top.

The 1st Royal Fusiliers and 4/6 Rajputana Rifles were in brigade reserve, and their role was to hold the original forward line and form a mobile reserve to support the attack with small arms fire by observation and assist in capturing any part of the objective which the attacking troops failed to capture. It was also to counter-attack if the Italians penetrated any part of the objective after its capture and exploit success in the direction of the Mogareh plain or Mt. Amba.

The 5th Indian Infantry Brigade consisted of 3/1 Punjab and 4 Sikh with the following under command :—

A and B Squadrons Central India Horse
Mortar Troops Central India Horse
Detachment 1 MMG Group SDF (eight guns)

---

[5] 4th Indian Division Operation Instruction No. 34, dated 11 March 1941.
[6] 11th Indian Infantry Brigade Operation Instruction No. 16, dated 11 March 1941.

The brigade was to attack Mt. Samanna with 4 Sikh and to capture its objectives-Left, Centre and Right Bumps-successively.[7] The brigade reserve was to consist of 3/1 Punjab with the following under command :—

    A and B Squadrons Central India Horse
    Mortar Troops Central India Horse
    Detachment 1 MMG Group SDF (eight guns)
    Two 3-inch mortars 4 Sikh

The role allotted to the reserve was to secure the positions already held on the line Mt. Jepio-Pt. 1572-Pt. 1710-Pt. 1702 and to give fire support to the attack by 4 Sikh.

The 5th Indian Division Plan

The 5th Indian Division was to capture and hold Mts. Dologorodoc and Zeban, and then exploit eastwards with the object of completing the elimination of all Italian forces in the Keren area.[8] The commander of the division had planned the operation in four phases. The first phase was the capture of Mt. Dologorodoc and the second, the capture of the line Falestoh Ridge (spur running north-west from Mt. Falestoh) Pt. 1552-Pt. 1717. The 9th Indian Infantry Brigade was to carry out both these attacks. The third phase was the capture by 29th Indian Infantry Brigade of Mt. Zeban and cross roads. In the last phase, exploitation was to be carried out by the 10th Indian Infantry Brigade which was to be in reserve in the first three phases.

Brigade Plans

The 9th Indian Infantry Brigade was composed of 2nd West Yorkshire Regiment, 3 Mahratta and 3 Royal Frontier Force Regiment less one company, at the time of this operation, and 2nd Highland Light Infantry from the 10th Indian Infantry Brigade was put under its command. The objectives allotted to the brigade were Mts. Dologorodoc, Falestoh and Zeban. It was to exploit on the northern slopes of Mt. Zeban. The Brigade plan was to attack with the 2nd Highland Light Infantry with brigade mortar platoons under command and capture Pinnacle, White Rock Hill and Dologorodoc Fort. The attack was to start at 1030 hours from the west bank of the water course south of the bend but it was not to be launched until the capture of Mt. Sanchil by the 4th

---

[7] 5th Indian Infantry Brigade Operation Order No. 4, dated 12 March 1941.
[8] 5th Indian Division Operation Order No. 8, dated 13 March 1941.

Indian Division. After the capture of the Fort by the 2nd Highland Light Infantry, 3 Mahratta was to attack from the line of the main road west of the Fort, pass through the 2nd Highland Light Infantry and capture Mt. Falestoh and the ridge running to the north-west. This unit was to commence movement from the starting line at zero hour plus 90 minutes. Lastly, the 2nd West Yorkshire Regiment was to start from the road west of the Fort at zero hour plus 120 minutes and capture Mt. Zeban.[9]

The 7th Indian Infantry Brigade operating from the north under the orders of Headquarters Troops Sudan was to cut the line of Italian communications east of Keren on the Keren-Asmara road.

From the information then available it appeared that *9th Colonial Battalion* and *105/106th Colonial Battalion* (amalgamated) were on Mt. Ab Aures ridge from the Anseba to the northern slopes of Ab Aures (Pt. 1620). General Lorenzini was reported to have his Headquarters on a jebel in the above area. He feared the infiltration of British troops through the mountain paths of the Ab Aures range and had placed his troops accordingly. It appeared that the Anseba would be defended by artillery. These were probably secondary positions for troops established on heights commanding the Keren-Asmara road.

Air Support

The air situation had improved steadily since the start of the advance and, by 10 March, the Royal Air Force had established its superiority over Keren. Commencing four days before the day fixed for the attack, the air force was asked to increase steadily its bombing programme over Keren with the task of dealing with any Italian artillery which might be seen firing. By 14 March, the day before the attack, it was to have bombers over the area continuously from 0500 to 1800 hours. In addition, fighter and bomber air support was arranged for each divisional attack.

A Difficult Task Ahead

The British and Indian troops were deployed for the attack on Keren on 15 March 1941. A difficult task lay ahead of them for the Italians were not only numerically superior but they had also the advantage of terrain. They had, at Keren, thirty-three battalions (possibly thirty-four) including the *Savoy Grenadier Division*, the best troops in the whole of Italian East Africa, over one hundred

---

[9] 9th Indian Infantry Brigade Operation Order No. 7, dated 13 March 1941.

and twenty guns and a larger number of mortars and machine guns. During the course of the battle they were to bring up another nine battalions. Against this the 4th and 5th Indian Divisions disposed between them nineteen battalions and about one hundred and twenty guns. In addition there was one squadron of "I" tanks (Matildas), but it could not be used until the road block was cleared. Though the Royal Air Force had gained local air superiority it was feared that the Italians would concentrate all their air strength to break it.

As regards position on the ground the advantage lay with the Italians. On the Allied side the hills rose high and steeply from the Ascidira valley. Mt. Sanchil was an almost sheer rise of 2,412 feet, while Mt. Dologorodoc, the lowest hill in front of the troops, was 1,475 feet, above the valley. Mts. Beit Gabru and Amba were even higher. The climbs were steep on the craggy slopes, with great boulders and outcrops of cliff-like rock. The Italians had prepared a very strong defensive position on this natural barrier. They had erected a continuous wire fence from Acqua Gap to Mt. Beit Gabru. It varied in thickness from a single fence to ten parallel belts in the areas likely to be attacked.

The Italians had some other advantages as well. The Keren valley was 1,500 feet higher than the Ascidira valley. Motorable roads ran up to Fort Dologorodoc and the foot of Mt. Amba. They held all the high features in the area and had constructed mule tracks to the top of these features. A pipeline for water had also been laid up to Mt. Sanchil. Yet, in spite of all these drawbacks, the British and Indian troops were to win a splendid victory at Keren. Their attack was planned upon a large scale with artillery and air support and carefully devised administrative arrangements. The capture of Keren was as vital to the British as its defence was to the Italians. A decisive British success here presaged far-reaching consequences. It pointed to the early fall of Asmara and the rapid collapse of Italian East Africa. The Italians were known to be staking a great deal on holding Keren. They had concentrated a high proportion of their best troops there and were expected to put up a determined resistance and fight hard before giving in. Previous encounters with the Italians, however, had shown that if they were subjected to relentless pressure they were liable to crack and in the withdrawal they became disorganised. The attack on Keren was therefore to be pressed home with full vigour and the Italians were to be hit hard to prevent them from carrying out an orderly withdrawal.

CHAPTER VIII

The Battle of Keren

The plan of operations, as outlined in the previous chapter provided for joint attack on Keren by the 4th and 5th Indian Divisions, the former to operate on the north and west of the road and the latter to the east of it. The initiative was to be taken by the 4th Indian Division, whose objectives included the series of hills from Mt. Sanchil to Mt. Samanna. The divisional plan was based on a two-brigade attack which was to be launched by the 11th and 5th Indian Infantry Brigades, and the date fixed was 15 March. In the paragraphs below the operations of the two brigades are narrated separately.

Attack by the 11th Indian Infantry Brigade

The 11th Indian Infantry Brigade was deployed for the attack with three battalions: on the right 2 Camerons was directed on Mt. Sanchil and Brig's Peak, in the centre 1/6 Rajputana Rifles headed for Hog's Back, and on the left 2/5 Mahratta Light Infantry was directed on Flat Top. On 14 April stores were carried to the dump. At 1900 hours, 2/5 Mahratta moved to the assembly area on the left of 1/6 Rajputana Rifles getting into position at 2130 hours. At this hour, 2 Camerons began its move up from the railway line to its assembly point and 1/6 Rajputana Rifles got into position. The assembly was carried out without incident or interference by the Italians. The night passed quietly and by 0600 hours, the next morning, the 11th Indian Infantry Brigade was in position according to plan. The attack was timed for 0700 hours on 15 March.

The attack went in as timed. The artillery bombardment opened at 0700 hours, but as the leading troops went forward the Italian defensive fire caused a number of casualties. Heavy artillery and machine gun fire from Mt. Sanchil and Brig's Peak was directed against 2 Camerons, which nevertheless continued to advance slowly, with C Company directed on Brig's Peak and B Company on Sanchil. By 0815 hours, C Company almost got to the top of Brig's Peak but failed to drive out the Italians. However, B Company encountered very stiff opposition and failed to make much headway in securing Sanchil. At 0850 hours one company and at 1030 hours another company of the 1st Royal Fusiliers came under command of 2 Camerons. But, in spite of these reinforcements, 2 Camerons failed to capture Sanchil and Brig's Peak, as the Italian opposition was quite determined. *Savoy Grenadiers* poured machine gun fire, mortars and grenades down the slopes. In consequence, by 1600 hours, 2 Camerons had suffered heavy casualties and was unfit for further fighting. At that hour at Brig's Peak only a few men of C Company (2 Camerons) had survived from the grim ordeal; the only survivors of the company of 1st Royal Fusiliers were the Commander and eight men. The Commander of B Company 2 Camerons with about eight men had reached the top of Sanchil but had been driven off. No further progress was possible with the depleted forces, hence it was decided to use the rest of the 1st Royal Fusiliers to complete the capture of Sanchil. The attack by the Royal Fusiliers on Sanchil passed the forward company positions of 2 Camerons at 1815 hours. At 2300 hours, this attack was reported to be going on slowly but little headway could be made against the strong Italian positions. Thus not much progress was made either at Sanchil or Brig's Peak. The terrain in this area was very difficult, consisting of boulders and small trees and intersected by small Khors which made observation of movement at times impossible.

On the left of 2 Camerons, 1/6 Rajputana Rifles was directed on Hog's Back. Its objective was from excluding Brig's Peak to including Hog's Back. The plan was for B Company to secure Hog's Back, on the capture of which A Company was to pass through to capture Bich Hill on the right. C Company was to move approximately 400 yards behind A Company. It was to be ready to assist A Company on to its objective and to capture Saddle. D Company was to be in reserve. One section Mortar Platoon was to assist B Company on to its objective whilst the second detachment was to follow behind B Company and to be prepared to cover A Company on to its objective. The Carrier Platoon was placed under the command of A Company.

The battalion came under defensive fire, which the Italians put down when the British guns opened up. It suffered several casualties even before crossing the start line. However, by 0830 hours, it was able to capture Hog's Back though not without suffering severe losses. Three companies had been committed to secure this objective. At this time the Commander of the 11th Indian Infantry Brigade felt that the battalion was not in a fit state to attack Bich Hill and Saddle. He, therefore, ordered the battalion to consolidate on Hog's Back. A rough estimate showed that, of the three forward companies, most of one, half of the second and a good proportion of the third had been knocked out.

At 1030 hours, the Italians put in a counter-attack on Hog's Back from the direction of Saddle but it was repulsed. At 1230 hours, C Company and one platoon of B Company 4/6 Rajputana Rifles were placed under the command of 1/6 Rajputana Rifles, which kept them in reserve and used up its fourth company to strengthen Hog's Back. Throughout the early part of the night and again at 0430 hours next morning the Italians made repeated counter-attacks against Hog's Back but were driven back by 1/6 Rajputana Rifles.

To the left of 1/6 Rajputana Rifles, 2/5 Mahratta attacked Italian defences on Flat Top. The objective of 2/5 Mahratta was from exclusive Hog's Back to inclusive Flat Top. The plan was for C Company on the left to secure Flat Top (from including prominent tree to including boulder) and D Company on the right to secure Slab Rock (from including prominent tree to including Slab Rock). A Company was to advance behind D Company, pass Slab Rock on the west and secure the saddle of low ground between Hog's Back and Flat Top (excluding prominent rocks to including prominent tree on the east edge of Flat Top). B Company in reserve was to move up immediately in the rear of the Battalion Headquarters to the area south of Slab Rock feature. Its role was to capture Mole Hill, about 400 yards north of Flat Top.[1]

The attack was launched in accordance with the plan at 0700 hours. Heavy defensive fire from the Italian artillery and mortars came down forward of the starting line and caused considerable losses in all companies advancing on the objectives. The Commander of D Company and some of his headquarters men were wounded but the company continued to advance and seized its objective, the Slab Rock feature, without much difficulty at 0720 hours.[2] A Company advancing behind D, passed Slab Rock on the west and moved on towards its objective—the saddle of low ground between Hog's Back and Flat Top. After hard fighting the company captured its objective by 1030 hours. It had to cross three belts of wire before it could get into the Italian positions. C Company, detailed as the left forward company with Flat Top as the objective, advanced at 0700 hours. It approached Flat Top from the south-east but was held up when only fifty yards from it. Further efforts were made to get into the position round the west flank but were unsuccessful. The company suffered heavy casualties in the process.

---

[1] 2/5 Mahratta Operation Order No. 1, dated 12 March 1941.
[2] It was commanded by Subedar N. Palao.

The battalion plan was based on saving the reserve company for the capture of Mole Hill, but when the situation deteriorated around Flat Top, D Company was sent in to attack that feature from the east. In this the company suffered severe losses, particularly from an Italian medium machine gun which opened up at twenty yards' range as the company advanced towards the crest of Flat Top. This machine gun was, however, ultimately silenced and by 1440 hours, the objective had been captured. The casualties sustained by the two companies, engaged on Flat Top, were so heavy that the idea of advancing on to Mole Hill was given up and the companies were ordered to consolidate their position on Flat Top. At 1600 hours, the total strength of the two companies on Flat Top had been reduced to one British officer, two Viceroy's Commissioned Officers and thirty-four Indian other ranks. Italian sniping from Mole Hill continued until dark. At dusk, considerable Italian artillery and mortar fire was opened up and caused more losses to the Indian troops.

At 1600 hours, the 11th Indian Infantry Brigade was informed that 3 Royal Garhwal Rifles was being put under its command forthwith, but that it could only be used in a static role. Hence the Brigade Commander ordered 3 Royal Garhwal Rifles to relieve 4/6 Rajputana Rifles which was then to come into brigade reserve. In addition, it was decided to use all available men from battalion and brigade B Echelons to thicken up the defences. They were sent up at 1730 hours and formed into two composite platoons (one British and one Indian). The British platoon was placed under the command of 1/6 Rajputana Rifles and occupied a feature to the south of Hog's Back, called Near Feature. The Indian platoon came under the command of 2/5 Mahratta for a counter-attack on Flat Top. Thus at nightfall on 15 March, the 11th Indian Infantry Brigade had made some progress in the teeth of opposition. Though heavy casualties had been sustained, Hog's Back had been captured and 1st Royal Fusiliers was on the move forward to attack Sanchil. Flat Top had also been taken and a way opened for further advance.

Attack by the 5th Indian Infantry Brigade

The 5th Indian Infantry Brigade detailed 4/11 Sikh to capture Mt. Samanna. The leading company advanced from Pt. 1710 at 0700 hours to capture Left Bump. This feature was secured without much difficulty for the attack was made before the Italians could recover from the artillery concentration. Then the other two companies moved on to their respective objectives—Middle

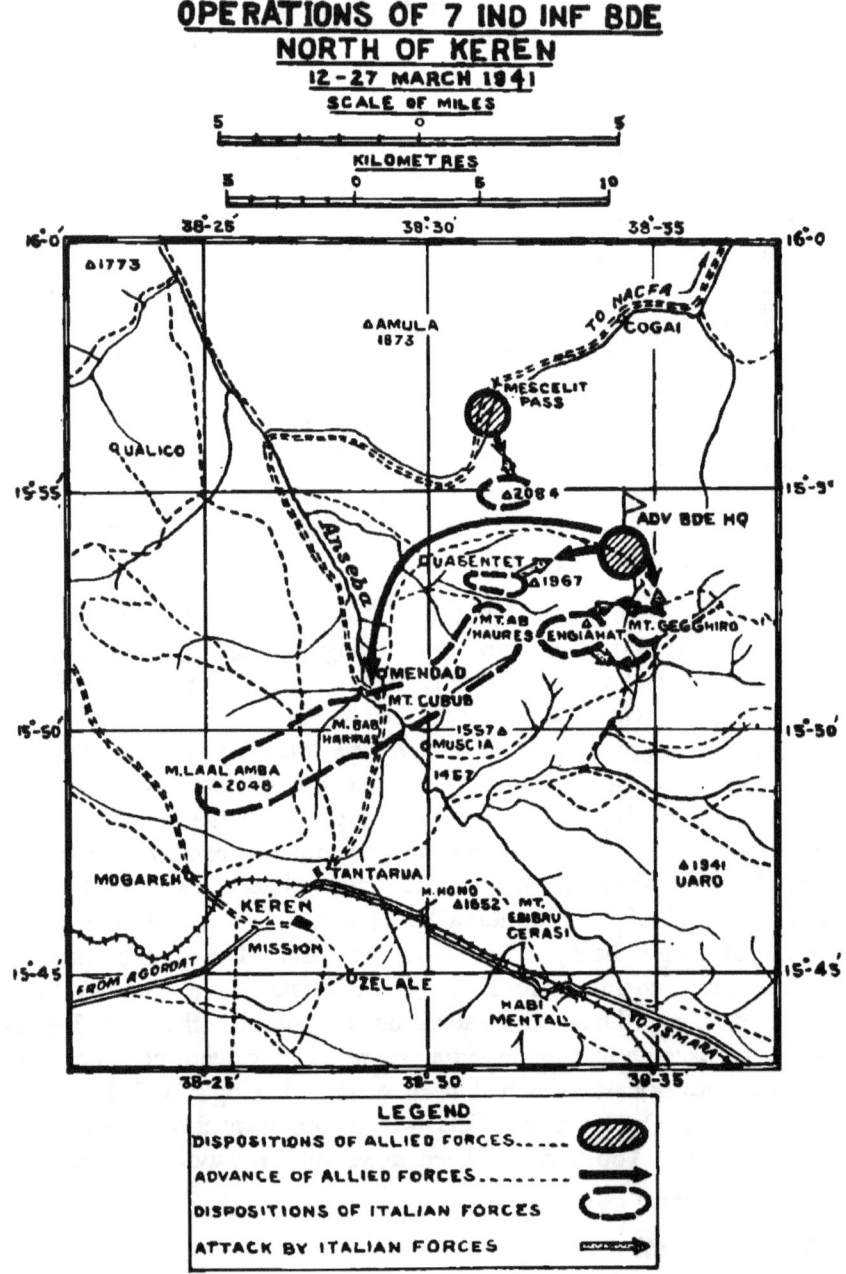

Bump and Right Bump which were held by *1st Alpini Battalion 10th Savoy Grenadier Regiment*. By about 0830 hours, the second company had reached within 200 yards from the crest of Middle Bump but was held up by determined resistance. Meanwhile the third company pushed on to Right Bump but was held up about 400 yards from the top. *1st Alpini Battalion*, which held these features, offered stubborn resistance and held up the advance of 4/11 Sikh. Further efforts to capture Middle Bump were unsuccessful, although the reserve company was also committed. It was then decided to abandon the attack on Right Bump, which had been found to be very strongly held by about four hundred Italians. The company in front of Right Bump was withdrawn successfully and ordered to assist the attack on Middle Bump. This attack, supported by artillery, was put in at 1335 hours but failed. Plans were made to attack during the night using the reserve battalion, 3/1 Punjab. This proposal was not accepted by the Commander of the 4th Indian Division, owing to the necessity of keeping this flank secure. It was, therefore, decided to withdraw 4/11 Sikh from the area of Middle Bump. The situation at nightfall was that 4/11 Sikh had captured Left Bump, but had failed to secure Middle Bump and Right Bump. It had suffered about 120 casualties during the day.

Diversionary Operations of the 7th Indian Infantry Brigade North of Keren

The leading troops of the 7th Indian Infantry Brigade had arrived south of the Mescelit Pass on 3 March. After that there lay between the brigade and Keren only the range of formidable hills covering the pass south of Mendad. At that time the Italians had six battalions in that sector. They were increased to seven by 12 March. The role of the brigade was to operate in the north to prevent the Italians from moving troops from that sector for use in the main battle in the south. Also it was to cut the line of Italian communications east of Keren and to interfere with their movements. The preliminary operation was the capture by the 1st Royal Sussex of Pt. 2084 ridge as far as the line of the water course running east and west to the south of Vasentet. This operation was to be completed by the evening of 13 March. Royal Sussex was then to patrol vigorously in the plain to attract Italian attention and to pay particular attention to the protection of its right flank. Then the main operation was to be carried out in two phases. In the first phase, 4/16 Punjab was to capture the line from Pt. 1557 to Pt. 1457 and to consolidate on this line and support further operations by fire. In the second phase, the Free French units (3rd Chad Battalion and 14th Battalion Foreign Legion) were to capture and consolidate the line Mt. Hono (Pt. 1652) Mt. Ebibru, Cerasi. From this line they were to send patrols to the Keren—Asmara road and prevent the passage of Italian troops and vehicles along it.

On 12 March, Advanced Brigade Headquarters and 4/16 Punjab moved from the bivouac area at Cogai to an area two miles to the north-east of Mt. Engiahat. It was hoped to accomplish the task set for 4/16 Punjab by surprise. The next day, reconnaissance groups spotted from Mt. Gegghiro some Italian troops on Pt. 1967. An observation post party sent at 1200 hours from 4/16 Punjab to Mt. Gegghiro, ran into an Italian observation post, which had been established there and all the men of the Indian party were killed or captured. Thus surprise was lost. On the same day, the 1st Royal Sussex encountered Italians on the Pt. 2084 ridge. The advance was held up and all efforts to reach their objectives on the ridge during the day failed.

When the presence of the Italians on Mt. Gegghiro became known, D Company 4/16 Punjab was detailed to drive them from there. It reached a spur running north from the feature but could not get any further. 14th Battalion Foreign Legion was, therefore, ordered to capture the feature before first light on 14 March. After the capture of Mt. Gegghiro, the latter battalion was to continue the operations in the area and capture Engiahat, it was hoped, before the Italians could reinforce it further. Mt. Gegghiro was captured by 0100 hours on 14 March, but the attack on Engiahat was not successful. One company of the 14th Battalion Foreign Legion, which was sent round the south-east flank, came under fire from the Italians and suffered very heavy casualties.

A reconnaissance party of 4/16 Punjab found that the Italians were holding the ridge running west of Pt. 1967. In view of this it became vital for the security of the line of communication to hold Pt. 1967. A and C Companies of 4/16 Punjab were therefore sent up in the afternoon to occupy it. They went up the five-thousand-foot climb with good speed. A party of the Italians, which was trying to occupy a feature to the north-east of Pt. 1967, was surprised and withdrew to Engiahat. Pt. 1967 was then occupied by the Punjab troops.

15 March was D day for the main attack on Keren. The role of cutting the Italian line of communication, however, had to be abandoned until the opposition at Engiahat was overcome. 4/16 Punjab sent out a patrol during the day to locate the Italian positions on Engiahat and to ascertain their strength. It was found to be

strongly held with machine guns. The ground already captured was, therefore, consolidated. The Foreign Legion battalion occupied Mt. Gegghiro, while the artillery registered Engiahat.

At 1300 hours, on 16 March, A and C Companies 4/16 Punjab attacked Engiahat, preceded by artillery fire. The Italians put up a strong resistance. The attacking companies reached the lower slopes of Engiahat, but then ran out of ammunition and had to withdraw. Meanwhile 1st Royal Sussex had failed to make any progress on the Pt. 2084 ridge.

The capture of Engiahat became difficult. On its spurs the Italians had constructed a series of fortified positions nearly a mile in depth. The only approaches to it were along two narrow ridges not permitting more than six men to pass at a time. The Commander of the 7th Indian Infantry Brigade made the following appreciation of the situation :—

(a) As Engiahat dominated the line of communication for the area of intended operations towards the Keren—Asmara road, its capture was essential before an advance in that direction was undertaken.

(b) It was necessary to build camel tracks up the hill side to a height of five thousand feet above the valley and to dump supplies, rations and ammunition before starting operations for the capture of Engiahat.

(c) Air photographs were required to enable definite objectives to be allotted to the different units. (This proved to be very difficult as, for many days, the air photos supplied seemed just to miss out the area required).

All these factors caused delay and further operations were not undertaken until 27 March.

5th Indian Division Operations

The plan of operations had allotted the capture of Mts. Dologorodoc and Zeban to the 5th Indian Division which had intended to execute it in four phases with the aid of two brigades, the third being in the reserve till these objectives had been secured. Accordingly, early in the morning of 15 March, the 9th and 29th Indian Infantry Brigades concentrated behind the lower slopes of Cameron Ridge. The assault on Fort Dologorodoc was to be carried out by 2nd Highland Light Infantry which was to approach its objective from a south-westerly direction. The attack was not to start until Mt. Sanchil and Brig's Peak had been secured by the 4th Indian Division. It was calculated that these objectives would be taken by 0900 hours. The exact time of attack depended on when the artillery supporting the 4th Indian Division might be spared to support the 5th Indian Division. By 0945 hours the situation on the 4th Indian Division front appeared to be sufficiently satisfactory for the 5th Indian Division to start its attack. At this time it was not known whether Brig's Peak and Mt. Sanchil had been captured though it seemed that they would be taken shortly.

Attack by the 9th Indian Infantry Brigade

The 2nd Highland Light Infantry, leading the attack, crossed the start line (west bank of the water course south of bend at 368858) at 1030 hours in order to capture Pinnacle, White Rock Hill and Dologorodoc Fort. The leading company was unable to cross the road owing to very heavy Italian artillery and mortar concentrations, and also enfilade machine gun fire from the top and the eastern slopes of Sanchil. The remaining companies tried to capture Pinnacle and Razor Hill from the south. But no progress was made. At 1500 hours, it was decided that further progress by daylight was not possible. The 2nd Highland Light Infantry was ordered to consolidate the ground gained and a new plan was formed. Preceded by heavy artillery concentrations on Pinnacle, Pimple and Fort Dologorodoc, 3/5 Mahratta was to attack Pinnacle from the south. 3 Royal Frontier Force Regiment was then to pass through and capture Pimple. Finally, after the first two objectives had been secured 2nd West Yorkshire Regiment, preceded by a further artillery concentration, was to pass through 3 Royal Frontier Force Regiment and capture the Fort. The first phase of this attack was originally planned to start at 1630 hours, but was later postponed to 1700 hours.

Crossing the start line at 1700 hours, 3/5 Mahratta encountered strong opposition. Yet by 1800 hours, it had reached Pinnacle, where a dogged fight ensued and the objective was not finally secured until 2000 hours. 3 Royal Frontier Force Regiment, less two companies, then passed through and captured Pimple at 0005 hours on 16 March. Touch was lost with the two forward battalions at this stage. The Commander of the 9th Indian Infantry Brigade, however, ordered 2nd West Yorkshire Regiment to move up to the low ground between Pinnacle and Pimple, in preparation for the attack on Fort Dologorodoc. At 0400 hours, the Italians put in a strong counter-attack on Pinnacle and Pimple. This met the whole of the 9th Indian Infantry Brigade in line and was beaten off.

The plan for the final phase of the attack had been for 2nd West Yorkshire Regiment to go through 3/5 Mahratta and 3 Royal

Frontier Force Regiment and assault the Fort under cover of a timed artillery programme. In the confusion caused by the counter-attack mentioned above, communications broke down and it was not possible to stop the artillery concentrations which came down on the Fort as planned. In fact, this proved to be most fortunate. The Italian counter-attacking forces found themselves between the small arms fire of the 9th Indian Infantry Brigade and the artillery fire falling on their own fort behind. They broke and were pursued by 2nd West Yorkshire Regiment into the Fort, which reached there at 0615 hours and immediately exploited for eight hundred yards beyond.

Subsequent 4th Indian Division Operations

On 16 March, on the 11th Indian Infantry Brigade front, 1st Royal Fusiliers and 4/6 Rajputana Rifles attacked Sanchil and Brig's Peak respectively while the Italians launched strong counter-attacks on 1/6 Rajputana Rifles at Hog's Back and on 2/5 Mahratta at Flat Top. 1/6 Rajputana Rifles and 2/5 Mahratta were counter-attacked a number of times during the night of 15/16 March. The forward positions had only been partially wired and the Italians managed to penetrate them many times and had to be ejected at the point of bayonet. A large number of high explosive grenades were used in repelling these attacks. The first counter-attack came simultaneously on both the battalions at 2230 hours on 15 March. Defensive fire was called for and the attack was repulsed by 2315 hours. The second counter-attack was on 1/6 Rajputana Rifles only. It lasted from 2315 hours on 15 March to about 0015 hours on 16 March, when it was driven back. At 0430 hours, on 16 March, there was a third counter-attack on 2/5 Mahratta and 1/6 Rajputana Rifles. In the Mahratta area, all the forward posts except one were recaptured by the Italians. This one post consisting of one officer and seventeen other ranks held on to the south-west edge of the position. A counter-attack by one Mahratta platoon was put in but was held up. Then a composite platoon from B Echelon under the command of an adjutant put in another counter-attack and, by 0515 hours on 16 March, had cleared the Italians from Flat Top at the point of bayonet.[3] The Italian counter-attack on 1/6 Rajputana Rifles at Hog's Back was less severe. The battalion held its ground until first light at 0500 hours on 16 March, when the Italians withdrew.

---

[3] A short description of the attack by 2/5 Mahratta on Flat Top and col between Flat Top and Hog's Back by Commander 2/5 Mahratta, dated 15 March 1941, Appendix III, War Diary 2/5 Mahratta.

While 2/5 Mahratta and 1/6 Rajputana Rifles were busy in repelling strong Italian counter-attacks, 1st Royal Fusiliers, reinforced by 4/6 Rajputana Rifles, attacked Italian positions at Sanchil and Brig's Peak. As mentioned earlier, the attack of 1st Royal Fusiliers on Sanchil had passed the forward company positions of 2 Camerons at 1815 hours on 15 March. At 2300 hours, on 15 March, this attack was reported to be progressing slowly but little headway could be made against the strong Italian positions. At 0245 hours, on 16 March, the Fusiliers were about two hundred yards below the top of Sanchil. At 0430 hours they launched a vigorous attack to drive out the Italians from Sanchil. The attack progressed slowly against strong opposition. By 0600 hours, the forward elements of the Fusiliers managed to get through the wire on to the top, but were driven back by superior numbers and mortar fire. At 0750 hours, the Commander of the Fusiliers was wounded and the second-in-command was sent up to take over and make a final effort for the capture of Sanchil. At 0015 hours, he reported that the Fusiliers were unfit to put in an attack on Sanchil as they had suffered heavy casualties, and the strength of the battalion at the time had fallen down to less then ninety men. Thus the Fusiliers had failed to drive out the Italians from Sanchil.

4/6 Rajputana Rifles attack on Brig's Peak was also not successful. This battalion had been relieved by 3 Royal Garhwal Rifles and had concentrated at Rajputana Hill for an attack on Brig's Peak at 0430 hours on 16 March. The plan was for B Company less one platoon to capture Brig's Peak. D Company was to secure Middle Bump and A Company to capture Sugar Loaf (the peak at the north-west end of Brig's Peak). Advanced Battalion Headquarters with C Company and one platoon B Company in reserve was to follow as soon as possible in the rear of the forward companies. The artillery support arranged for this attack was defensive fire to be put down on previously registered lines on Brig's Peak and Saddle, at half-hourly intervals from 0300 hours to 0500 hours, by which time it was hoped the leading troops would be nearing the objectives. However, the attack did not make much progress. Italian opposition was very strong and the Indian troops suffered heavy casualties. The leading elements could not get nearer than two hundred yards from the peaks, by 0800 hours. Another attack was put in at 0830 hours, using the reserves of the forward companies, but was no more successful. A further attack was arranged to take place at 1015 hours with air, mortar and machine gun. At 1005 hours, information was received that there would be no air co-operation, but that the attack was to go in at 1030 hours. It

Despatch riders in the Amba Alagi area

A truck of a mechanised column of an Indian cavalry regiment about to start on a patrol in the Amba Alagi area

A Bren-gunner and a rifleman in a stone sangar at an observation post, Ethiopia

A squadron section post and observation post beyond Amba Alagi

Road block partly cleared for the trucks to carry supplies to the forward troops in Ethiopia

Panorama of the country on the southern side of the Falaga Pass in Ethiopia

Members of the Jammu & Kashmir Mountain Battery at work camouflaging their guns

With bayonets fixed a platoon of Sikhs attack the enemy position up a mountain in Ethiopia

was, then, too late to change the original orders. Therefore, the attack was put in at 1015 hours, without support of any kind. It had not made much progress when it was brought to a halt by machine gun fire.

At this stage the 10th Indian Infantry Brigade was placed under the command of the 4th Indian Division for exploitation into the plain west of Keren. This brigade was ordered to move up to Cameron Ridge area in readiness for an attack starting from the line of the col between Sanchil and Brig's Peak. The attack was to start at 2100 hours. In view of this the 11th Indian Infantry Brigade was told to hold on to the ground gained and to continue the forward pressure.

On the 5th Indian Infantry Brigade front, no operations were undertaken on 16 March. 4/11 Sikh consolidated its position on Left Bump. It was subjected to intermittent mortar and artillery fire.

5th Indian Division Operations

On the 5th Indian Division front, on 16 March, the 9th Indian Infantry Brigade consolidated the ground gained. As mentioned earlier, Fort Dologorodoc had been occupied at 0615 hours on 16 March by 2nd West Yorkshire Regiment. The Italian reaction to this success was violent. The first counter-attack on the Fort came at 1005 hours. Defensive fire was called for; artillery engaged the Italian assembly area and the attack was broken up. The next attack came not long after. At about 1150 hours, a large number of Italians were observed to be forming up to the east of the Fort, evidently for a counter-attack. Two field regiments engaged the target and the Italians, estimated at three battalions, were scattered. In view of the impending counter-attack, air support, in the form of two fighter aircraft for strafing ground targets outside three hundred yards radius from the Fort, was arranged and the guns of both divisions were laid on. When, after all, the attack did develop at 1330 hours, it was repulsed. Although there were no further counter-attacks during the day, the troops holding the Fort were constantly shelled and sniped by the Italians who had complete observation of the area from Sanchil, Zeban and Falestoh.

Estimate of the Progress of Operations (15-16 *March*)

During these two days of fighting British and Indian troops had made some important gains. On the 5th Indian Division front, Fort Dologorodoc had been captured and held against persistent Italian counter-attacks. The capture of Fort Dologorodoc was of great importance since it afforded, for the first time, observation on to the Keren plain. On the 4th Indian Division front, the British and Indian troops, in spite of strenuous efforts, had failed to drive out the Italians from Sanchil and Brig's Peak. Further to the west, however, Hog's Back and Flat Top had been captured and held against strong counter-attacks. On Samanna, the Left Bump had been captured and held, though efforts to capture Middle and Right Bumps had been unsuccessful, and had finally been abandoned. The Italians still held all the dominating features and, while this state of affairs lasted, the British and Indian troops were exposed to heavy machine gun, mortar and artillery fire.

The Italians had offered stout resistance and inflicted severe casualties on the British and Indian troops with the result that some of the units were rendered unfit for immediate action. In addition to the determination shown by the Italians in the fighting, the failure of the British and Indian forces in gaining objectives, was due to the unfavourable weather and physical conditions. During the two days of the hard fighting, the weather was extremely hot and oppressive. Speaking of the operations on 15 March General Platt observed "Some of the efforts of the troops that day were defeated almost as much by heat and heat exhaustion as by hostile opposition".

Operations on 17 March

As the British and Indian troops in the forward line had suffered heavy casualties it was necessary to employ fresh troops for launching another attack. An attack on both the divisional fronts to break through to the Keren plain was now undertaken. On the 4th Indian Division front, the 10th Indian Infantry Brigade was ordered to break through between Brig's Peak and Mt. Sanchil and advance as far as the line of the water course running west from the railway and water course junction at 378883. This attack was to start from the line of the col between Sanchil and Brig's Peak at 2100 hours on 16 March. The Commander of the 10th Indian Infantry Brigade planned to carry out the operation in two phases. In the first phase, 3 Royal Garhwal Rifles was to capture Sanchil and 4/10 Baluch on the left was to capture Brig's Peak. In the second phase, 2nd Highland Light Infantry was to attack the col between Sanchil and Brig's Peak and break through on to the Keren plain and secure up to the line of the water course running west from the railway crossing over the water course at 378883.[4]

---

[4] 10th Indian Infantry Brigade Operation Order No. 1, dated 16 March 1941.

On the 5th Indian Division front, the 9th Indian Infantry Brigade was to consolidate its position in the Fort area and the 29th Indian Infantry Brigade was to attack forward of the Fort and capture Falestoh Ridge—Pt. 1552—Zeban—cross roads 402883. The attack was to start from the Fort and the time for it was to be approximately 2200 hours on 16 March. The actual time was to be decided by the Commander of the 29th Indian Infantry Brigade, after reconnoitring the approach and considering the state of the moon.[5] This operation was also conceived in two phases. In the first phase, the 1st Worcestershire Regiment on the right was to capture Falestoh Ridge up to Pt. 1552, and 3/2 Punjab on the left was to capture Zeban Minor up to Pt. 1717. The attack of the 1st Worcestershire Regiment was timed for 2230 hours on 16 March and that of 3/2 Punjab for 2245 hours. In the second phase, 6 Royal Frontier Force Rifles was to capture the remainder of Zeban and cross roads 402883. This attack was to start at 0300 hours on 17 March.

Attack by the 29th Indian Infantry Brigade (17 March)

The concentration of the 29th Indian Infantry Brigade in the area of the Fort prior to the attack was very seriously delayed. The climb up the Hill was very difficult, the track being narrow and having large quantities of cable laid across and along it. The last battalion did not reach the Fort area until 0100 hours on 17 March. The zero hour for the attack was, therefore, changed to 0230 hours. The artillery fire in support of the attack opened at 0230 hours on 17 March. The delays in this attack, however, were not yet over; 1st Worcestershire Regiment miscalculated the time needed to get to its start line and was one and a half hours late. However, once it had crossed the start line, it made good progress and by 0730 hours had established itself on a little feature, a hundred yards to the south of Pt. 1552, on Falestoh Ridge. All attempts to get to the top of Mt. Falestoh were, however, unsuccessful and the battalion suffered heavy casualties—23 killed, 55 wounded and 7 missing.

On the left, 3/2 Punjab made some progress. The plan was for D Company to move north of the Fort track and secure Zeban Minor. C Company following D Company in the rear was to secure Pt. 1717. A Company following C Company in the rear was to secure the col north of Pt. 1552 on the left flank of 1st Worcestershire Regiment. Battalion Headquarters and B Company were to move behind A Company. The attack took place according

---

[5] 5th Indian Division Operation Instruction No. 18, dated 16 March 1941.

to plan and D Company crossed the start line at 0230 hours on 17 March. D Company, not being fired at from M.G. ridge (a small feature immediately below the Fort), moved on towards its objective. Hardly had it gone 800 yards when it met the Italians in a strong position just east of a small nullah. This position was attacked at once by D Company from the front and by the two other companies following (C and A Companies) from the right and the left. Although Italian machine guns on the flanks caused heavy casualties, the attack was pressed home with determination and the position was captured.

At 0600 hours, the Italians put in a counter-attack on the forward positions. This was repulsed. In order to help in repulsing this counter-attack, B Company 6 Royal Frontier Force Rifles was placed under the command of 3/2 Punjab and was ordered to move up on the left flank. The ground over which it had to pass was swept by machine gun fire from Sanchil and Railway Bumps. The company, however, rushed across this area and eventually captured forty prisoners. Its own losses were three killed and five wounded. At the same time some Italian troops were seen creeping up the northern slopes of the Fort. They were engaged by fire and forced to withdraw. The advance of the forward companies was held up by heavy machine gun fire from M.G. ridge. B Company, in reserve, engaged the Italians in position on M.G. ridge and the machine gun fire from this ridge was neutralised by Bren and mortar fire. The advance on Zeban was resumed again. By 0730 hours, the forward troops had reached the bend in the track. Further advance was held up by heavy fire from Zeban Minor and col. This situation remained unchanged until 1300 hours. Then the Brigade Major was sent forward to get exact information about the situation. The weather continued to be hot and the maintenance of the forward troops with water and ammunition was found difficult. The forward troops had been moving and fighting for nearly twenty hours, and their positions were very exposed. The Commander of the 29th Indian Infantry Brigade appreciated that all the above factors had combined to break the impetus of the attack. As no fresh troops were available to carry on it was decided to withdraw the forward troops to less exposed positions after dark.

At 1600 hours, British aircraft dropped supplies of food and ammunition on the two forward battalions. A great volume of hostile fire from the ground greeted the aircraft and the supplyd rop was not a success. Owing to faulty packing the ammunition was bent and many of the supplies fell so far away from the battalion areas that they could not be recovered.

At 1900 hours, B Company 6 Royal Frontier Force Rifles was counter-attacked again. This was a very strong effort by the Italians, but the Company fought gallantly and held its ground at the cost of over a third of its total strength. Heavy casualties were inflicted on the Italians also, and the attack was finally repulsed. During this attack two platoons from C Company 6 Royal Frontier Force Rifles reinforced B Company. Captain Anat Singh Pathania displayed great courage in this keenly-contested engagement. Although wounded in the face and both legs he rallied his men to a final charge and pushed out the Italians at the point of the bayonet from his company's position where they had succeeded in penetrating.

The withdrawal started at 2300 hours on 17 March and the 1st Worcestershire Regiment moved back to a position on the slope south-east of the Fort (Big Rock area). The movement was covered by 3/2 Punjab, which retired to a position about 800 yards in front of the Fort.

Attack by the 10th Indian Infantry Brigade

To conform with the 29th Indian Infantry Brigade operations, the attack by the 10th Indian Infantry Brigade was so timed that the leading troops would reach their objectives about 0330 hours on 17 March. The two leading battalions, 3 Royal Garhwal Rifles and 4/10 Baluch, therefore, moved from their assembly areas at 0130 hours. 3 Royal Garhwal Rifles was led by guides provided by 1st Royal Fusiliers to within one hundred and fifty yards of the top of Sanchil. The attack was launched at 0300 hours with D Company on the right and B Company on the left, C Company being in reserve. Although the troops fought well the advance was held up by heavy machine gun fire from Brig's Peak and by grenades and mortar fire. A dogged fight continued until 0700 hours but no progress was made. The Garhwalis suffered heavy casualties.

Meanwhile 4/10 Baluch too had not made much progress. The battalion moved off from Granite Peak (3585) behind the Garhwal Rifles, crossed the col and reached the lower slopes of Brig's Peak. The attack was launched with C Company on the right and B Company on the left, D Company being in reserve. The attack was met by heavy machine gun and mortar fire and could not get nearer than three hundred yards from the objective. At 0530 hours, the Italians put down defensive fire, artillery and mortar, and inflicted severe casualties. Under their accurate fire it became difficult to get the wounded away. The forward companies were withdrawn to about a third of the way from the Brig's Peak feature at 0700 hours.

Throughout the day the two forward battalions, 3 Royal Garhwal Rifles and 4/10 Baluch were subjected to heavy fire. By the evening of 17 March, it was clear to General Platt that the attack had failed and that the 10th Indian Infantry Brigade would have to be withdrawn. The Italian strength on Sanchil-Brig's Peak had been underestimated. The forward troops had suffered heavy casualties. They could also not be maintained due to heavy fire. Success was not likely to be gained even if the weak 2nd Highland Light Infantry (the only remaining battalion of the 10th Indian Infantry Brigade) was committed to battle. A further assault, in the face of strong opposition, would have probably resulted in the destruction of the 10th Indian Infantry Brigade, the only reserve force available. He, therefore, decided to withdraw the 10th Indian Infantry Brigade, leaving the 11th Indian Infantry Brigade to hold on to Hog's Back and Flat Top. The 10th Indian Infantry Brigade was to be concentrated again as Force Reserve.[6] The withdrawal was carried out during the night of 17/18 March without incident (2nd Highland Light Infantry remained on Cameron ridge until withdrawn on the night of 18/19 March). The 10th Indian Infantry Brigade had suffered heavy casualties in the operations of 16/18 March. The casualties of 4/10 Baluch were 123—16 killed, 105 wounded and 2 missing. The casualties of 3 Royal Garhwal Rifles were 193—10 killed, 174 wounded and 9 missing. These figures are indicative of the intensity of the struggle.

The attacks on both the divisional fronts had thus spent themselves and the British and Indian troops were still in the hills with a hostile force, severely mauled but unbroken, between them and Keren. The attack by the 10th Indian Infantry Brigade on Brig's Peak-Sanchil had left no reserves with which to make further advance, once the 29th and the 10th Indian Infantry Brigades had been held up. A period of reorganisation was therefore necessary. A week passed during which the British and the Indian troops held the ground gained, while the Italians counter-attacked a number of times to recapture Fort Dologorodoc.

5th Indian Division Front

Between 18 and 22 March the Italians attacked Fort Dologorodoc no less than seven times. These attacks were beaten off and the British and Indian troops fought with courage and determination. On 19 March Italian General Lorenzini was killed on this front.

---

[6] Platt's Despatch on Operations in Eritrea and Abyssinia, dated 11 September, 1941.

He was respected by his troops and his death was a severe blow to them. Active patrolling was carried out during this period and efforts were made to start work on the road block to open the road to Keren for the passage of mechanised forces.

The 29th Indian Infantry Brigade had withdrawn from the area of Falestoh and Zeban early in the morning of 18 March. At 0230 hours, the Italians made a counter-attack from the direction of Railway Bumps and Falestoh. It was directed on the Fort and 2nd West Yorkshire Regiment had to bear the brunt of the attack. By first light, the attack had been beaten off and the Italians suffered several casualties in the fighting.

Again at 1645 hours, the Italians launched another attack on the Fort. It was preceded by heavy artillery concentrations, but was repulsed without difficulty.

At 0400 hours on 19 March, the Italians again made an attack. It was carried out by *10th Alpini Battalion* which had assembled in the depression of the valley to the west of the Fort. From there, two companies moved direct towards the Fort while one went round the north to the Hill (367860). They could get to within seventy yards of the Fort and were then driven back. The Italians reformed and made a more determined effort. They were repulsed again, and this time pursued with bayonets and grenades. They abandoned two pack guns, some mortars and machine guns.

A regrouping of British and Indian forces on Mt. Dologorodoc was ordered on 19 March. It was to be completed by the midnight of 19/20 March. The various features in the Dologorodoc area were to be held by two brigades. A forward brigade was to be responsible for holding the Fort and ridges four to six hundred yards north of it. In the south, its area was to extend as far as, but excluding the features at 382856 and 376860. It was also to be responsible for the protection of the working parties engaged in clearing a way through the road block. The 9th Indian Infantry Brigade was to take over this area.

The rear brigade was to hold the area 382856—376859-Pinnacle 375857. It was to be responsible for the protection of both flanks. It also had the role of operating astride the railway in the event of the Italians attacking in force from that direction. The 29th Indian Infantry Brigade was ordered to pull back and take over this area.

The relief was completed without incident. 3 Royal Frontier Force Regiment, less one company, relieved 3/2 Punjab on the features to the north of the Fort. The company of 6 Royal Frontier Force Rifles which was under the command of 3/2 Punjab passed to the command of 3 Royal Frontier Force Regiment. 3/5 Mahratta took over the Fort and 2nd West Yorkshire Regiment came out of the Fort to the area between the Fort and 376859.

After the relief, the dispositions of the 29th Indian Infantry Brigade were as follows:—

Brigade Headquarters	—Pinnacle
1st Worcestershire Regiment	—Area Pinnacle— 376859 - 382856.
3/2 Punjab	—Area Pinnacle.
6 Royal Frontier Force Rifles	—South of the peak.

The Italian counter-attacks had not exhausted themselves yet. On the night of 20/21 March, a patrol from 3 Royal Frontier Force Regiment found a party of Italians collected in a water course preparing for an attack on the left flank of the battalion area. The patrol attacked this party and dispersed it, capturing thirteen prisoners. At 2300 hours, a party of the Italians attacked the left forward company of 3 Royal Frontier Froce Regiment. The attack was preceded by a very heavy artillery and mortar concentration. This attack was beaten off, but was soon followed by a battalion attack on the right forward company of the same unit. This larger attack was supported by three light tanks and was pushed home in a very determined manner. After a sharp action lasting about twenty minutes, the Italians were again driven back at the point of the bayonet. They were pursued with grenades, and artillery fire took a heavy toll of them as they withdrew.

On 18 March, the 5th Indian Division planned an operation to make a way for 'I' tanks and carriers over the road block. The plan was to lay explosive charges and blow them up on the night of 18/19 March. During the night of 19/20 March, the maximum number of working parties was to be used to clear the debris and make a way for the tanks and carriers.[7] On the completion of this task a force, consisting of B Squadron 4th Royal Tank Regiment less one section, and with carriers in support, was to pass over the road block and exploit to Keren.

On 18 March, the sapper demolition party, with an infantry escort, went out after dark to work on the road block. The party contacted the Italians near the road block and had to withdraw.

---

[7] 5th Indian Division Operation Instruction No. 19, dated 18 March 1941.

However, it was reported that these Italians were only part of a counter-attacking force which was forming up in the area for attacking Fort Dologorodoc. Therefore, it was decided to repeat the attempt the next night.

During the night of 19/20, the Sappers were escorted by a platoon of 6 Royal Frontier Force Rifles. Some Italians were met with in the area of the road block again and the escort suffered nineteen casualties. The operation was, therefore, abandoned until such time as an attack could be arranged to clear the Italians from the ground from which small arms fire could be brought to bear on the road block.

At 1130 hours on 20 March, two "I" tanks reconnoitred along the road as far as the road block. The Italians opened with artillery and mortars, covering the demolition on both sides of the road.

Operations on the 4th Indian Division Front

After the withdrawal of the 10th Indian Infantry Brigade during 17/18 and 18/19 March the dispositions of the 4th Indian Division were as follows:—

11th Indian Infantry Brigade

Cameron Ridge	4/6 Rajputana Rifles (less two companies)
Excluding Cameron Ridge to Near Feature 353877	2 Camerons
Excluding Near Feature to Hog's Back	1/6 Rajputana Rifles plus two companies 4/6 Rajputana Rifles
Excluding Hog's Back to including Flat Top	2/5 Mahratta
In reserve	1st Royal Fusiliers

5th Indian Infantry Brigade

Left Bump	4/11 Sikh
Pt. 1710	3/1 Punjab and Brigade Headquarters

At 0440 hours on 19 March, 4/11 Sikh put in an attack on Middle Bump preceded by an artillery concentration. The attack was made on a two-company front. Some of the Italian machine gun posts on top held on in spite of the heavy artillery fire and barred the advance of the infantry when about two hundred yards from the objective. Italian troops on the feature were then reinforced. At 0800 hours, when the failure of the attack was apparent, the Commander of the 5th Indian Infantry Brigade ordered a withdrawal, which was completed by 0910 hours. 4/11 Sikh had eleven men killed and sixty wounded.[8]

On 19 March, two men of 3 Royal Garhwal Rifles, who had not received the withdrawal order on the night of 17/18 and had got left behind in the area of Sanchil, were brought in by an officer's patrol of 2 Camerons.

On 21 March, 3 Royal Garhwal Rifles was ordered to move into Happy Valley to achieve the following purposes:—

(1) to secure the flank of the 5th Indian Division,
(2) to protect the artillery in Happy Valley,
(3) to persuade the Italians to believe that an attack on Acqua Gap was being planned.

No other major events occurred before 24 March and the Italians continued to enjoy the advantage of complete observation over British and Indian positions held by both the divisions. The forward troops were shelled, machine gunned and sniped constantly. On the night of 19/20 March, the 11th Indian Infantry Brigade had arranged a programme of harassing artillery fire to cover the movement of the 5th Indian Division troops in the Dongolaas Gorge, but the Italian fire in return was so intense that the programme had to be cancelled.

As the time passed the weather warmed up and became very unpleasant for the troops in the valleys. As a result of preparations, however, during this period the administrative position improved considerably. There were more mules and more tracks for them

---

[8] Three new ideas were tried in this attack :—
(a) A proportion of the leading infantrymen carried corrugated iron shields as protection against the Italian hand grenades. The shields were not popular on account of their bulk and weight, but it was considered that the idea had potentialities and should be developed. One enthusiastic individual said that no less than six grenades had bounced off this shield and had left him only with a headache.
(b) In the artillery support programme the guns fired smoke shells in the last five minutes. The idea was not to obtain smoke effect, but to enable the infantry to approach near to the artillery fire while giving the Italians the impression that the bombardment was still going on. This idea also showed great promise, but on this occasion the infantry did not take full advantage of it, probably for want of training.
(c) In the middle of the artillery programme, the guns observed two pauses of five minutes' duration each. It was hoped thus to make the Italians think that the artillery had lifted and that the infantry attack was coming in, and to induce them to leave cover. It was not possible to assess the effect of this.

to use than before; still there was a good deal of manhandling to be done though the problem had ceased to be serious.

Air Situation

During this period of reorganisation, the Italian Air Force became active after a long spell of inactivity. Their fighters carried out a large number of patrols but were unwilling to engage British Hurricanes, unless in superior numbers and when operating from a position of initial advantage. British aircraft kept up their attacks on Asmara in addition to the standing patrols over the battle area. These patrols performed offensive, air photo and reconnaissance work.

During this period too the Royal Air Force received its first call for artillery reconnaissance. The first attempts were not successful owing to the lack of experience of pilots and gunners and some equipment difficulties. But within a few days very successful shoots were conducted.

5th Division Plan to break through the Road Block

From Mt. Sanchil a spur ran to the north-east. The railway ran along the east side of Sanchil and, after going round this spur, it turned west. At the level of the railway this spur flattened out into small broken hills, which were called Railway Bumps—which ended at the junction of two dry stream beds. The main stream bed was that of a water course which ran down the Dongolaas Gorge. A subsidiary one came in from the north-west. At the junction, the banks of the latter were very steep, the south-west bank being the Railway Bumps and the north-east one Railway Ridge. Machine guns on Railway Bumps and Railway Ridge commanded Dongolaas Gorge, the east side of Sanchil, the west side of Mt. Dologorodoc and the road block.

The attempt to secure protection for the Sappers working on the road block (380868) on the nights of 18 and 19 March had failed because of Italian positions in the area Railway Bumps—Railway Ridge—spur 384871 (East Gate Spur)—Hillock 'A' 377863—Hillock 'B' 380866. An operation was, therefore, planned,

> first, to secure ground from which close range small arms fire might be brought to bear on the road block area, next to prepare a way across the road block for the passage of tracked vehicles; and finally, to exploit towards Keren.

All these operations were to be carried out by the 5th Indian Division which had under its command B Squadron 4th Royal Tank Regiment (less one troop), ten carriers of 3/1 Punjab and one Field Company Royal Indian Engineers. In addition, the 4th Indian Division artillery was to fire in support of the 5th Indian Division and to distract Italian attention from the latter by sending fighting patrols in Brig's Peak area.

The divisional plan was to carry out the operation in four phases with some preliminary moves, and finally to exploit with a mobile force. The preliminary moves were to consist of:—

(1) Concentration of the 10th Indian Infantry Brigade less 3 Royal Garhwal Rifles in the area of Cameron Tunnel on 24 March.

(2) Sending of reconnaissance patrols on the night of 23/24 March to the area of Hillocks 'A' and 'B', and East Gate Spur.

(3) Despatch of fighting patrols by 3 Royal Garhwal Rifles on the nights of 23 and 24 March towards Acqua Gap.

The main operation was to be carried out in four phases. In the first phase, the 9th Indian Infantry Brigade with 28 Field Regiment in support was to capture Hillock 'A' by 0430 hours on 25 March. In the second phase at the same time, the 10th Indian Infantry Brigade less 3 Royal Garhwal Rifles was to advance on and capture Railway Bumps. It was then to exploit to hill 376882, if the situation so demanded. Simultaneously, the 9th Indian Infantry Brigade was to capture Hillock 'B'.

At 0445 hours, Sapper working parties were to advance to the area of the road block and commence work on clearing a way through it. It had been estimated that this task would take thirty-six to forty-eight hours.

In the third phase, the ground captured was to be consolidated. If necessary, for the protection of the right flank of the 10th Indian Infantry Brigade, the 9th Indian Infantry Brigade was to be prepared to secure the ridge west of 385876 (Railway Ridge).

In the fourth phase, the 29th Indian Infantry Brigade was to capture Zeban Minor. This was not to be executed before 26 March. Fire programme for this attack was to be arranged mutually between the brigade commander and the commander Royal Artillery.

Exploitation by a Mobile Force

A mobile force called Fletcher Force[9] was detailed for exploitation. The task allotted to this force was to advance down the main road to Keren in co-ordination with an attack by the 29th Indian

---

[9] The force was commanded by Lt. Col. B.C. Fletcher.

Infantry Brigade on Zeban Minor. It was to cut Italian communications and destroy guns, headquarters, rearward services and capture or destroy Italian forces in the Keren area.[10] During the exploitation phase, the 10th and 29th Indian Infantry Brigades were to co-operate in accomplishing the above tasks as opportunity offered.

The 4th Indian Division was to hold its positions and try to distract Italian attention from the operations of the 10th Indian Infantry Brigade by active patrolling and harassing the Italians. It was also to be prepared to exploit towards Sanchil-Brig's Peak-hill 358880, when ordered.

The 7th Indian Infantry Brigade was to co-operate, to the full, by exerting pressure on the Italians from the north.

The Attack

At 1745 hours on 24 March, 3 Royal Frontier Force Regiment reported that Italian artillery was registering Hillock 'A' (377863). At 2330 hours that night, a patrol from 2nd West Yorkshire Regiment occupied the feature and by 0430 hours two companies were established on it without the pre-arranged artillery support. Following this, 3/5 Mahratta advanced at 0430 hours and captured Hillock 'B' (380866) against strong opposition. By 0655 hours, it had taken a part of East Gate Spur. This came as a surprise to the Italians who retaliated by heavy and accurate shelling and mortar fire on 3/5 Mahratta and the road block, where the Sappers were already at work.

The attack by the 10th Indian Infantry Brigade started at 0430 hours on 25 March according to the plan and made good progress. The Italians had been expecting an attack from the direction of the Dologorodoc Fort, hence they were completely taken by surprise. Although they fought hard their opposition was overcome easily.

The objective of Railway Bumps had been divided into six separate points called 'A', 'B', 'C', 'X', 'Y' and 'Z'. Going from west to east, 'A', 'B' and 'C' were along the southern edge and 'X', 'Y' and 'Z' along the northern edge. By 0700 hours, 2nd Highland Light Infantry had captured 'A', 'B' and 'C' and 4/10 Baluch 'Y' and 'Z'.

3/2 Punjab had been placed under the command of the 10th Indian Infantry Brigade and was directed to capture Railway Ridge

---

[10] 5th Indian Division Operation Instruction No. 21, Dated 23 March 1941.

KEREN - THE

15-27 M

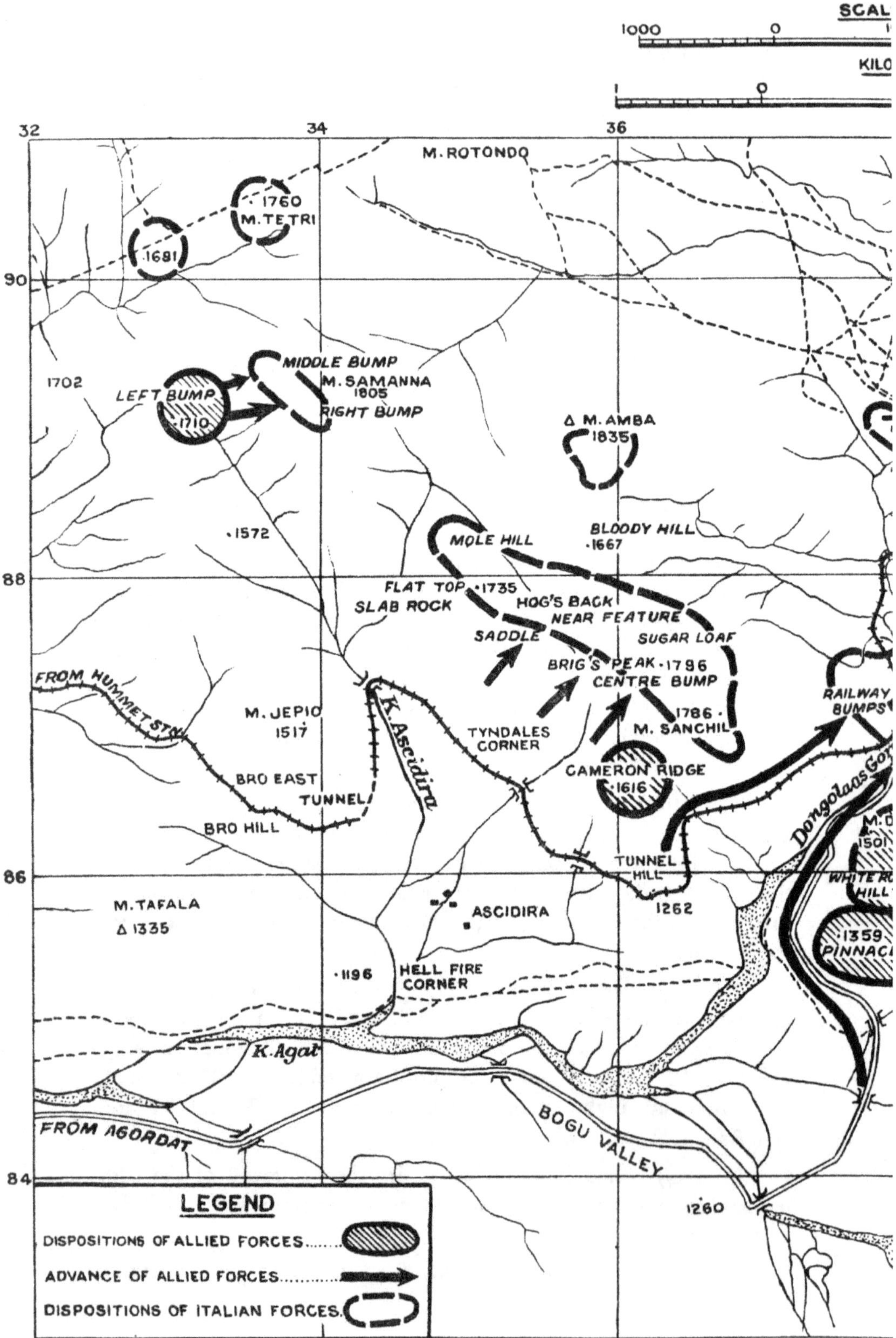

FINAL BATTLE
MARCH 1941

(383876), starting at 0945 hours. By 1025 hours, it had secured that objective.

The situation on East Gate Spur remained unsatisfactory for some time. 3/5 Mahratta reached its objective but was forced off it by enfilade fire which inflicted heavy casualties. The battalion put in another attack at 0945 hours, in conjunction with an attack by 3/2 Punjab. By 1045 hours, the situation had improved with 3/5 Mahratta consolidating on Red Hill, a part of East Gate Spur. In all, this battalion was counter-attacked four times but held its ground in spite of heavy losses.

Work on the Road Block

The tasks allotted to the Sappers during this operation were :—

(a) To clear mines from the road and railway as far as the forward troops might advance.

(b) To construct anti-tank obstacles and mine the road north of the road block to cover the troops working on the demolition.

(c) To clear a way for "I" tanks and carriers across the road block as soon as possible.

(d) To send a Sapper party with the mobile force to assist in removing obstacles and mines during the exploitation phase.

The Sapper plan was for the 2 Field Company to advance at 0445 hours behind the artillery barrage and start work on the block as soon as possible. The first task on the block was to demolish the large boulders. At 1830 hours, the 20 Field Company was to relieve the 2 Field Company on the block and carry on work until 2330 hours when it would be relieved by the 21 Field Company. An officer from B Squadron 4th Royal Tank Regiment was detailed as liaison officer with the commander Royal Engineers 5th Indian Division to advise him on the extent of work required to make a way for "I" tanks and carriers to pass.

The 2 Field Company advanced at the fixed time and commenced work on the road block. Although the Italians kept up a heavy fire on the road to the south of the block, the work on the actual site proceeded without much interference, and satisfactory progress was made throughout the day. Italian shelling on the road block increased in the evening, but work continued throughout the night and, by 1430 hours on 26 March, a way for "I" tanks and carriers had been cleared.

The Operations

At 1350 hours on 25 March, the Commander 10th Indian Infantry Brigade reported that the Italians were massing for a counter-attack at 390877 and asked for artillery to engage them. Thereupon the artillery engaged the Italian force and dispersed it. At 1340 hours, white flags were reported on Sanchil. Forward troops asked for artillery fire to be stopped but the General Officer Commanding 5th Indian Division ordered the fire to continue until the fire from Sanchil on the road block had stopped. The reports about the white flags, however, did not seem to be correct as the Italians continued to hold out. There were also reports of white flags on Zeban Minor but they were not confirmed.

During the night of 25/26 March, minor counter-attacks were put in by the Italians against 4/10 Baluch, in the Railway Bumps area, but were easily repulsed. Another counter-attack had been planned by the Italians to take place on the 3/5 Mahratta positions on Red Hill at 0500 hours. While the counter-attack troops were assembling the Mahrattas got scent of them and the attack was broken up by artillery and machine gun fire.

Also Italian movement eastward across the Mogareh plain was detected. All this seemed to indicate that they were preparing to withdraw. At 0725 hours, a patrol from 4/10 Baluch met a party of Italians who put up their hands. But on the approach of the patrol, they threw bombs at it and then ran away into the hills.

In planning for attack on Zeban the Commander of the 29th Indian Infantry Brigade had suggested that it would be best to attack at dawn on 27 March to save the troops from exhaustion from the stiff climb up to the objective. General Officer Commanding the 5th Indian Division, however, decided that, if the way across the road block was cleared, the 29th Indian Infantry Brigade was to be prepared to move at 1200 hours on 26 March. In his opinion a delay of several hours was likely to affect the subsequent operations adversely and the mere danger of the troops being exhausted was not enough justification for postponing the attack till the 27th.

It was however finally decided to start the attack at 0430 hours on 27 March. 3 Royal Garhwal Rifles was placed under the command of the 29th Indian Infantry Brigade for the operation. 3 Royal Garhwal Rifles had been relieved in Happy Valley on 25 March by the Central India Horse, which had, on that date, been placed under the command of the 5th Indian Division. The Commander of the 29th Indian Infantry Brigade had planned to attack on a two-battalion front. 1st Worcestershire Regiment was to capture

Zeban Minor and 3 Royal Garhwal Rifles, on the left, to capture the cross roads at 402883 and then to secure the line of the road Mission—Mogareh to the west of the main road. This would allow the main road to the north of the road block to be cleared of the mines. 6 Royal Frontier Force Rifles was to be in reserve.

The attack started at 0430 hours on 27 March with artillery support. When the infantry went in, very slight opposition was encountered and both the battalions had captured their objectives by 0600 hours. 6 Royal Frontier Force Rifles was ordered to advance through 1st Worcestershire Regiment and capture Mt. Zeban. This was done without opposition at 0730 hours.

It was now clear that the Italians had evacuated Keren. 6 Royal Frontier Force Rifles was ordered to exploit up to Mt. Canabai which was occupied at 1030 hours. Patrols were then sent out to round up the stragglers.

On the 4th Indian Division front, patrols, out during the night of 26/27 March, reported that the Italians were still holding their positions. At 0540 hours, 3/2 Punjab reported white flags on Sanchil. This was confirmed from more than one source by 0600 hours and arrangements were made to take over the positions. They had all been taken over by 1000 hours.

Operations of Fletcher Force

Fletcher Force was composed of following troops :—

B Squadron 4th Royal Tank Regiment (less one troop)	(eight tanks)
Carrier Squadron Central India Horse	(seventeen carriers)
Carriers 9th Indian Infantry Brigade	(thirteen carriers)
Carriers 10th Indian Infantry Brigade	(thirteen carriers)
Carriers 3/1 Punjab	(ten carriers)

At stated above, the task allotted to this force was to break through in conjunction with the 29th Indian Infantry Brigade attack and destroy all Italian communications, headquarters and guns in the Keren area. Fletcher Force's plan was to move with an advanced guard of one carrier Central India and one troop "I" tanks directed on to cross roads at 402883 as first objective and area 410895 as second objective. Of the main body, two troops carriers of Central India Horse were to move at the head and join the advanced guard on the second objective. Two "I" tanks and one light tank were to go to the Mission. Two Central India Horse troops carriers were to go to the area 410895 and thence to the Nacfa Road. The 9th Indian Infantry Brigade carriers were to go to Tantarua in the north-east quarter of the town, while the carriers of 3/1 Punjab were to remain at the cross roads at 402883.

Crossing the start point at the bridge at 377846, at about 0500 hours on 27 March, the advanced guard got as far as the road block. In trying to cross it the leading carrier got stuck on an incline where the engine failed and it had to be cleared back. The "I" tanks then tried and the leading one got across at about 0600 hours, and the second at 0620 hours, while the third and last of the advanced guard crossed at 0640 hours. At 0700 hours, orders were issued to Fletcher Force stressing the importance of advancing up the Nacfa road and trying to cut the retreat of Italian troops in that area, opposing the 7th Indian Infantry Brigade. It was also told to try to advance on Habi Mantel from the north.

The 10th Indian Infantry Brigade was allotted the responsibility of looking after Keren.

At 0730 hours, Sudan Defence Force armoured cars were sent forward with orders to follow up the withdrawal of the Italians along the road. They were to be launched under orders of the General Officer Commanding 5th Indian Division as soon as he could get them across the road block.

By 1000 hours, the mobile force had got across and was well on the way in pursuit of the Italians. At 1230 hours, the leading elements of this force were reported to be about one mile west of Habi Mantel. All the available aircraft had been put on to harass the Italians in their withdrawal.

7th Indian Infantry Brigade Operations

Owing to repeated delays in obtaining air photos it was not possible for the 7th Indian Infantry Brigade to attack until 27 March. In the intervening period continuous artillery fire was kept up on the Italian positions on Engiahat. Finally, an attack on Engiahat was planned in conjunction with the operations of the 5th Indian Division. Because morning mist prevented artillery observation, this attack could not be timed to start before 0730 hours. 4/16 Punjab pressed this attack with great vigour, the Chad Battalion co-operating on the left flank. The Italian resistance, however, was slight and it was soon clear that they had withdrawn the bulk of their forces during the night of 26/27 March. The Foreign Legion

Battalion was therefore immediately directed to advance into the Anseba valley to cut the retreat of the Italians and to establish contact with the 5th Indian Division. This was accomplished before dark and many prisoners were taken. 4/16 Punjab was ordered to advance to Mt. Cubcub and join up with 1st Royal Sussex, which was told to open the road to Keren.

Thus, after a siege of fifty-three days British and Indian troops entered Keren. The strategic possibilities of this position had been appreciated by the Italians for many years, and it was here that they had decided to make their main stand. They had concentrated the bulk of their forces in Eritrea in this area. From the build up of their forces and the statements of their prisoners it was clear that they were staking a great deal on holding this fortress. They feared that if Keren fell, Asmara, the capital of Eritrea, would also be lost. The selection of Fort Dologorodoc as an objective was very sound. Its capture put British and Indian troops in a strong position. Although it was overlooked by Sanchil and Falestoh, and was a very difficult position to hold, it was a key position in the system of the Italian defences. They wanted it back and their keenness was so great that, during the days following its capture, they made repeated efforts to take it and wore themselves out in a series of unsuccessful counter-attacks. In all, the Italians were estimated to have employed at Keren a total of thirty-nine battalions and thirty-six batteries. During the whole battle they used over thirty thousand infantry and one hundred and forty-four guns. Many of these were fresh troops.

General Frusci in his reports, admitted to having lost three thousand men at Keren including General Lorenzini. The total Italian losses probably were about ten thousand. He made much of the fact that he had managed to withdraw from Keren the bulk of his infantry and guns; but the fall of Keren had finally shattered the morale of the Italian Army. At the end of the battle of Keren there were only three battalions and few batteries uncommitted between Keren and Asmara. Practically all had been staked on holding Keren.

The British and Indian troops had fought hard and won. The battle was described by General Platt as "a ding-dong battle, a soldier's battle, fought against an enemy infinitely superior in numbers, on ground of his own choosing which gave him every bit of observation against the movement of our troops, the positions of our guns and the approaches of our transport". And it was won by "the tenacity and determination of commanders and troops, by whole-hearted cooperation of all ranks, whether forward or back, of whatever race or creed, and by the continuous support given to infantry by the Royal Artillery...". The British casualties were not light. Some 500 officers and 3,000 men had been killed and wounded. The 4th Indian Division was particularly hard hit. Yet the determination of the British and Indian troops to fight to victory was to leave its mark upon the Italians and to affect their conduct in the subsequent operations. They were never really to stand to fight again in the same spirit. The outcome of the contest in Italian East Africa was no longer in doubt. There were to be more battles and more victories before Italian East Africa was conquered, but Keren had broken the back of Italian resistance and subsequent operations were easier.

The conduct of the 4th and 5th Indian Divisions won them ready applause from several quarters. "The whole Empire", wrote the British Prime Minister to the Viceroy of India shortly after the victory at Keren, "has been stirred by the achievement of the Indian forces in Eritrea.........". He also congratulated Generals Platt and Cunningham upon "this timely and brilliant culmination of your memorable and strenuous campaign".[11] Lord Wavell, who had been awaiting the outcome of the battle with anxiety and had flown to the Sudan on 26 March to confer with General Platt, was evidently relieved. He found the victory "a fitting climax to the great work in Eritrea of the 4th and 5th Indian Divisions ably commanded by Major-General N. M. de la Beresford-Peirse and Major-General L. M. Heath respectively". He could now well think of transferring some of the forces from this theatre to the more important areas of war. Eritrea had ceased to present a military threat to the Allies.

---

[11] Churchill. *The Second World War*, Vol. III *The Grand Alliance*, 79-80.

CHAPTER IX

The Advance Continues

The Italians had managed to withdraw considerable artillery and some of the infantry from Keren. They were now to be pursued by the British and Indian troops and the advantage gained over the Italians at Keren pressed home. After Keren the Italians made little serious effort to defend Eritrea and within a fortnight of the capture of that fort both Asmara and Massawa fell. This removed Italian threat to the Allied shipping through the Red Sea and secured the strategic object of the campaign in Italian East Africa, namely, to make the Red Sea supply route safe and immune from an Italian attack.

The 4th Indian Division

After the fall of Keren the 5th Indian Division took up the pursuit of the retreating forces. The 4th Indian Division was detailed to clear the area of the battle, bury the dead and salvage British and Italian stores and equipment. The 5th Indian Infantry Brigade was ordered to go to a rest area. The 11th Indian Infantry Brigade was detailed to carry out the above job. On 29 March the 5th Indian Infantry Brigade was ordered to move at six hours' notice by mechanical transport. It moved next day to Agordat on way to Kassala. On 30 March, the 11th Indian Infantry Brigade was concentrated in a rest area and only small working parties were left to finish the clearing work. 25 Field Regiment less one battery and 1 Anti-Tank Troop Royal Horse Artillery left the 4th Indian Division and came under the command of the 7th Indian Infantry Brigade.

The 4th Indian Division remained in the Keren area doing garrison and cleaning up jobs until 17 April when it moved to Port Sudan en route for Egypt and the desert again. The liberation of the 4th Indian Division except its 7th Indian infantry Brigade from further fighting in the Eritrean campaign showed the decisive character of the battle of Keren. It also showed British confidence in their ability to beat the Italians in East Africa with a smaller force.

Pursuit by the 5th Indian Division

On 27 March, once it was over the road block, Fletcher Force went straight through Keren and on, pursuing the retreating Italians. By 1050 hours, it was eight kilometres beyond Keren and by 1320 hours it had covered another twelve kilometres. At 1830 hours the same evening, orders were received from General Platt putting the 5th Indian Division in charge of the pursuit operations. It was ordered to advance on Ad Teclesan and Asmara. The following units were placed under its command for this operation :-

Fletcher Force
68 Medium Regiment
41 Light Anti-Aircraft Battery
A Troop Light Artillery Battery
1 Motor Machine Gun Group (Sudan Defence Force).

The town of Asmara lay in the centre of a plateau about 7,000 feet high. The road from Asmara to Keren fell steeply from Ad Teclesan down to the level of Keren, a drop over 2,000 feet. Between kilometre 56 and Ad Teclesan the country consisted of big rounded hills, less rocky than those at Keren. Ad Teclesan was naturally strong, even stronger than Keren, for the approach wound through an even narrower valley and there was no room for the deployment of artillery which had played an important part in the battle of Keren. The railway took a different route south of the road but even along the railway there were very few places where wheeled vehicles might be deployed off the railway track itself. Had the Italians not been beaten so effectively at Keren the advance of the British and Indian troops would have been very difficult.

At 2100 hours on 27 March, General Officer Commanding 5th Indian Division issued orders for the formation of a mobile force under Brigadier J. C. O. Marriott. It consisted of the following units:—

Headquarters 29th Indian Infantry Brigade
Central India Horse (less one squadron)
B Squadron 4th Royal Tank Regiment (less one troop)
2 M. I. Company Sudan Defence Force
Other S. D. F. units on arrival
28 Field Regiment
3/2 Punjab in lorries
6 Royal Frontier Force Rifles in lorries
20 Field Company (less one section).

This force was to pursue the Italians along the Keren-Asmara road with the utmost vigour.[1] Fletcher Force was disbanded and taken over by the 29th Indian Infantry Brigade on the morning of

---

[1] 5th Indian Division Operation Instruction No. 24 dated 27 March 1941.

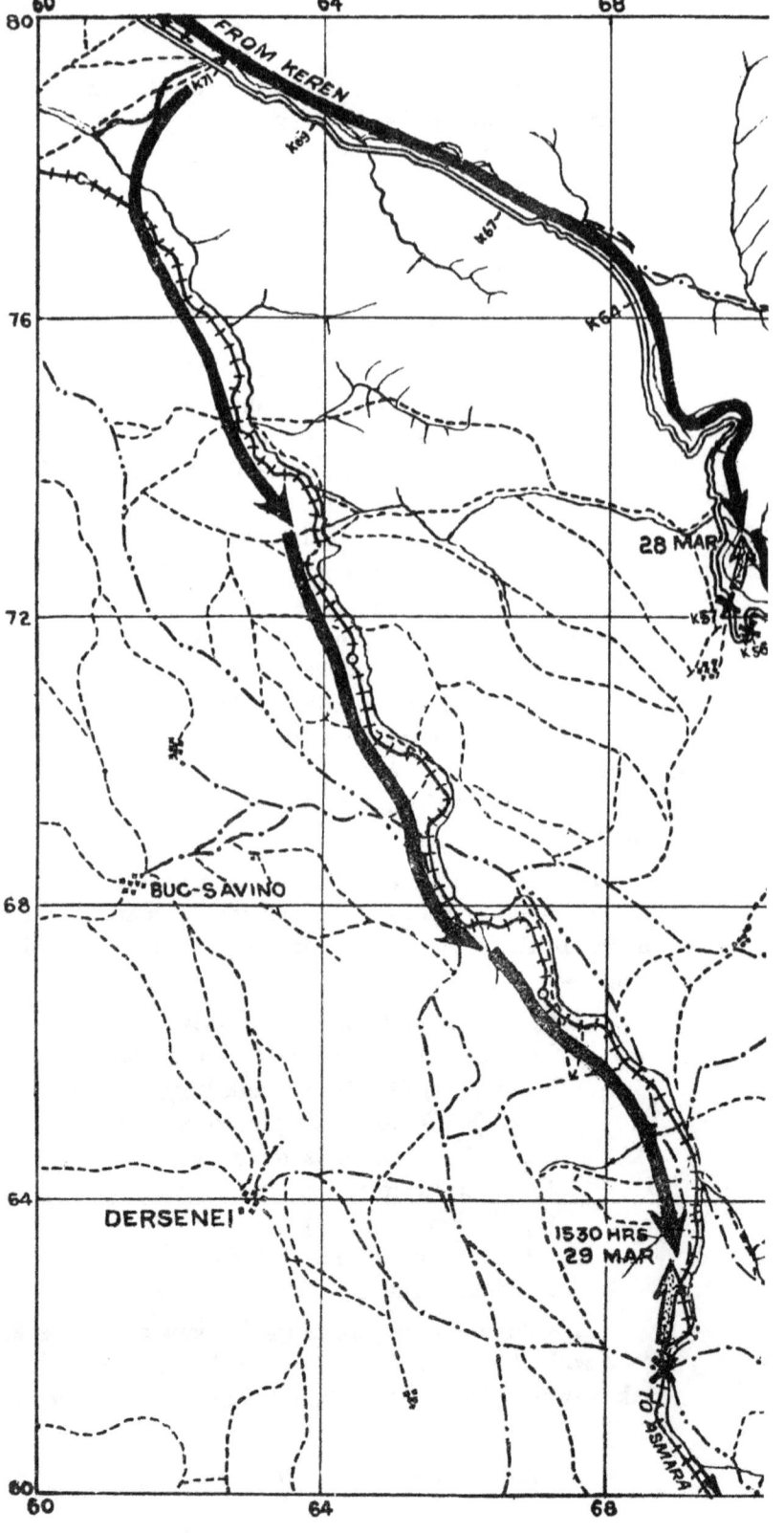

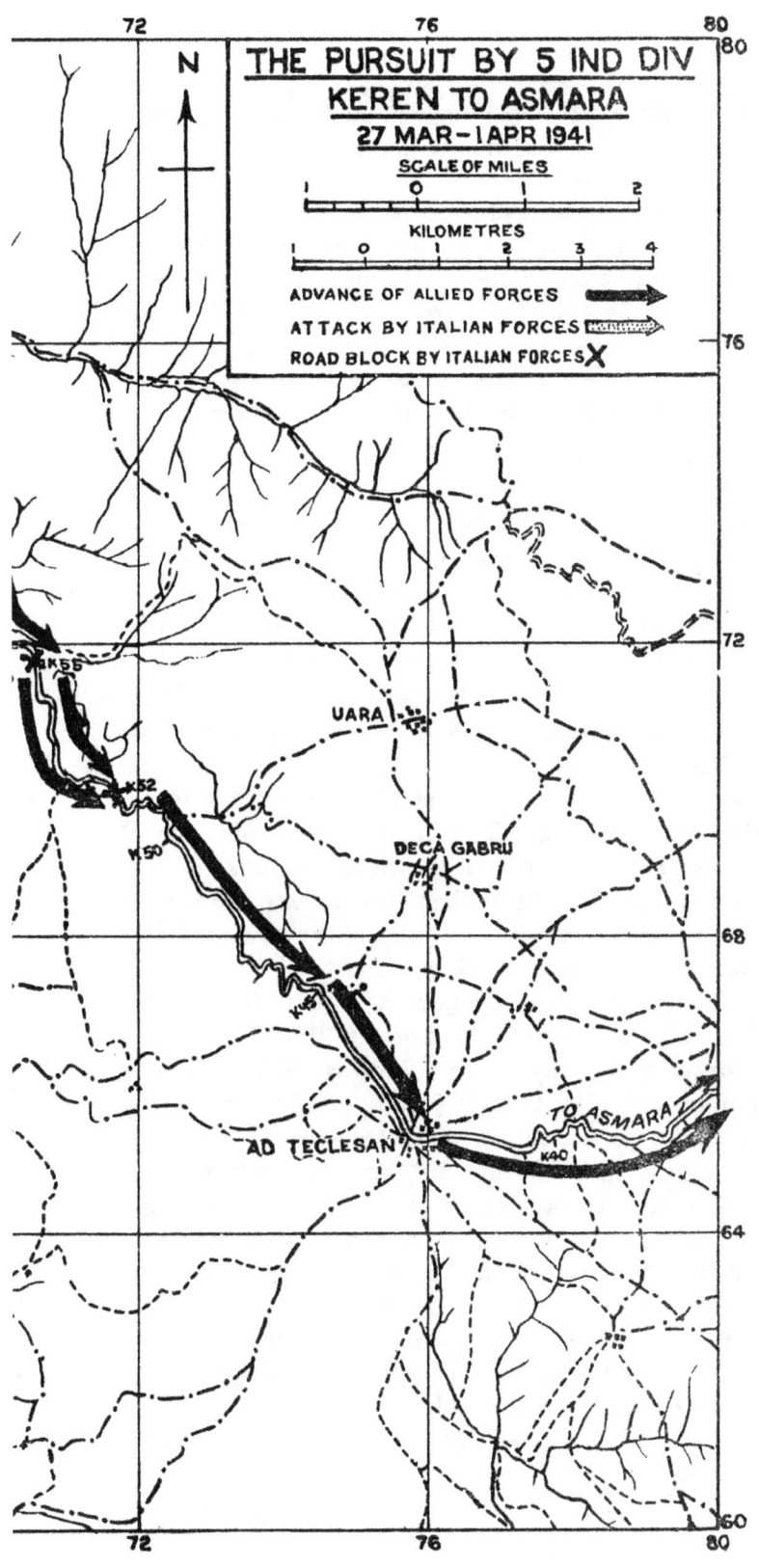

28 March. On the same day, 3/2 Punjab and 6 Royal Frontier Force Rifles concentrated forward and after reconnaissance launched an attack at 1445 hours. Except for one or two rounds from a pack battery and some machine gun and rifle fire on 6 Royal Frontier Force Rifles, no opposition was encountered and by 1630 hours both the battalions had captured their objectives, high hills overlooking the road block on both sides of the road. British light machine guns engaged Italian gunners trying to load up their guns. Eventually the Italians had to abandon these guns (seven) and withdraw; and so also did the Italian troops in the area south of kilometre 56.

The road block was cleared and the advance resumed at 0530 hours on 29 March with "I" tanks leading. Another road block was met at kilometre 55 (705718). Sappers were immediately employed and they cleared it for tracked vehicles by 1500 hours. In the meantime, 3/2 Punjab had also been advancing on both sides of the road. It met only slight opposition from the Italians and by 1500 hours had reached positions level with kilometre 55. This movement had also provided cover to the Sappers on the road block.

On 29 March at 1500 hours a mobile force consisting of one squadron from Central India Horse with three "I" tanks, seven armoured cars and two Bren vans of Sudan Defence Force under command, passed through the road block. It got as far as kilometre 52 (714701) where it was halted by heavy fire from Italian pack guns covering yet another road block. The Italians also attacked the armoured cars with bombs from high ground. One of the armoured cars and an Italian lorry which had been placed so as to block the road, were set on fire. By 1600 hours, 3/2 Punjab had also started advancing with the object of capturing the ridge from Pt. 2160 (7269) to Pt. 2129 (7270). Heavy fire was met from the Italians holding positions astride the road at kilometre 50. Pt. 2129 was captured and an attack on Pt. 2160 ordered in conjunction with the advance of the tanks. But, as the tanks were soon held up, this operation could not be completed. By this time it was getting dark. The mobile force which had come under the command of 3/2 Punjab was, therefore, withdrawn to the area between 54 and 55 kilometres for the night. One company 6 Royal Frontier Force Rifles was placed under the command of 3/2 Punjab and moved forward to strengthen the battalion's position. 3/2 Punjab had thus made good progress during the day. It had covered considerable ground against Italian opposition in a country well suited for defence. It had suffered only two casualties, one killed and one wounded, but captured about sixty prisoners, all from a fresh battalion of the *Savoy Grenadiers* which had been sent up hastily from Addis Ababa. Considering the natural strength of Italian positions they had not put up strong resistance and were driven back with comparative ease.

During the night of 29/30 March, the Italians put in only one counter-attack on Pt. 2160. It was easily repulsed. The night otherwise was quiet except for some shelling by the Italians.

The 10th Indian Infantry Brigade had been ordered forward of Keren on 29 March. It had moved up as far as the area of kilometre 71 the same day. The next day it moved up to kilometre 64, and the 9th Indian Infantry Brigade proceeded to kilometre 71. Air reconnaissance on the morning of 30 March revealed another serious demolition in the area of kilometre 45. From the heavy anti-aircraft and artillery fire it was apparent that this was the main Italian position.

At 0900 hours on 30 March another reconnaissance of the forward area was carried out by the General Officer Commanding 5th Indian Division along with the Commander of the 9th Indian Infantry Brigade. It was followed by a conference and orders were thereafter issued for the 9th Indian Infantry Brigade to attack the ridge astride the road at 726694 at 1630 hours. The 9th Indian Infantry Brigade, however, could not assemble in time. The attack was therefore postponed to 0445 hours on 31 March.

Advance along the Railway

On 29 March, when the advance along the road was being constantly interrupted, the Commander of the 10th Indian Infantry Brigade suggested an advance along the railway to outflank Italian positions on the road. With a mechanised column of one company 3 Royal Garhwal Rifles he moved along the line of the railway from the area of kilometre 71 (6279) on the road. At 1530 hours, this force reached a point about 22 miles from Asmara. Strong Italian opposition was met here and a defensive position was taken up at dusk. Reports by patrols indicated that Italian strength in this area was about a battalion and that a block had been erected on the railway by blowing it up at 690620 where it crossed a steep face of the hill.

On the next morning, 30 March, this detachment of the 10th Indian Infantry Brigade was reinforced with one company Highland Light Infantry, one squadron Central India Horse, and one Motor Machine Gun Company (Sudan Defence Force). But the Italian positions and the road block in front had effectively cut the line of advance. On 30 and 31 March efforts were made to find alternative routes around the flanks but they were unsuccessful. These efforts were still being continued on 1 April when news was received that Asmara had been taken.

Operations along the Road

On 31 March, 2nd Yorkshire Regiment of the 9th Indian Infantry Brigade made an attack on the ridge at 726694. It started at 0445 hours. The first objective was captured by 0603 hours and the second by 0715 hours. Four hundred and sixty Italian prisoners including 19 officers were captured. Most of them belonged to *1/10 Grenadier Regiment*. Further fighting continued during the day in which 1 Worcesters advanced a little after heavy fighting. At 1800 hours, 3 Royal Frontier Force Regiment attacked and captured Italian positions covering the area of the demolition on the road against slight opposition. At 0530 hours on 1 April Italian envoys with a white flag arrived from Asmara. They were from the civil authorities and stated that the military forces had evacuated Asmara and that the civil authorities wished to hand over the city. They said that there had been rioting during the night of 31 March/1 April by *50* and *51 Colonial Battalions* and that they needed British help to restore order.

The 10th Indian Infantry Brigade was ordered to move to Asmara by mechanical transport and entered the town at 1040 hours. The 9th Indian Infantry Brigade was ordered to move to Ad Teclesan. Headquarters 5th Indian Division also moved to Asmara the same evening.

After the occupation of Asmara, the civil administration of the city was reorganised. It was no mean task. The people were mostly armed and the occupation forces had no surplus police or troops for running the administration. The supply situation had also to be improved before a further advance could be undertaken. The task was well performed. There were no major disorders or serious attempts at sabotage.

Advance to Massawa

After the fall of Asmara the next British objective was the capture of Massawa with its harbour and shipping intact. It was the main port of Eritrea on the Red Sea and its possession was necessary to make the Red Sea a safe supply route. Along with the advance to Massawa a pursuit of the Italians along the two main roads leading south from Asmara was also organised. The 29th Indian Infantry Brigade was ordered to send a mobile force to reconnoitre the Zahafalam-Zagher-Massawa road. The force was commanded by Major G. P. Coldstream and consisted of two companies 6 Royal Frontier Force Rifles, two sections medium machine guns and one section carriers. It moved off at 1400 hours on 1 April. By the evening it had advanced fifteen kilometres from Zahafalam when it came up against a road block and halted for the night. The next morning it discovered that there were three big road blocks in the area of 15-17 kilometres. This was reported to the 5th Indian Division Headquarters and they ordered the force to withdraw. The force rejoined the 29th Indian Infantry Brigade at Ad Teclesan on 3 April.

On 2 April, a message was sent to the Italian commander of Massawa informing him of the British occupation of Asmara and of the impending advance on Massawa. He was called upon not to scuttle any ship in the harbour and was warned that, if he did so the British would not be responsible either for feeding the Italian population in Eritrea and Ethiopia or for its removal from those countries.[2] The Italian commander could not give any assurance on British demands and the negotiations therefore were broken.

Attack from the North

The 7th Indian Infantry Brigade (which after the fall of Keren had been ordered to concentrate in the area of Chelamet) was ordered to move eastwards. Preparations were also made to open a port at Mersa Cuba for maintaining supplies to this force when it reached the sea coast. On the capture of Asmara the 7th Indian Infantry Brigade received orders to send a mobile column, in addition to Free French, to Massawa to prevent sabotage there. This column consisted of 1st Royal Sussex, one battery 28 Field Regiment, one Anti-Tank troop and one platoon 7th Brigade Anti-Tank company. It was to advance through Mersa Cuba. Although tactically this route was not the best it was chosen in order to avoid coming into conflict with the advance of the Free French Column[3]. The British column moved on the night of 1/2 April and reached Mersa Cuba by 0930 hours. Its further advance was held up as vehicles got stuck into the sand. An advance guard, however, pushed forward for another fifteen miles. Then it came to a bridge which had

---

[2] Almost three fourth of the power available in Asmara was generated at Massawa and in the event of Massawa electric supply being cut off the electricity and water position in Asmara would have been imperilled.

[3] The Free French Column after the fall of Asmara was directed to proceed first to Ailet and then to Asmara-Massawa road between Ghinda and Dogali.

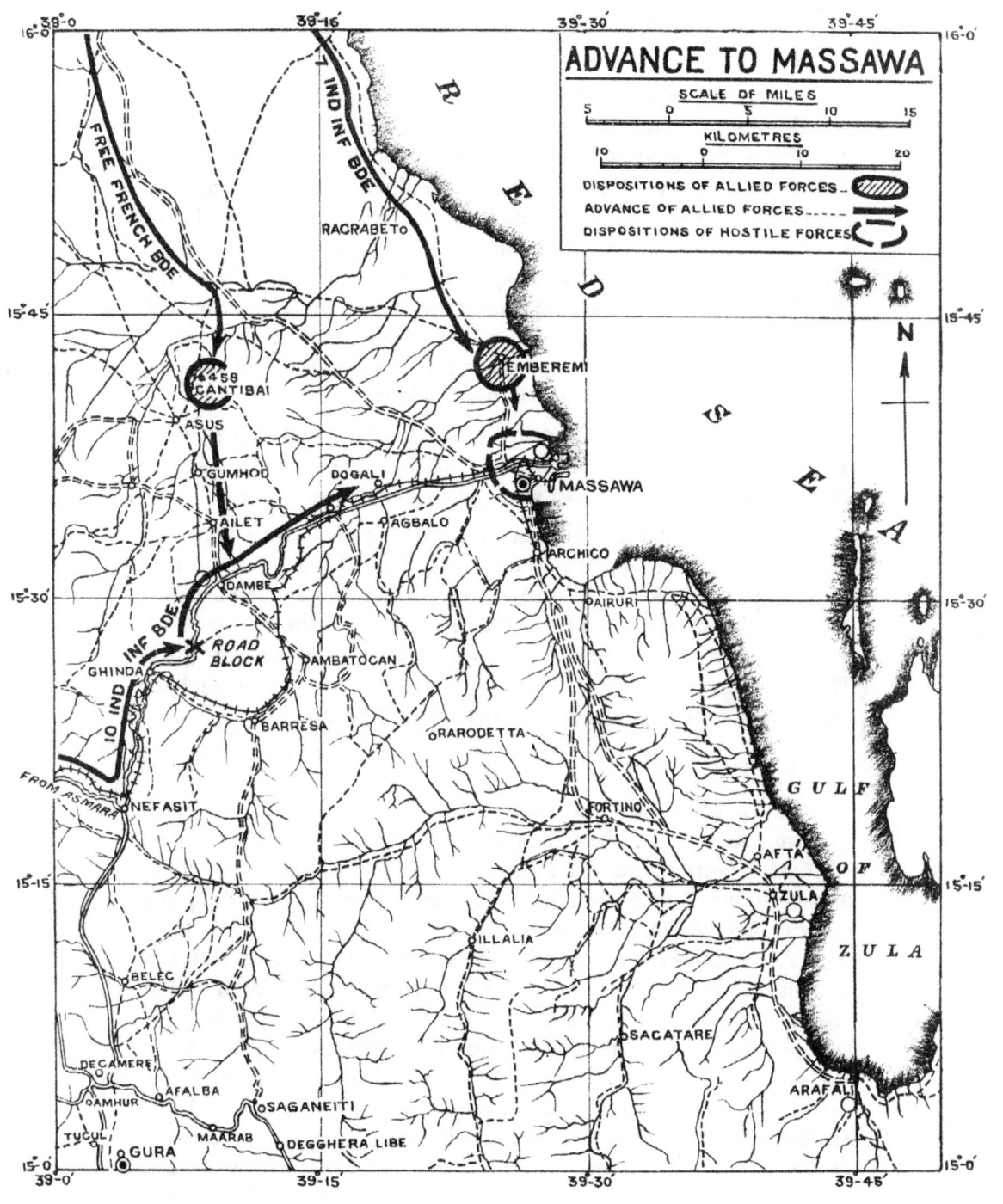

been burnt by the Italians. A diversion was found but the guns could not get across the bridge and the column had to halt for the night for the bridge to be rebuilt.

The advance was continued the next morning. The advanced guard passed through Embremi, six miles north of Massawa. Mine clearing work was started and went on unhampered for some time. From here Italian wire outside Massawa could be seen and it appeared from the lack of opposition met so far that the Italians did not intend to make a stand at Massawa either. But, suddenly, some thirty guns opened fire simultaneously. But as the Italians had been completely surprised their fire was uncoordinated. They had evacuated the outpost positions and still seemed to be under the impression that British advance was taking place along the Obellet road and not along the coast track from Mersa Cuba.

1st Royal Sussex was detailed to hold defensive positions covering the points where observation posts had been established and cover the positions where British guns had come into action.

On 4 April, the 7th Indian Infantry Brigade, which had been placed under the command of the 5th Indian Division was ordered to remain in the Embremi area to reconnoitre Italian defences and gauge Italian strength. The Chad battalion was sent to the Cantibai area to reinforce the Foreign Legion which was already there. The remaining units of the brigade group were ordered up and the whole force was concentrated in the area of Embremi.

The 5th Indian Division

The Asmara-Massawa road had been blocked at kilometre 18 from Asmara. By the midnight of 3/4 April the block was cleared. Orders were issued the same night for the 9th Indian Infantry Brigade to take over station duties in Asmara and for the 10th Indian Infantry Brigade to move to Massawa on 4 April. At 0530 hours on 4 April, the Free French Brigade reached the Asmara-Massawa road and found a road block about four miles east of Ghinda. The Free French Brigade had been warned of the advance of the 10th Indian Infantry Brigade which had left Asmara at 0615 hours but was held up for two hours at a road block at kilometre 30. In the evening Brigade Headquarters and 3 Royal Garhwal Rifles reached the road block at kilometre 55, four miles east of Ghinda. This road block was cleared by the evening of 4 April. On 5 April the 10th Indian Infantry Brigade moved to Dogali and found another road block at kilometre 10. By the evening a diversion had been made for the cars to pass.

Parleys

After the breakdown of negotiations with the Italian Admiral commanding Massawa on 2 April, as stated above, further parleys took place on 5 April. At 1300 hours a lorry with a white flag was seen in Asmara. An observation post, Sudan Defence Force Battery, which did not notice the white flag engaged the lorry with artillery fire. This was, however, stopped quickly and a party sent out to ascertain whether the Italians meant to surrender. The party was taken blindfold to the Admiral in command of Massawa. He asked for terms of surrender, which he said, he would signal to the Italian High Command. Same terms as before were sent to him. He passed them on to Rome but they were refused and hostilities were resumed at 1300 hours on 6 April.

Plan of Attack on Massawa

A plan for attacking Massawa was formulated on 7 April. The 5th Indian Division was put in command of the following forces for this operation :—

7th Indian Infantry Brigade
Brigade d' Orient Free French Forces
B Squadron 4th Royal Tank Regiment
233 Battery 68 Medium Regiment
2 Motor Machine Gun Group Sudan Defence Force
4 Motor Machine Gun Company Sudan Defence Force
A and B Troops Light Artillery Battery Sudan Defence Force.

The attack was planned to take place on 8 April. The 10th Indian Infantry Brigade with 21 Field Company under command and B Squadron 4th Royal Tank Regiment (less one section) in support was to capture in succession :—

Signal Hill	142071
Hill 36	143071
Swedish Mission	144071

The attack was to start from the line 140 north and south grid of square 140072 at 0400 hours.

The 7th Indian Infantry Brigade was to start from the east and west grid line 077 at the same time and capture the line Fort Otumlo-Fort (149071)-Abdel-Kader Peninsula (151071). It was to have 25 Field Regiment in support and, in addition, it was to make direct arrangements with the Royal Navy for support.

The Brigade d' Orient was to advance on the orders of the General Officer Commanding 5th Indian Division and capture Moncullo-Fort Moncullo-Fort Vittorio Emanuele. It was intended to launch this operation when the effect of the attack by the 10th Indian Infantry Brigade was felt by the Italians in or south of the squares 140070, 140071, 141070 and 141071.

B Squadron 4th Royal Tank Regiment (less one section) was to support the attack of the 10th Indian Infantry Brigade by moving along Wadi Boo-Tombe to the north of Signal Hill feature. After the general line of 145 north and south grid had been secured B Squadron 4th Royal Tank Regiment (less one section) was to pass on and attack Italian Headquarters and reserve positions and to advance on Massawa via the causeway. One section B Squadron 4th Royal Tank Regiment was to remain in divisional reserve and was to assist the Brigade d' Orient if it experienced difficulty in reaching its objectives.

Operations

Massawa was attacked from the north and the west. The 10th Indian Infantry Brigade moved forward during the night of 7/8 April and occupied part of the ridge running west and slightly north of Signal Hill without opposition. At first light the attack started with artillery support. The Italians were strong in artillery and made some show of defence but their troops had little heart. Although the Italian defences were elaborate a large number of them surrendered and became prisoners. The 10th Indian Infantry Brigade pushed on steadily and took Signal Hill and Pts. 66 and 51. The 7th Indian Infantry Brigade had some difficulty in the beginning as it encountered heavy artillery fire. However, it managed to get on along the sea coast and its carriers were the first to enter Massawa. The attack of the Brigade d' Orient was launched at 0630 hours and by 1120 hours Fort Vittorio Emanuele was captured. Massawa surrendered soon after and at 1400 hours the Admiral commanding Massawa made submission to the General Officer Commanding 5th Indian Division. All the ships in the harbour were found scuttled and harbour installations badly damaged. Guns and tanks had been run into the sea. Nine barges were seen by the air throwing their goods overboard. The scuttling, however, had been bungled and the ships were later recovered. On the Italian side, 10,000 men were taken prisoners. They included Admiral Bonetti commanding Italian Forces in Massawa. There were also a large number of deserters.

By the reduction of Massawa and the Italian fleet, the Red Sea ceased to be dangerous to British shipping. "All organized opposition in Eritrea was now over; all the Italian warships had been accounted for, and the handful of aircraft remaining in Ethiopia presented no danger. The strategic object of the East Africa campaign, which was to remove the threat to shipping through the Red Sea had thus been attained".[4] On 11 April President Roosevelt declared that the Red Sea and Gulf of Aden had ceased to be combat zones. This meant that American ships could now travel with war material to the Middle East and thus ease the strain on British shipping. "The reinforcement of British forces in Egypt thus received an incalculable impetus at the hour when the triple test in Crete, in Syria and in the Western Desert was drawing near". Another result of these victories was that a threat to the British main route of aerial reinforcement to Egypt, which now came from West Africa through the Nile valley, was removed. "The Mohawks and Tomahawks, the Glenn Martins and Liberators could roar to Cairo through aerodromes unaffected by war".[5] In short, the disintegration of the Italian forces in East Africa was growing apace after the capture of Keren, and Asmara and Massawa were easily taken. The Italians were being beaten and pushed back from the north and the south. In the south, the East Africa Force had reached Addis Ababa[6] and the patriotic forces and the advance of the Emperor had forced the Italians to evacuate Debra Markos. The Italians were now concentrating on holding Amba Alagi in the east and Gondar in the west.

After the fall of Keren the Italians had still held many strong defensive positions. If they had fought hard the British and Indian troops would have been hard put to capture them. But the Italians made feeble resistance and were driven back with comparative ease. This showed the crumbling of their morale which also accounted for large-scale desertions and the way in which large number of persons were captured and transported. Whole units were ordered to move to Asmara without escorts in their own transport and in some cases bearing their arms. It seemed they did not resent going into captivity and no trouble was reported from the use of such unorthodox methods.[7]

---

[4] Playfair, op. cit. p. 442.
[5] *The Abyssinian Campaigns*, pp. 51-52.
[6] Addis Ababa was taken on 6 April. General Cunningham's forces in a campaign of two months captured over 50,000 prisoners and occupied some 360,000 square miles.
[7] See Appendix IV for estimated Order of Battle of the Italian Northern Army, the units liquidated and those still to be dealt with, as on 10 April 1941.

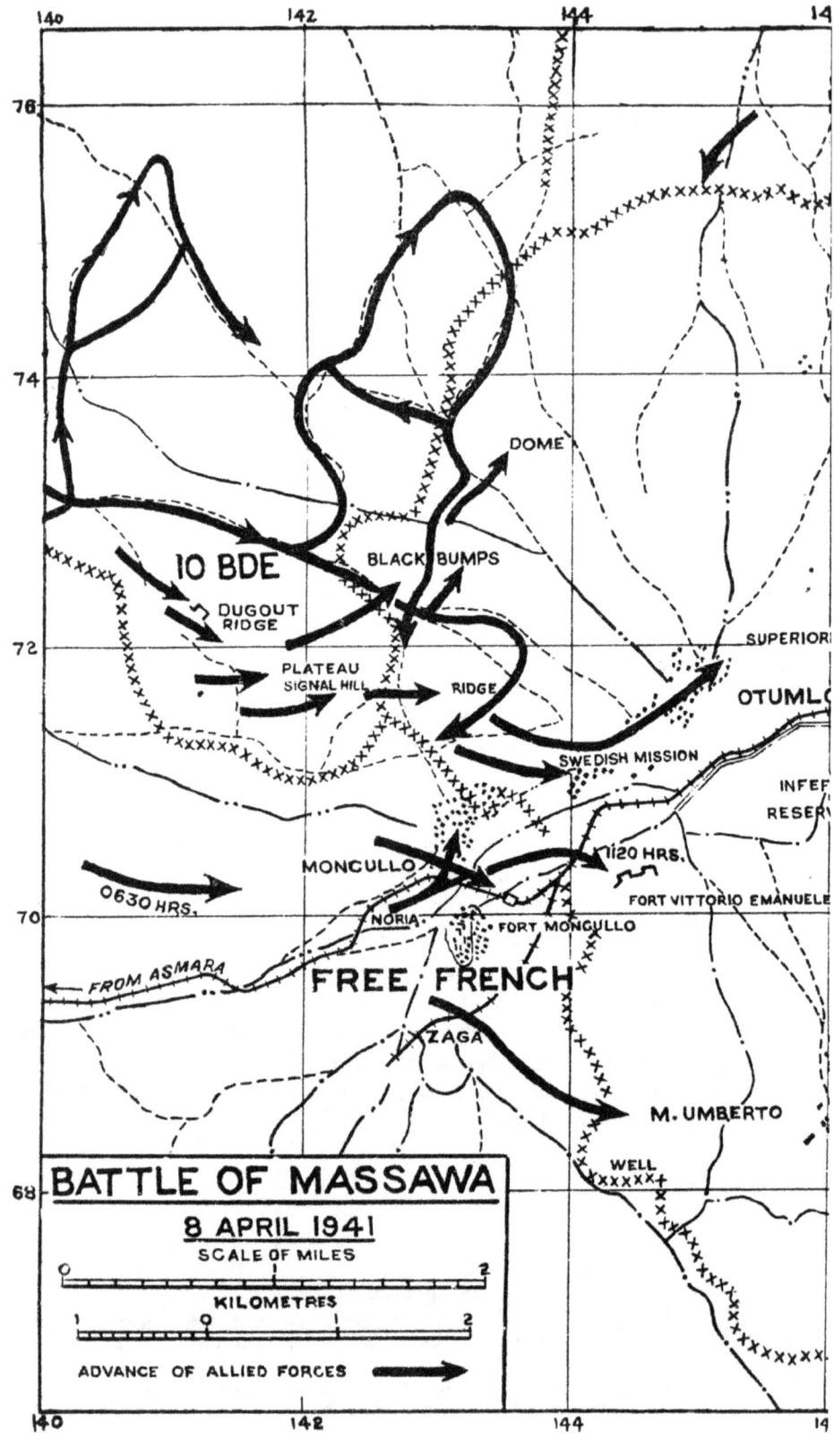

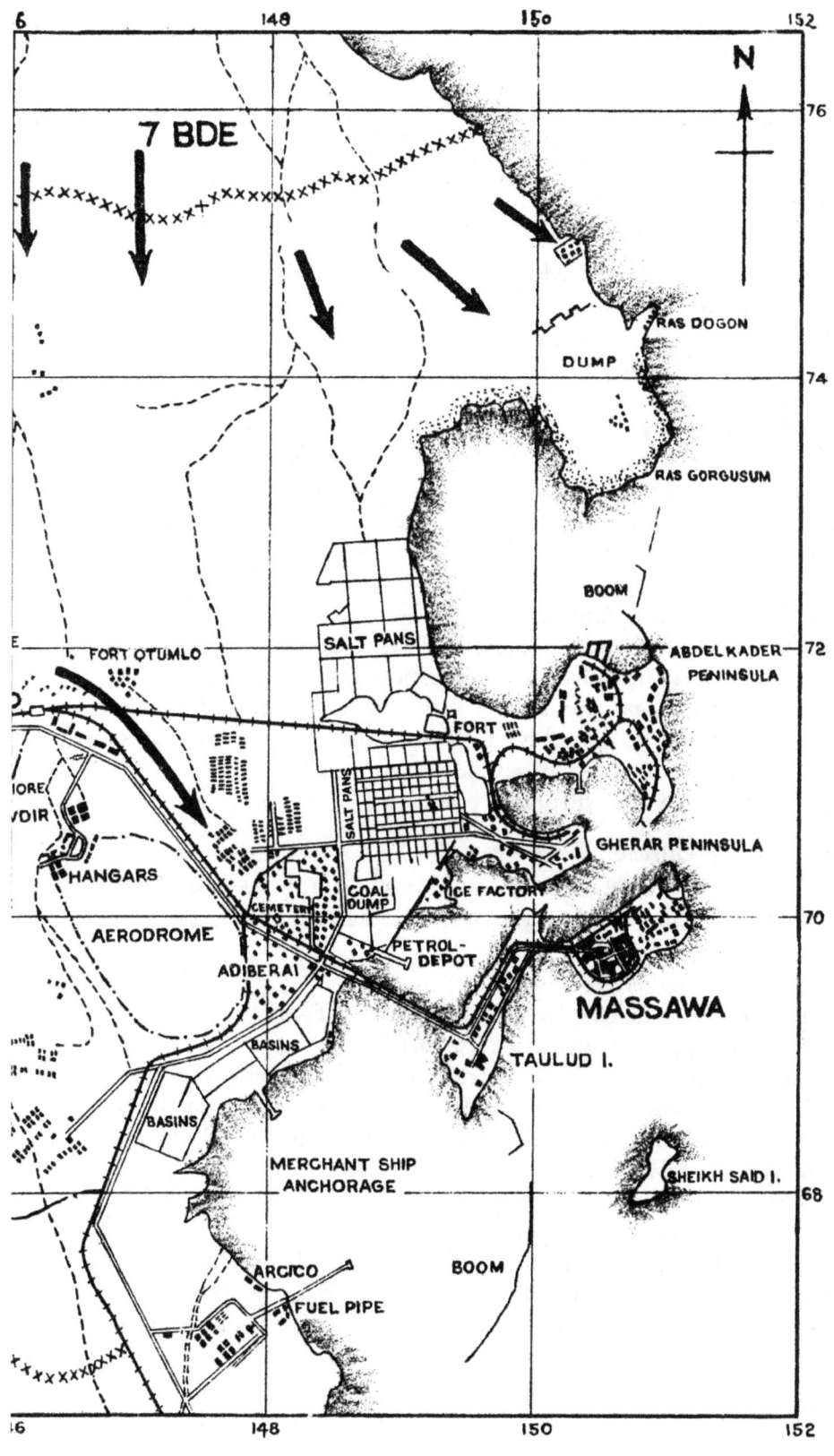

CHAPTER X

The Capture of Amba Alagi

After the capture of Massawa, the two main Italian centres of resistance left in Northern Ethiopia were Amba Alagi and Gondar. The remnants of Italian armies from Eritrea had retreated along the two main roads from Asmara to these areas, and for some time previously the Italians had also been preparing a defensive position to hold Toselli Pass. Gondar had always been a big military station, the centre of the Italian military organization in the country north and west of Lake Tana. On the other side, at this time commitments elsewhere had made it imperative for General Wavell to withdraw as many forces as possible from Eritrea. The policy laid down by him was that no major operations should be undertaken in Eritrea and Northern Ethiopia which would interfere with the withdrawal of troops to the Middle East. Nevertheless, though the Italian forces which had withdrawn southwards were no longer a menace to the Sudan and though they had little chance of staging a counter-offensive to recapture Eritrea, their continued presence in the country was a source of possible future trouble. It was desirable therefore that they should be eliminated.

Pursuit South of Asmara

On 2 April, after the fall of Asmara a Flit Force was formed for pursuing the Italians south of Asmara. It consisted of the following troops :—

Central India Horse
1 Motor Machine Gun Group Sudan Defence Force
A Troop Light Artillery Battery (SDF)
Det Sappers (Sufficient for three mine-clearing parties).

This force was to pursue the Italians and prevent them from moving on Addis Ababa and to determine their strength and locations on the Asmara-Addis Ababa and Asmara-Gondar roads.[1]

The Commander Flit Force left Asmara at 1200 hours on 2 April with 1 Motor Machine Gun Group with the object of reaching Adowa the same evening. Another column of Flit Force consisting of Central India Horse was directed along the Decamere-Saganeiti-Adi Caieh road. 1 Motor Machine Gun Group, in ad-

---

[1] 5th Indian Division Operation Instruction No. 25 dated 2 April 1941.

vancing towards Adowa made contact with the British force operating in the Arresa area, which had also followed up the Italians on their withdrawal. At Adi Ugri an Italian camp for prisoners of war was found and 187 prisoners were released. The Italians at Adi Ugri were apprehensive of rioting and asked for British help and protection.

Central India Horse advanced against slight opposition. On 3 April it was ambushed at a place eighteen kilometres north of Adi Caieh. It was not found to be a serious obstacle. 47 men and 2 heavy machine guns were captured. Although some road blocks were met on the way, Central India Horse continued to advance. It reached Adi Caieh at 1225 hours. By evening it had passed Senafe and spent the night three miles south of that place. Also, Headquarters Flit Force with 1 Motor Machine Gun Group continued to advance on the Adowa road and Adowa was reached the same day. From there Headquarters Flit Force with one company of Motor Machine Gun Group moved to Adigrat which was reached at 1700 hours. The rest of the Motor Machine Gun Group was left at Adowa. When Indian troops entered Adigrat, *140 Colonial Battalion* was on the point of leaving in lorries and the whole of it was captured.

Addis Ababa Road

Central India Horse reached Adigrat on 4 April at 0755 hours and made contact with Headquarters Flit Force. Flit Force continued its operations and its locations during the night of 4/5 April were as follows :—

Headquarters Flit Force
Central India Horse (less one squadron) } Adigrat
1 Motor Machine Gun Group (less one company)

One company 1 Motor Machine Gun Group} Adowa

One squadron Central India Horse} Ten miles north of Quiha.

On 5 April Central India Horse Squadron entered Quiha without opposition. The remainder of the regiment also arrived there at 1040 hours. Here reports were received that the Italians were preparing for a final stand at Amba Alagi. Next day one squadron Central India Horse moved south but it could not get very far being held up by artillery fire and a road block three miles south of Mai Mescic and thirty miles south of Quiha.

On 6 April orders were received for the relief of Central India Horse by 1 Horse. Central India Horse was ordered to revert to

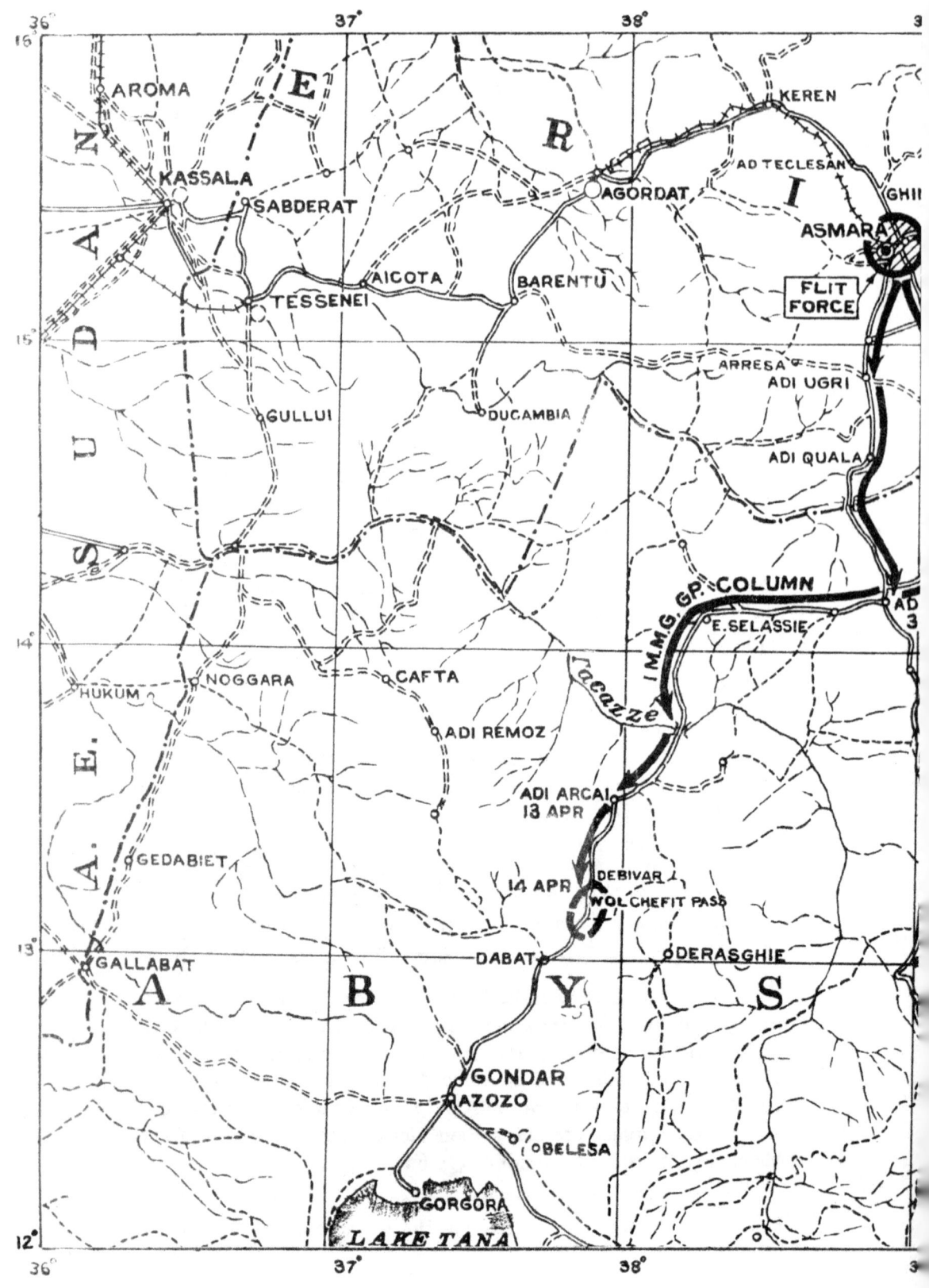

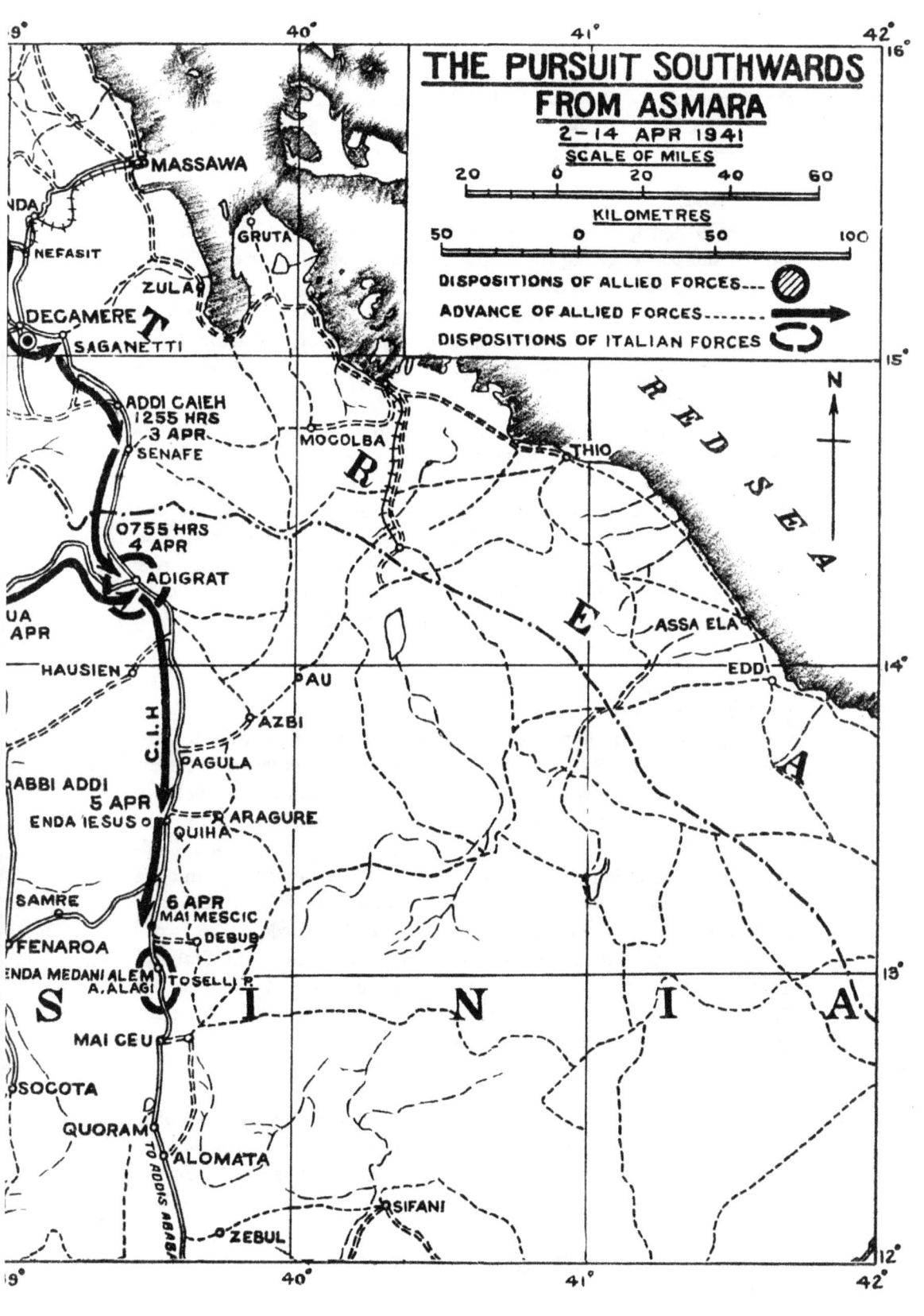

the command of the 4th Indian Division. This relief was completed by 0900 hours on 8 April. Central India Horse moved back the same day to rejoin the 4th Indian Division.

Gondar Road

On 9 April, 1 Motor Machine Gun Group which had advanced unopposed along the Gondar road reported a series of undefended road blocks. The advance went on slowly and by 13 April the forward troops reached Adi Arcai. At this stage 2 Motor Machine Gun Group was ordered to join 1 Motor Machine Gun Group. On 14 April, the leading elements were ambushed in the area of Debivar.

The Italians were holding Wolchefit Pass[2] about three miles to the south of Debivar in some strength. It was difficult to estimate their numbers at this stage. But some indication was available from their having engaged British and Indian troops with rifle and machine gun fire and also with artillery of several calibres. They had also used Breda anti-aircraft guns against British aircraft flying over the area. The ground in the area of the pass was very difficult, vehicles not being able to get off the road at all.

SITUATION ON 15 APRIL

5th Indian Division

The forward troops were in contact with the main Italian positions at Wolchefit Pass on the Gondar road and Toselli Pass, near Amba Alagi, on the Addis Ababa road. The Italians were holding both these naturally strong positions in considerable strength, and it was realized by General Officer Commanding 5th Indian Division that the forcing of them would be a major operation, outside the scope of the light pursuit forces in contact with the Italians at both these places. These forces were therefore ordered to consolidate the ground gained and to keep contact with the Italians. In the meantime, plans for further operations to reduce these last Italian fortresses were considered and reconnaissances were made to gauge the exact Italian strength.

East Africa Force

Advancing from the south the East Africa Force had captured Harar on 25 March, Dire Dawa on 29 March and Addis Ababa on 6 April. After this event it had sent the 1st South African Brigade northwards. On 15 April, this brigade was in contact with an Italian

---

[2] The garrison at Wolchefit surrendered on 28 September.

force holding Combolcia Pass, to the south of Dessie. The pass was captured on 22 April and Dessie on 26 April.

Patriot Forces of Emperor Haille Selassie

The emperor of Ethiopia had forced the Italians out of Debra Markos, which was occupied on 6 April. After that little remained to be done by his forces. Addis Ababa had fallen on the same day and the Italian forces were either deserting in large numbers or were on the move towards Dessie and Amba Alagi. All the local chiefs, those who had helped the Patriot Forces as well as those who had sided with the Italians, were hurrying to pay respects to the Emperor. Such little mopping up, as was necessary, was in hand.

By 15 April the Italian air force had been forced away from nearly all its bases and airfields. Combolcia, the last base, was to fall a few days later. There was then little left of the Italian air force.

Forces Available

The forces available for operations against Amba Alagi and Gondar and for internal security duties in the whole of Eritrea were :—

5th Indian Division
1 Motor Machine Gun Group (SDF)
2 Motor Machine Gun Group (SDF)
51 Commando
One battery 68 Medium Regiment (RA)
Two Companies Mounted Infantry (SDF).

These forces were not sufficient for simultaneous operations against both Gondar and Amba Alagi.[3] One of them had to be taken first. Amba Alagi was chosen as success there would open the road to Addis Ababa and allow the transfer of the forces to the Middle East through Massawa. The task of attacking Amba Alagi was entrusted to the 5th Indian Division.

Topography

Amba Alagi has an altitude of about 11,282 feet above sea level. The road from Eritrea into Ethiopia crossed a spur of this mountain at Toselli Pass (also called Alagi Pass) which was defended by a fort. The approach from the north was steep and winding and for some miles the road worked its way through a narrow valley, overlooked on both sides by commanding heights. The general run of the high ground, which culminated at Amba Alagi was north-west

---

[3] Gondar was captured on 27 November 1941.

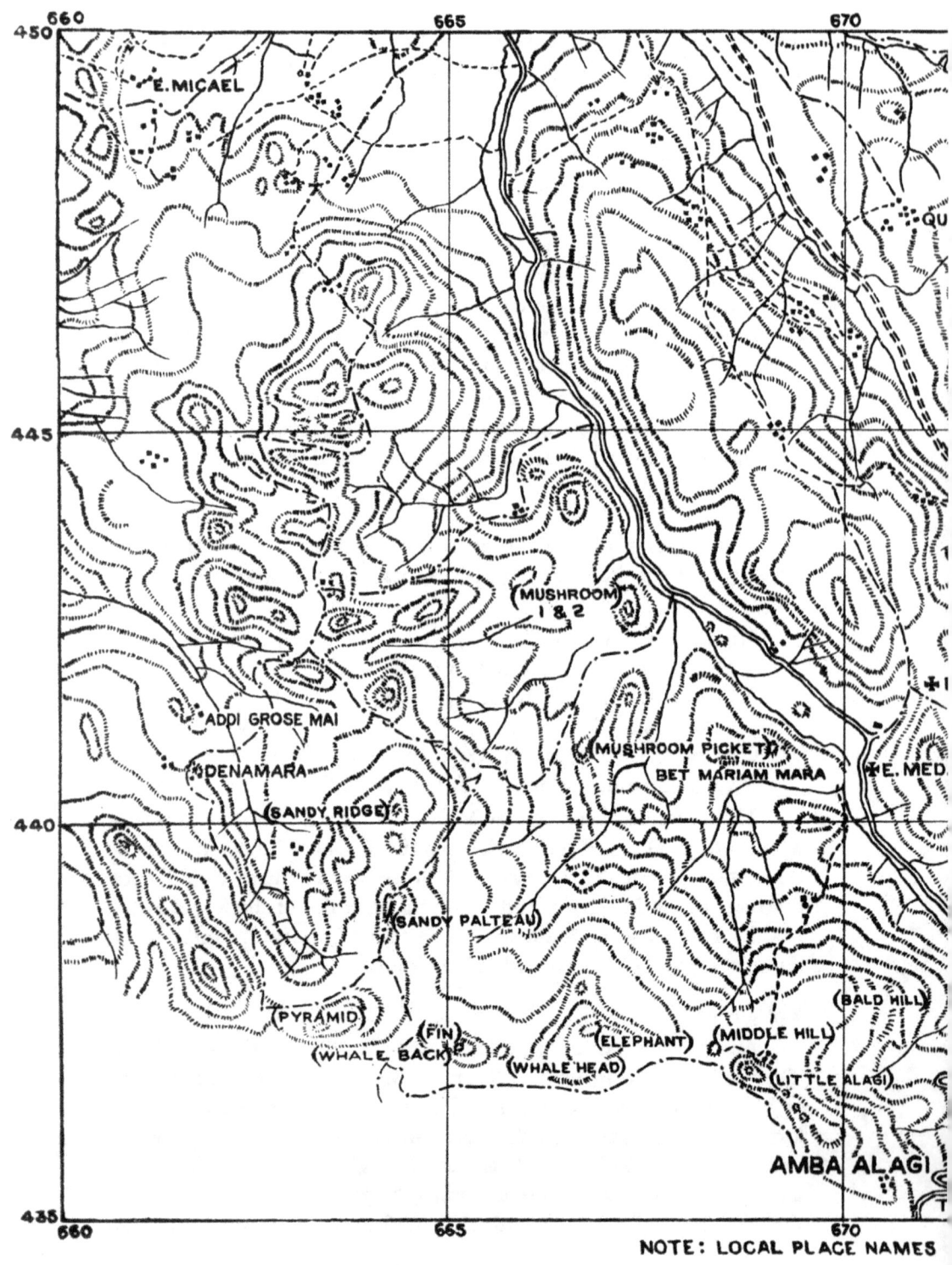

NOTE: LOCAL PLACE NAMES

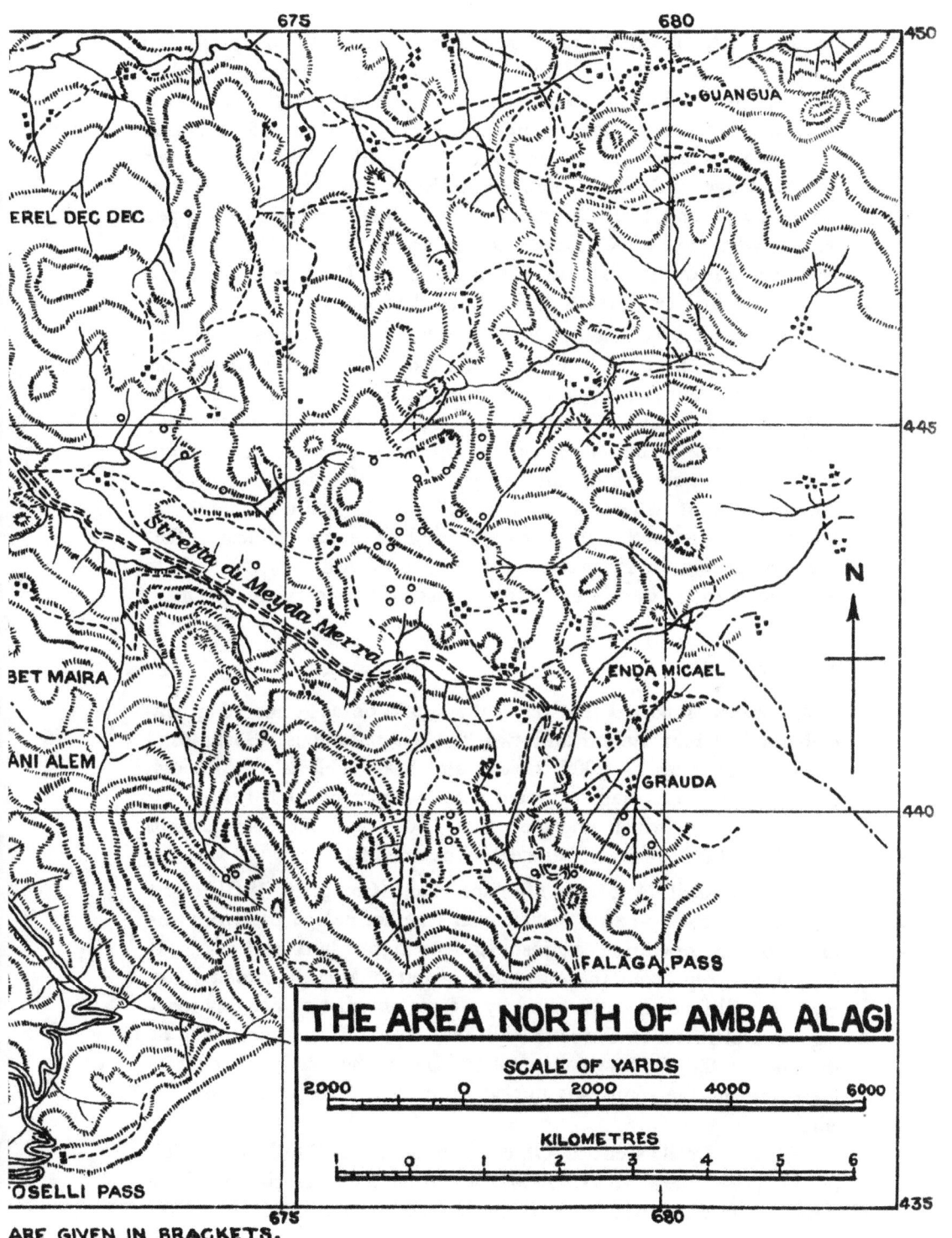

to south-east. North-west of Amba Alagi itself is a long range with a number of peaks on it. These were named as Little Alagi, Middle Hill, Elephant, Pyramid and Sandy Ridge. All these peaks were prominent features of tactical importance. South-west from Amba Alagi ran a narrow ridge culminating in a hill. These were called Castle Ridge and Castle Hill respectively. Almost due north of Amba Alagi and Little Alagi was Bald Hill, a high flat-topped feature with precipitous sides. South-east of Amba Alagi and on the other side of the pass, two prominent hills, Triangle and Gumsa, intervened between Toselli and Falaga Passes.

The road over Toselli Pass was a good all-weather, graded main road. The road to Falaga Pass took off from the east of the main road about thirty kilometres north of Amba Alagi. This road was in a bad condition, just good enough for one-way motor traffic for some distance beyond Debub. This was the route the Italians had used themselves in the final stages of the Ethiopian war in 1936. Just opposite of where the Falaga road left the main track another track led to the south-west through the hills as far as Socota. This was practicable for mechanical transport with difficulty, but there was no road or track from Socota eastwards, to rejoin the main road.

Italian Strength

Deserters reported that the Italian garrison at Amba Alagi was composed of four Italian and two *Colonial* battalions. Their total strength was given as 4,000 Italians and 1,000 *Colonials*. Although Italian propaganda had suggested a total figure of 30,000 the highest suggested by British informers was 7,000. Of the *Colonial* units *25th Colonial Battalion* was believed to be one of them.

On 21 April, 4 Motor Machine Gun Company (SDF) went out on a three-day patrol to ascertain whether Falaga pass could be used for an operation against Italians' right flank and rear. It was also to report on the possibility of outflanking the Amba Alagi position still further to the east, by a force on wheels, possibly moving via Debub on to Corbetta and Mai Ceu. The report made at the end of the reconnaissance stated that without a great deal of improvement the route was not suitable for a force of any size on wheels.

On 24 April, General Officer Commanding 5th Indian Division Major-General A. G. O. M. Mayne in an appreciation of the situation stated that, in view of the requirements of internal security and the length and vulnerability of the Allied line of communication, it was not possible to maintain a powerful striking force in the forward area. He intended the following force to be concentrated forward:—

Advanced Headquarters 5th Indian Division
29th Indian Infantry Brigade
3 Royal Garhwal Rifles
51 Commando
28 Field Regiment
144 Field Regiment
233 Medium Battery
41 Light Anti-Aircraft Battery (less one troop)
1 Horse
1 Motor Machine Gun Group
A Troop Light Artillery Battery SR (Sudan Defence Force)
2 Field Company
20 Field Company.

In the air, 237 Squadron was to be moved forward with seventeen aircraft, including three bombers. But as there were no all-weather advanced landing grounds, the value of this force was to depend on the weather to a considerable extent. Transport also was short and it was necessary to dump both for the battle and maintenance. General Officer Commanding 5th Indian Division did not consider it possible for the above-mentioned force to be concentrated before 30 April. After that reconnaissance and detailed planning would take some time so that no major operation could be launched before 3 May. He feared that contingencies of weather, numerous road blocks and other unforeseen hindrances might delay the operation even further. On the prospects of exploitation he found that if the Italians broke up and started withdrawing, the lack of transport on the British side would be a serious handicap and would make a pursuit of the Italian force in any strength quite impossible.[4]

In the meantime, steps were taken to improve the position. On 26 April 3 Royal Garhwal Rifles occupied Sandy Ridge without opposition. The same evening orders were issued for forming a column consisting of 1 Horse, 51 Commando, A Troop Light Artillery Battery SR, and one section Field Company.[5] This force was to develop a strong feint against Falaga Pass and, if possible, to outflank the Italian positions at Amba Alagi and still further round the east.

---

[4] 5th Indian Division War Diary Situation Report dated 24 April 1941, Appendix G 172.
[5] The column was commanded by Lt. Col. I.F. Hossack.

1 Horse advanced along the road towards Falaga Pass on 27 April but was held up by a second road block. Pickets were placed to the south-west of the ridge in the face of Italian artillery fire, and work to clear the road block commenced. On 29 April a track for one way traffic was cleared and a reconnaissance patrol was sent through towards Debub. Debub was reached and found unoccupied on 30 April.

On 28 April General Officer Commanding 5th Indian Division reviewed the situation again and formulated a plan of attack on the Italian positions. In the south, Dessie had been captured by East Africa Force on 26 April and Sudan Defence Force and Patriot Forces had occupied Socota on the same day. He estimated Italian forces at Amba Alagi at 5,000 men, with thirty guns in post. Having lost Dessie and being marooned between that place and Amba Alagi, their stock of food and war material was expected to be limited. The Patriot Forces having obtained a notable success at Socota were expected henceforth to harass the Italians on all sides. General Mayne thought that the Italians might be impressed by the comparative strength of British and Indian troops concentrated on their front and decide to surrender. On the other hand, he also considered the possibility of the Italians deciding to fight. The Axis successes in the Balkans and Libya and the exaggerated accounts put out by the Axis propaganda machine were expected to encourage the Italians in their resistance in Ethiopia and tone up their morale. Taking both these possibilities into account, General Mayne was inclined to believe that the Italians might not surrender at once. But once they were convinced of the overwhelming strength of British and Indian troops they might decide to do so. There was always a possibility of their holding on till the opening of the main attack. But, at any rate, he did not expect the Italians to fight with the same determination as at Keren.

Italian Positions

The Italian positions extended from the west of Pyramid (Togora 663437) to the Falaga Pass road. They were thus extended over a front of ten to twelve miles, a wide frontage for some five thousand men to hold. No information was available about any artificial defences that they might have constructed, but their natural position was very strong. General Mayne assessed its value for defence as twice that of Keren. Assault on any point in the Italian line would have had to go up the precipitous hills, over long distances from truck-head and under Italian observation. It would certainly have been arduous. But it was also certain that the Italians were not strong at all points along their very extended line, and Mayne hoped, by deception and feints, to find a fairly soft spot for the major assault to go in. The Italians were presumed to hold the forward posts lightly, as had been their practice, and to trust to counter-attacks by their reserves in the event of a breakthrough by the Indian troops. It was also expected that they would be anxious about the centre of their position and also about their right flank, Falaga Pass. On the whole, Mayne had hoped to gain a measure of surprise for his attack by keeping the Italians in a state of uncertainty over a front of more than ten miles. His plan of attack was to start a demonstration against Falaga Pass at once which was to be developed into a fully convincing feint on D minus 1 day. This operation was to be undertaken by Fletcher Force[6] consisting of

Headquarters
1 Horse
One Troop Field Artillery (25 pdrs)
A Troop Light Artillery Battery SR
51 Commando
One Company 3 Royal Frontier Force Regiment
One Section Sappers
One Troop medium artillery in support for a limited period.

Secondly he wanted a feint attack under strong artillery support astride the main road and in the direction of Amba Alagi. It was to be staged in the afternoon of D minus 1 Day. The main attack on the Italian left was to be launched at dawn with maximum artillery support by the 29th Indian Infantry Brigade, except one troop field artillery and A Troop Light Artillery Battery remaining under command of Fletcher Force. The movement of battalions to battle positions (in Sandy Ridge Area) was

---

[6] Fletcher Force was first formed in the last days of the battle of Keren with the role of breaking into Keren and interfering with the Italian communications and headquarters. It was subsequently used in a pursuit role in the initial stage of the pursuit from Keren. It was then dissolved. It was reconstituted on 29 April to take charge of operations in the Falaga Pass sector. Lt. Col. Fletcher was in the meantime appointed to the officiating command of 9th Indian Infantry Brigade. As the battle in the Falaga Pass sector developed and the administrative situation became complicated a proper headquarters was required to conduct it. Therefore Headquarters 9th Indian Infantry Brigade moved from Asmara and took charge of the Falaga Pass sector operations. After this the force was sometimes referred to as Fletcher Force and at others as 9th Indian Infantry Brigade.

Fletcher Force, however, should not be confused with Flit Force, a mobile force constituted on 2 April, also under command of Lt-Col. B. C. Fletcher, with the role of conducting the pursuit south of Asmara along the Gondar and Addis Ababa roads. It was dissolved in front of Amba Alagi on 13 April on which date Fletcher was appointed to the officiating command of the 9th Indian Infantry Brigade.

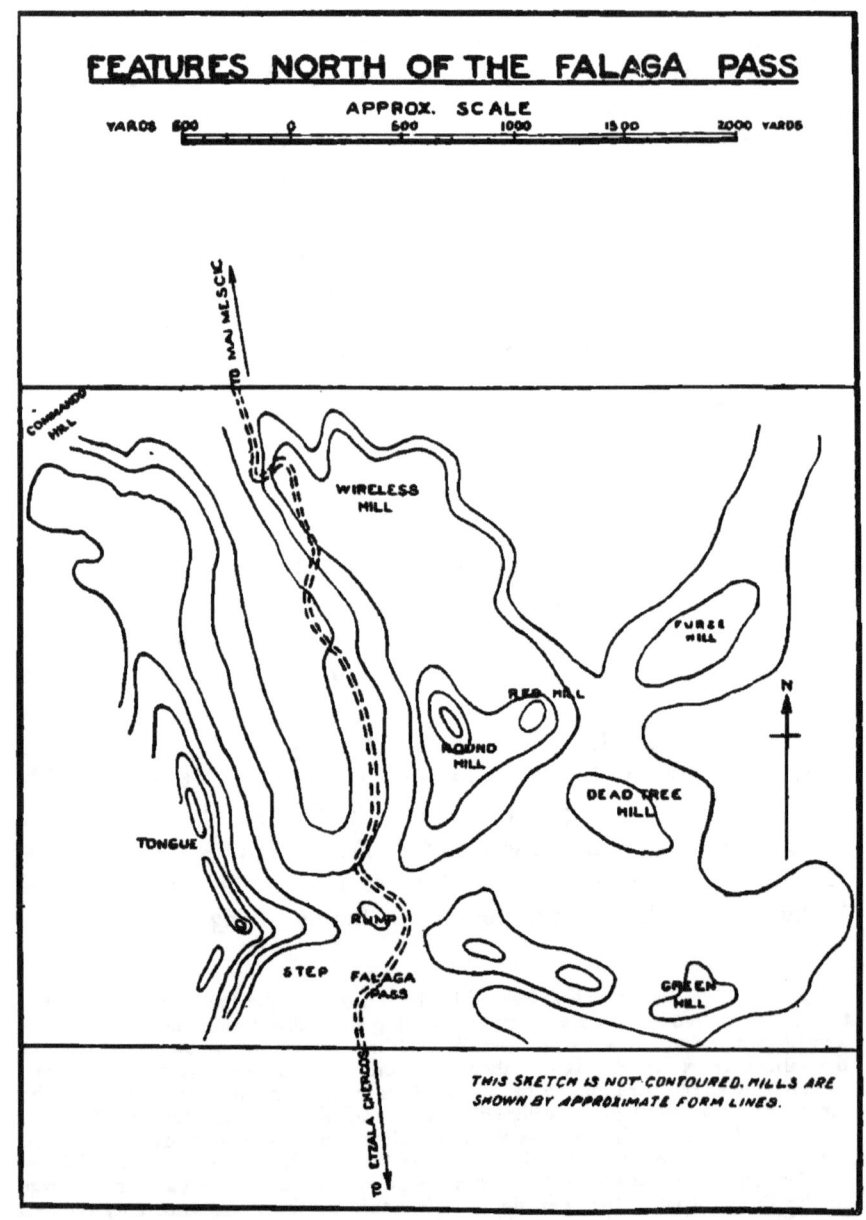

to start on 30 April. Attack was to go in at first light on 3 May.

This plan was discussed with General Platt who approved of it and consequently orders were issued to implement it. The only change from the outline plan was that another battalion from the 10th Indian Infantry Brigade was not used for the feint against Toselli Pass. 3 Royal Garhwal Rifles was detailed to carry out this task.

D Day for the main attack had originally been planned for 3 May but owing to transport and maintenance difficulties it was finally fixed for 4 May at 0415 hours.

OPERATIONS

Falaga Pass Sector

On 1 May, 51 Commando with one campany less one platoon 3 Royal Frontier Force Regiment attacked and captured Commando Hill after a long and difficult night march. Throughout the day hostile artillery, mortars and machine guns fired on British and Indian troops on the feature.

Wireless Hill, a feature to the east of Commando Hill, was captured on the morning of 2 May. The situation on this front appeared to be very promising. Further advance was made on 3 May and, by the evening, the leading elements had reached a position astride the track one mile north of Falaga Pass. The same day 4 Motor Machine Gun Company carried out a successful raid round the east flank of the Italian position and shot up a party of about 30 Italians who appeared to be in conference.

On the night of 3/4 May an attack on Falaga Pass was put in. The feature named Tongue on the west of the pass was captured, but the attack on the pass itself was held up about two hundred yards from the objective. Heavy fighting went on for three hours after which Indian troops withdrew. In the early hours of the morning on 4 May the Italians' counter-attacked Indian positions but were repulsed. Thus the operation in the Falaga Pass sector had been successful. It had not only contained the troops on the east of the main road but also succeeded in drawing some Italian troops from the west.

Toselli Pass Sector

The objective allotted to 3 Royal Garhwal Rifles was the line of the village Enda Medani Alem. The attack started at 1648 hours on 3 May and the battalion was able to secure its objective. The right forward company then advanced up the spur leading up to Bald Hill. This was found to be very strongly held. The company, therefore, withdrew to the line of the original objective.

The Main Attack

The 29th Indian Infantry Brigade was to capture the line—Pyramid-Whale Back-Elephant—on 4 May and then to exploit towards Amba Alagi. The brigade was to attack with 6 Royal Frontier Force Rifles leading, directed on Pyramid. 3/2 Punjab was to pass through 6 Royal Frontier Force Rifles and capture Whale Back and Elephant.

The attack opened with artillery fire at 0415 hours. The leading battalion followed up close to the barrage. Advancing at great speed it completely surprised the Italians and Pyramid was taken by 0545 hours. Passing through the leading battalion, 3/2 Panjab made for Whale Back and Elephant. The whole of the Whale Back feature was captured by 0635 hours, by which time the advance on Elephant was well on its way. The top of the feature was reached at 0720 hours and the ridge came into the hands of the Indian troops by 0735 hours. Reconnaissance at this stage revealed that only a narrow undulating ridge, completely devoid of cover and commanded by Bald Hill and Amba Alagi, joined Elephant and Middle Hill features. It was therefore decided to postpone further attacks until the early hours of the morning on 5 May. Throughout the rest of the day the Italian positions were engaged by British aircraft and artillery. Ten Italian officers and fifty-eight other ranks and seventy Colonial other ranks were captured. They included the Italian commander of the western sector and his staff who had in their possession orders and plans for the defence of Togora Pass. Indian casualties during the day in the main attack amounted to one Viceroy's Commissioned Officer and one Indian other rank killed and nineteen Indian other ranks wounded.

On 5 May, the forces carrying out the feint attacks in Falaga Pass and the main road sectors continued to exert pressure on their respective fronts. In the sector of the main attack 3/2 Punjab attacked Middle Hill at 0415 hours, and, after a fight with bomb and bayonet, the feature was taken by 0445 hours. 1 Worcesters then passed through and attacked Little Alagi. Wire was met and the battalion came under intense machine gun fire from Little Alagi and Bald Hill. It asked for artillery support but its further attempts to get forward were not successful.

At 0930 hours General Officer Commanding 5th Indian Division ordered the 29th Indian Infantry Brigade to hold Middle Hill and to withdraw 1 Worcesters to Elephant. The route for

A 25-pounder gun in action near Amba Alagi

On the level top of the hill men rushing forward, during an attack on a mountain feature in Amba Alagi area

Italian motor transport in Fort Toselli captured by Allied troops

The prisoners of war in Enda Medani Alem make a huge dump of arms

Indian troops on guard over what was left of Fort Toselli

The Duke of Aosta leaving Amba Alagi with British generals and staff officers after his surrender.

Maj.-Gen. Mayne with some officers after the Amba Alagi victory

Italian prisoners of war march down from Toselli Fort
to the bottom of Tosseli pass at Enda Medani Alem

the withdrawal of 1 Worcesters lay along the narrow bare ridge which was completely overlooked by Italian positions on Little Alagi and Bald Hill. The forward troops therefore had to hold the ground they had gained until dark. They withdrew at 1800 hours. The battalion suffered a few casualties during the day, 8 being killed and 28 wounded. One company 3/2 Punjab which had captured Middle Hill continued to hold it.

Further Planning

The General Officer Commanding 5th Indian Division had ordered the 29th Indian Infantry Brigade to hold Middle Hill on 6 May, to enable him to consider plans for further operations. The alternative courses open to him were to continue pressing with the attack on the west flank or to try to break through in the Falaga Pass area.

In the Falaga Pass sector Fletcher Force had reported on 5 May that although the Italians were building sangars and showing general activity they appeared to be withdrawing some troops from that sector to the other flank. The Commander of Fletcher Force was confident of success in breaking through on that flank. General Mayne, however, thought that a force strong enough for a decisive break-through on this front was not available. He also considered it difficult to get the guns forward in a long advance on this front.

On the western flank the Italians were holding strong positions. Their machine gun and mortar posts were sited in dug-outs, cut deep down or into the face of the rock which in most cases had proved impossible to be knocked out by artillery fire. The 29th Indian Infantry Brigade had already occupied Pyramid, Whale Back, Elephant and Middle Hill. Movement by daylight on the last named feature or between it and Elephant would immediately draw accurate machine gun fire from Bald Hill, Little Alagi and Amba Alagi. The only approach from Elephant to Middle Hill was along the cart track on the east side of the saddle of low ground separating the two features and was in full view of and within close range from Bald Hill. The approach forward of Middle Hill towards Little Alagi was along a narrow ledge with precipitous drops on both sides. Just to the west of Little Alagi there was a drop in the ledge. Little Alagi itself, though a big feature, was completely dominated by Amba Alagi. Thus the problem of capturing Little Alagi and Bald Hill was a very formidable one. It was not possible to force a way into the position merely on the strength of superior numbers, because there was not room enough on the ledge leading to it for the employment of large numbers. Nor was there any scope for manoeuvre because in moving along a route other than the ledge the attacking troops would lose height and would then have an almost unscaleable position to assault. On the other hand, the evidence gathered from captured Italian prisoners showed that Italians were badly shaken on account of continuous artillery bombardments and air action. The rank and file had no heart in the battle, and General Mayne rightly believed that the fall of Dessie and the advance of the East Africa Force and the Ethiopian Patriots from the south would further weaken their morale. He also thought it possible that if the Indian troops broke into Italian defences the Italians might give up without a fight. On these considerations he evolved the following plan of operations.

The Main Attack

Little Alagi was to be attacked and Bald Hill to be mopped up on the night of 7/8 May. It was to be a silent attack with no artillery support unless called for by pre-arranged signal. There was to be, if possible, a simultaneous attack by a small body of picked troops against Italian positions south of Alagi. The Royal Air Force was to bomb and machine gun targets immediately south of Amba Alagi and suspected Italian gun positions east of it. Subsidiary operations were to be launched by Fletcher Force and 3 Royal Garhwal Rifles. Fletcher Force was to carry out enveloping movements in the Falaga Pass sector. On the night of 6/7 May, one company 3 Royal Garhwal Rifles was to move round the Italians on the east flank and, on the morning of 7 May, 51 Commando was to make a wider movement round the same flank. This was to be followed the same day or during the night of 7/8 May by an outflanking move by 3 Royal Frontier Force Regiment (less one company) to gain ground affording observation of the Italian areas. Further operations to exploit the above were to be planned after these operations had been completed.

3 Royal Garhwal Rifles was to engage Bald Hill and the Alagi ridge on the night of 7/8 May from the east.

Operations

Fletcher Force

On 5 May, Battalion Headquarters and one company 3 Royal Frontier Force Regiment joined the force in the Falaga area, followed by another company on 6 May. On 6 May, 3 Royal Frontier Force Regiment took over Wireless Hill from 1 Horse and one squadron of the latter relieved a detachment of the former on Commando Hill. After dark, the same day, 3 Royal Frontier Force Regiment sent out a platoon to get on to Dead Tree Hill from the east.[7] This was to be accomplished without the Italians coming to know of it. About the same time a mortar was moved up to a position just under the east bank on Wireless Hill and laid to fire on Round Hill at 1600 hours. However the Italians opened machine-gun fire at about 1545 hours on Furze Hill. Thereupon Indian troops on Dead Tree Hill opened fire in return. Red and Round Hills were finally attacked and captured on 8 May. On the capture of these features the country beyond was found to be very complicated. An operation had been planned for 51 Commando to raid Italian guns in the area of the Falaga Pass. After a reconnaissance of the area this plan was amended. In the meantime, harassing fire on Italian positions on Rump and Step was kept up, which was so effective that these features surrendered at 1500 hours.

At this stage it appeared that the Italians had withdrawn from the Falaga Pass. This was reported to Headquarters 5th Indian Division who ordered the infantry of Fletcher Force to make for Mt. Gumsa and the motorised part of the force to try to get through to the Atzala Valley and so behind the Italian positions. There were, however, some immediate tasks for Fletcher Force to complete. 51 Commando was ordered to advance direct on the Pack Battery Col (a gun position in the Falaga Pass) during the night of 8/9 May. It was to be followed by 3 Royal Frontier Force Regiment which was asked to send one company on to Tongue at dawn on 9 May.

The night of 8/9 May was bitterly cold and in moving from Step towards Pack Battery Col 51 Commando lost direction in the clouds. By the time it and 3 Royal Frontier Force Regiment reached Pack Battery Col the Italians had abandoned the position and withdrawn. In the morning one company of 3 Royal Frontier Force Regiment went to Tongue which it had mopped up by 0900 hours.

3 Royal Garhwal Rifles

During the night of 7/8 May 3 Royal Garhwal Rifles demonstrated against the centre of the Italian position and the Italians were compelled to open fire in defence.

---

[7] The features called Dead Tree Hill, Furze Hill, Rump, and Step were small features in the hills to the north of the Falaga Pass.

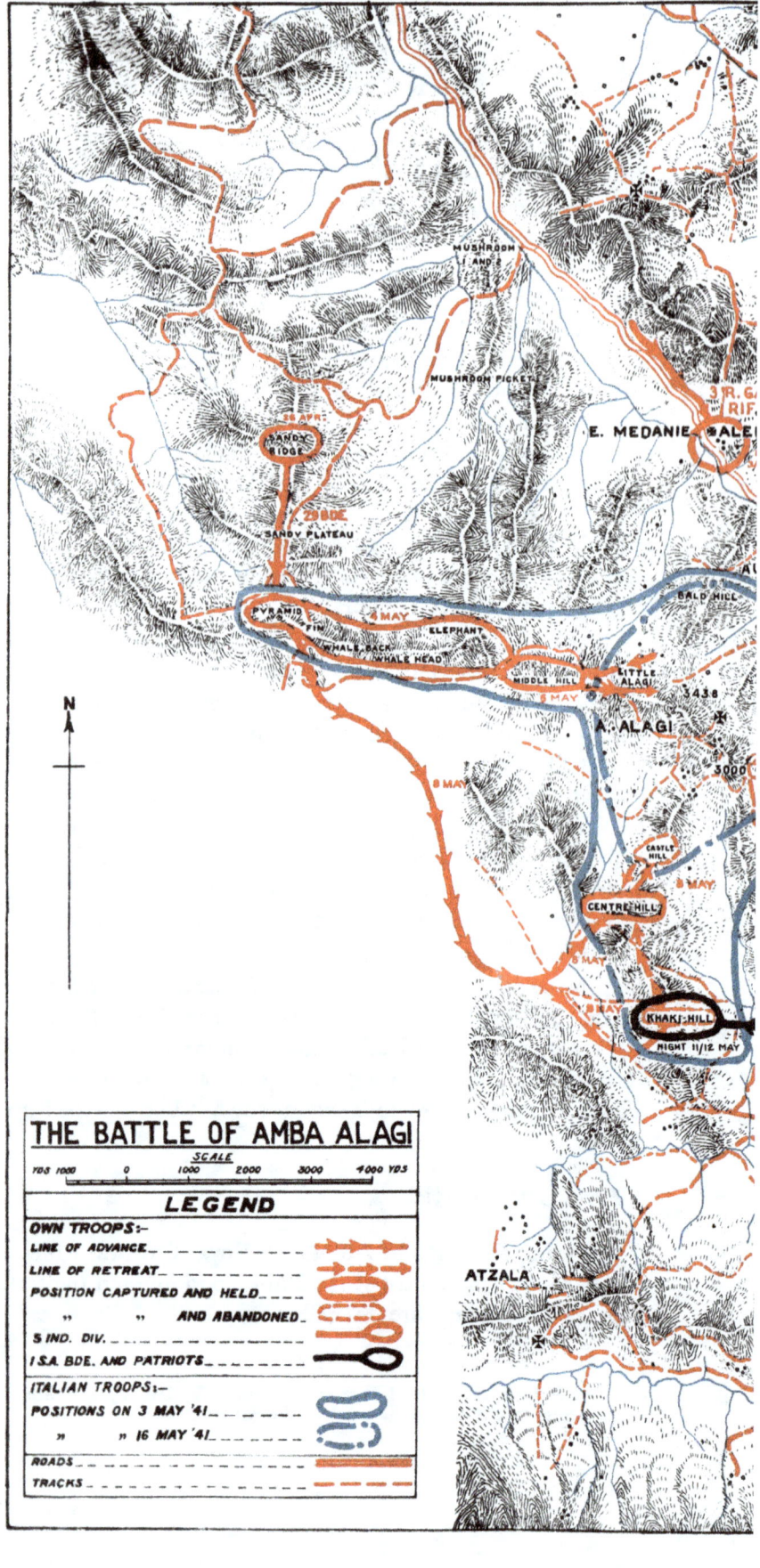

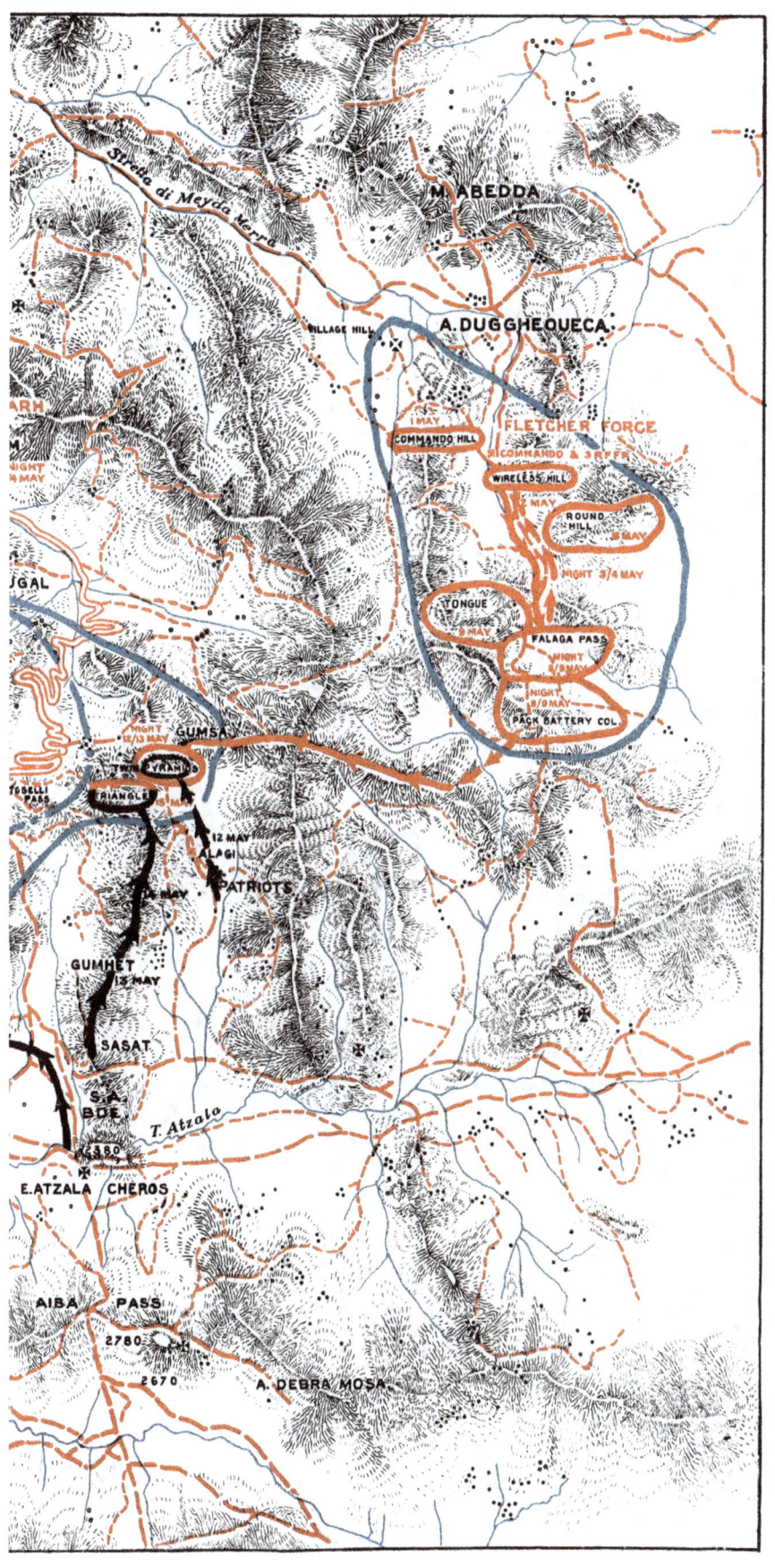

The Main Attack

The attack was put in according to plan.[8] Centre Hill was captured at 0515 hours and Khaki Hill at 0545 hours on 8 May. A Company attacking Castle Hill reached the southern end of the objective at 0530 hours after a very difficult climb. The Italians on the top of the hill displayed a white flag. When however Indian troops had almost reached the top to take it over and make the garrison prisoners, the Italians met them with a shower of bombs which caused a number of casualties. An attack was put in after this and the south end of Castle Hill was captured by 0600 hours. The Italians counter-attacked immediately, but were thrown back with heavy losses. They followed up with another counter-attack with stronger forces and supported by intense and accurate mortar and machine gun fire. Indian troops held the ground resolutely. However, the company had to withdraw in the end after it had run out of ammunition. It moved back to Centre Hill.

Khaki Hill was a long way from British positions and its maintenance proved very difficult. There was also a danger of its being isolated in the event of a counter-attack. Therefore at 0855 hours the Commander 29th Indian Infantry Brigade ordered the troops on it to be withdrawn.

Centre Hill was completely dominated by the Italian positions on Castle Hill. But in view of the expected advance of the East Africa Force the Commander 29th Indian Infantry Brigade decided to hold the ground gained.[9]

Throughout the rest of the day and the night of 8/9 May the Italian machine guns on Castle South were active as a result of which 6 Royal Frontier Force Rifles sustained some casualties. On the night of 9/10 May, 1 Worcesters relieved 6 Royal Frontier Force Rifles on Centre Hill. A certain amount of confusion was caused by an Italian counter-attack in the midst of the relief. However, defensive fire was called for and the attack was repulsed. 6 Royal Frontier Force Rifles moved back in the area of Fin Col to the northwest of Whale Back.

---

[8] The records of various units are not agreed as to whether the attack by 29th Indian Infantry Brigade on 8 May was a silent one or with supporting fire. In his appreciation the General Officer Commanding 5th Indian Division had planned for the attack to be silent and the records of 6 Royal Frontier Force Rifles also say that the attack was such. The war diary of the brigade headquarters, however, states that it was put in with artillery support.

[9] At this stage it was not certain how soon the 1st South African Brigade from the East Africa Force would be able to bring pressure upon the Amba Alagi position from the south. While liaison with the advancing troops from the south was being arranged the Commander 29th Indian Infantry Brigade was told by Headquarters 5th Indian Division to maintain his position on Centre Hill.

East Africa Force

Having captured Dessie on 26 April, East Africa Force had sent the 1st South African Brigade, with some Patriot Forces under command, in pursuit towards the north. The brigade had to cover 175 miles to reach Toselli Pass. By 7 May, Alomata, seventy-seven miles from Toselli Pass, had been captured and the advance from the south was held up at a road block ten miles to the north of that place. The same evening Mai Ceu, twenty-eight miles from Toselli Pass, was reached. The next day, the leading elements were moving towards E Atzala Cheros which was only eight miles south of Toselli Pass. The brigade came under the command of the 5th Indian Division at 1430 hours on 9 May.

Fletcher Force

On the night of 8/9, 51 Commando had occupied Pack Battery Col, which the Italians had abandoned before British and Indian troops could get there. 3 Royal Frontier Force Regiment had secured the feature called Tongue overlooking Falaga Pass by 0900 hours on 9 May. British and Indian troops on this feature had been fired upon by Italian machine guns during the day on 9 May from a feature called Four Bumps. That evening, 3 Royal Frontier Force Regiment was ordered to capture this feature during the morning of 10 May.

On the capture of Falaga Pass, it was found that the road through it was not complete and that it ended abruptly on reaching the top of the pass. It was therefore not possible to send motorised units through to the Atzala Valley. 1 Horse was ordered to the main road and its place was taken by 3 Royal Garhwal Rifles on 9 May.

The Investment of Amba Alagi on all Sides

On 10 May the leading battalion of 1st South African Brigade reached Mai Ceu and the next day the whole brigade less one battalion arrived there. On the morning of 11 May, 1st Royal Natal Carbineers reached the top of the Pass Di Aiba, from which a clear view of Amba Alagi, some eight miles away, was obtained. An armoured car patrol was sent forward to contact the Patriots operating in the Sasat area in the hills to the south of Toselli Pass.

On 11 May, the General Officer Commanding 5th Indian Division flew over the Italian positions to Alomata, to explain the situation to the Commander 1st South African Brigade. In the afternoon they went to the top of the Pass Di Aiba, and carried out a reconnaissance. On the east, the 9th Indian Infantry Brigade was operating towards Twin Pyramids, over extremely difficult knife-edge crests, and with a line of communication dependent on pack-transport forward of Falaga Pass. The 29th Indian Infantry Brigade was holding Middle and Centre Hills. British artillery had direct observation on Toselli Fort and was pounding the Italians unmercifully.

1st South African Brigade was ordered to occupy Triangle and Khaki Hill and gain touch with the 29th Indian Infantry Brigade on the west and the 9th Indian Infantry Brigade on the east. It was thus to complete the investment of Amba Alagi. The Patriots were to be withdrawn from the road up Toselli Pass and were to operate on the right flank of the 1st South African Brigade.

Khaki Hill

On the night of 11/12 May, 1st Royal Natal Carbineers occupied Khaki Hill. The artillery of the South African Brigade was deployed in the area of Khaki Hill and Pass Di Aiba on 12 May. This put the Italian artillery in a most difficult position, because the guns deployed on the southern slopes of Amba Alagi, against the 5th Indian Division, were exposed to the view of the artillery observation posts of the South African Brigade.

On 12 May, patrols from 1st Royal Natal Carbineers gained touch with 1 Worcesters occupying Centre Hill. The same day the telephone line from the 29th Indian Infantry Brigade to 1 Worcesters was extended to Headquarters 1st South African Brigade.

Triangle

The position of the Italians on Triangle (Mt. Corarsi) was very strong. Their men were well concealed in caves and trenches on ground overlooking the approaches. 'No Man's Land' was a fairly open slope ending in a cliff at the top, rising thirty feet with the Italians entrenched above it. There was no actual position on the summit of Triangle but an anti-aircraft gun was dug in there.

1 Transvaal Scottish was detailed to hold itself in readiness to move on the night of 12/13 May against Triangle.

12 May was spent in reconnaissance and planning. The Commander Fletcher Force flew over to Mai Ceu and visited the Commander 1st South African Brigade. They agreed that the South Africans should move up the south-east spur of Triangle. The Commander Fletcher Force on his part undertook to support this advance as best as he could, either by an advance on his own front or by fire.

While these matters were being discussed the Patriots entirely without warning to Indian forces first stormed Pyramid East and then Pyramid West. Their line of approach was up the precipitous southern slopes of the two Pyramids. The Italians put up a stout resistance on Pyramid West, but were overwhelmed. The Patriots then attempted to pass over to Triangle. The ridge from Pyramid West to Triangle was barred by two double apron fences of barbed wire and by a mass of fascines, all covered by machine gun posts, of which the nearest, White Rock, was not more than fifty yards away. British artillery did its best to knock them out, but they were too well dug in to be seriously affected. The Patriots failed in their very gallant effort to cross this heavily defended defile. They were forced to withdraw to Pyramid West where those on the north side were engaged by pack guns from Amba Alagi and those on the south by machine guns on Triangle. They had therefore to fall further back and took shelter on the lower slopes between the two Pyramids.

In order to make certain that the Italians did not reoccupy them, one company 3 Royal Garhwal Rifles occupied Twin Pyramids, without opposition, on the night of 12/13 May.

On 13 May, 1st South African Brigade occupied its first objective, Wade's Post, a feature on the lower slopes of south-east spur of Triangle. The same day the Patriots made another attempt to get to the top of Triangle, this time up the steep sides of the feature and not along the defile from the direction of the Pyramids. Their attempt failed, but it helped the South Africans in getting on to their objective. After the capture of Wade's Post, 1st South African Brigade continued its advance up the hill at about 1600 hours on 13 May. The second objective was a ridge further up the slope. Heavy rain, however, checked the advance and the objective was not reached.

On 14 May the rain had stopped before the morning and the advance was resumed at first light. A deep gully about two thousand yards from the top was successfully crossed and the advance continued. Artillery fire made many Italians leave cover and they were caught by the machine guns in the open. By midday 1 Transvaal Scottish was nearing the summit. The Italians put in a counter-attack at this juncture and African troops were forced back to the foot of the cliff. Further artillery support was arranged and, after heavy fighting, the leading troops were checked to the south and south-east of the Triangle.

3 Royal Garhwal Rifles on Twin Pyramids had been joined by large numbers of Patriots. 3 Royal Garhwal Rifles supported the attack of the South Africans on Triangle with machine gun fire. The Patriots once again tried to assault Triangle over the narrow

ridge leading from Pyramid West. However, they were held up by the wire and machine guns on the north-east corner of Triangle. The machine guns were finally silenced by British artillery in the evening and it was planned to blow a gap in the wire with Bangalore torpedoes (a type of explosive charge) during the night.

On the night of 14/15 May the wire on the ridge between Pyramid West and Triangle was blown successfully. The Italians abandoned Triangle during the night and withdrew to Amba Alagi.

A patrol from 3 Royal Garhwal Rifles found Triangle abandoned at dawn on 15 May. Patrols from 1st South African Brigade were also up soon after. The feature was occupied by 3 Royal Garhwal Rifles and the South Africans immediately took up operations to secure the ridge leading to the main road. Heavy fire was encountered from Amba Alagi and Toselli Fort and the advance was postponed until the night of 15/16 May.

Amba Alagi was now invested on all sides, on the north and east by the 9th Indian Infantry Brigade, on the south by the South Africans, and on the west by the 29th Indian Infantry Brigade.

1 Horse patrols moving up from the north in the area of the main road occupied Cannefat to the north of Twin Pyramids on the evening of 15 May and made contact with 3 Royal Garhwal Rifles.

The Final Assault

After the fall of Triangle the Italians were holding only Amba Alagi, Toselli Pass, Castle Ridge, Little Alagi and Bald Hill. An operation was planned in which the 1st South African Brigade was to attack Toselli Fort with a feint preceding the main attack, by the 29th Indian Infantry Brigade. The 9th Indian Infantry Brigade was to support the 1st South African Brigade and protect its right flank. Owing to the necessity of securing the ridge running down to the main road from Triangle and the difficulties of administration it was not possible to stage this attack before 17 May which was fixed as a provisional D Day.

The Surrender

At 0730 hours on 16 May the first Italian envoys arrived to ask if the General Officer Commanding was prepared to receive an envoy from the Duke of Aosta, the Viceroy and Commander-in-Chief of the Italian forces in East Africa to discuss terms of surrender. This was agreed to and after discussions the Italians agreed to surrender. They laid down their arms at 1200 hours on 19 May. They were granted the honours of war. A guard of honour consisting of representative sub-units from all units presented arms as the defeated Italians filed down the road to lay down their arms and pass into captivity. The next day, the Duke of Aosta personally surrendered with his staff to General Mayne.

Thus the battle of Amba Alagi in the heart of Ethiopia was won. Amba Alagi was a strong natural position and was considered by the Italians to be impregnable. It had been chosen by the Duke of Aosta as the stronghold on which to make a final stand. The Italian forces were surrounded on all sides and their power broken by a large pincer movement the northern arm of which consisted of forces based on the Sudan and the southern arm of forces based on Kenya under General Cunningham. The Indian troops coming from the north after the victory of Keren arrived on the scene first. The South African troops coming from the south had much further to travel and had to subdue the fortress of Dessie on the way. So the battle was first joined by the Indian troops alone. After a week's heavy fighting in mountainous country they had destroyed the Italian forward troops and forced their way, on the north, the east, and the west, to within striking distance of Italian innermost fortress defences. It was at this stage that the South African forces reached the battle-field. It fell to them to storm their way up precipitous heights against stiff opposition and to close the ring on the south. After the circle was closed the only question was how long it would take to overcome Italian opposition. As the net was tightened and the bombardment by air and artillery became more concentrated, the morale of Italian forces deteriorated rapidly and their surrender came soon after.

After the fall of Amba Alagi the remaining centres of Italian resistance were in the Galla-Sidama area in the south-west and in the Gondar area in the north-west. Some brilliant operations by the African divisions, assisted by a Belgian force from the Sudan resulted in the complete liquidation of all Italian resistance in the south-west of Ethiopia while the Italian outposts in the Gondar area were also cleared. The Gondar area itself was allowed to remain for the time being in Italian hands as it was considered to have no further influence on the operations and as General Wavell was anxious to transfer troops back to the main theatre in Egypt as rapidly as possible. The 4th Indian Division had been withdrawn to Egypt immediately after the fall of Keren. The 5th Indian Division followed after the fall of Amba Alagi.

During the operations by regular troops in the south and in the north, the west centre of Ethiopia was being cleared by some daring operations of Colonel Wingate's small regular force of Sudanese troops and bands of Ethiopian Patriots assisted by British officers,

The Emperor with Brigadier Sandford followed the operations of these troops and made a formal entry into his capital of Addis Ababa on 5 May.

Though Italian forces remained in Ethiopia even after the fall of Amba Alagi and kept two African divisions occupied all through the summer, Ethiopia had been freed of Italian domination. Indian troops which had played such an important part in the offensive in this area were now withdrawn in bulk to the more important theatres of war in the north. The British attention was now directed towards their north-western frontier and to the possibility of an advance by German and Italian troops from Libya against any of their communications along the Nile or west from Khartoum.

CHAPTER XI

Conclusion

Some weeks before the outbreak of the Second World War in 1939 the first Indian troops appeared in Egypt. They were to be the vanguard of the 4th and 5th Indian Divisions which won fame in the conquest of Italian East Africa. This conquest was effected in a short period of about five months from January to May 1941 and severe losses in men and material were inflicted on the Italians. The remarkable features of this campaign were the storming by British, Indian, Sudanese and South African troops of Keren and Amba Alagi positions which were considered by Italians to be impregnable. The Indian troops were in the thick of fighting and covered themselves with glory in most of the engagements fought in this theatre. Their courage and bravery were as clearly brought out as their high morale and fighting spirit. Together with forces from other countries they conquered Eritrea, Ethiopia and British Somaliland. In all, their record was an impressive one.

It is relevant to state the development of British strategy in this theatre.

The campaign in East Africa grew gradually from the progress of the operations. In September 1940, shortly after Italy had joined the war, General Wavell instructed the commanders in the Sudan and Kenya not to undertake any general offensive. General Platt was asked to prepare local attacks on Gallabat and at other places which were to be carried out on the onset of the dry weather. In Kenya, General Dickinson was asked to concentrate for the time being upon an active defence. He was, however, to make plans for a future offensive. As stated earlier in this narrative, General Platt's operations at Gallabat carried out early in November were hardly successful. Early in December General Wavell reviewed the whole situation at a meeting of the commanders at Cairo. He decided that the Patriot Revolt in Ethiopia was to be fostered by all possible means and that the Italians at Gallabat were to be harassed.

The rapid expulsion of the Italians from Egypt led the British Chiefs of Staff to decide at the end of December in favour of early operations in Ethiopia. As a German advance through Bulgaria appeared likely it was considered desirable to speed up the conquest of Italian East Africa. The British Prime Minister expressed the hope that by the end of April the Italian army in Ethiopia would have been smashed.

Earlier in January 1941 there were indications that the Italians were intending to withdraw from Kassala. Platt was therefore ordered to advance his operation to prevent the Italians from withdrawing. Before, however, he could attack, the Italians had evacuated Kassala. It was therefore decided to attack them as they retreated over the mountain passes of Eritrea. Wavell ordered Platt to press on to Asmara. Cunningham in Kenya also thought of taking an offensive and of attacking and capturing Kismayu early in February. He sought Wavell's permission for this attack. At this time operations in the Balkans and the Far East were influencing Allied strategy in this region and Wavell had to decide whether to continue operations against Italian East Africa or to start withdrawing troops to meet British commitments in the Balkans. He decided to continue operations in East Africa but ordered Platt to limit himself to occupying Eritrea and not to advance into Ethiopia. He warned him that some of his troops might be withdrawn after the conquest of Eritrea. Cunningham in the south was told to be prepared to part with the South African Division after his capture of Kismayu.

Towards the end of February 1941 Platt was fighting a long and difficult operation at Keren with two Indian divisions. Keren fell on 27 March. Massawa was taken on 8 April. By this time most of Cyrenaica had been recaptured by the Germans and so the withdrawal of British and Indian troops to Egypt became imperative. Wavell therefore ordered Cunningham to move north with a view to secure the main road from Addis Ababa to Asmara along which troops and material could pass on the way to Egypt. The result of this advance from the south was that the Duke of Aosta was encircled by the forces of Cunningham and Platt and he surrendered at Amba Alagi.

Thus in the course of a few months the British strategy had developed from a purely defensive into an offensive one. The British wrested successfully the initiative from the hands of the Italians and by fruitful planning and organisation made rapid advance and routed the Italians at Keren, Asmara, Massawa and Amba Alagi. "The ultimate pattern of the conquest", wrote Wavell later "was a pincer movement on the largest scale, through Eritrea and Somaliland converging on Amba Alagi, combined with a direct thrust through Western Abyssinia by the Patriot Forces—this result was not foreseen in the original plan but arose gradually through the development of events. It was in fact an improvisation after the British fashion of war rather than a set piece in the German manner". Wavell's task in complying with a rapid succession of instructions and suggestions[1] from his superiors was a difficult one. But by his perseverance and ability he ensured British victory in this region.

Among the causes of the Italian failure may be set down the unpreparedness of Italy for a long war in 1940, the failure of the Italians to exploit their early successes and their general defensive policy, and the Patriot rising in Ethiopia. When Italy joined the war on the side of Germany in June 1940, she counted on a very short war which, with the collapse of France, appeared to have been already won. But she herself was not ready for a long conflict. Her economic condition was difficult. Her balance of trade was unfavourable and an armament race for her could only be ruinous. In the army there were shortages of weapons and equipment and of officers and instructors. Neither her air force nor her fleet was ready for a major war. During the negotiations for the Pact of Steel of May 1939 Mussolini told Hitler that Italy could not take part in a European War before 1942. When suddenly told in August 1939 that Germany was about to invade Poland, he presented a long list of requirements—coal, steel, oil and wood and other articles, that Italy required before she could join. On learning he could not have these things Mussolini decided to stay out of the war. This lasted for nine months. During this period Italian capacity to wage war for a long stretch of time increased but little. To the British Government, however, it gave some valuable time for improving their defences. After Italy had joined the war her position was to become worse as Italian East Africa was cut off from Italy by land and sea and there were not stocks enough to support her warfare in this theatre.

Because of her unpreparedness Italy was led to adopt a defensive strategy even in the early stages of the war when the British forces in Kenya and the Sudan were very limited and when the time was propitious for the Italians to launch a vigorous offensive. The Italians were in a strong position in the opening of 1940 campaign and the odds were heavily against the British. They controlled the southern entrance to the Red Sea. They could have taken advantage of their superior position to conquer the Sudan. If the Italians had conquered the Sudan it would have rendered the British position difficult. The British would have lost the supply lines to the Middle East up the Red Sea and across Africa from Tako-

---

[1] Playfair, *op. cit.*, Vol. 1, p. 396.

radi to Khartoum. Egypt itself would have been insecure. But the Italians sought to achieve no such advantage from their stronger position and lost a good chance. They also did nothing serious to interfere with the arrival of British reinforcements at Mombasa and Port Sudan. "Lack of enterprise in the air was matched at sea, and the destroyers and submarines based at Massawa were inactive. Thus the strategic asset of Italian East Africa's geographical position on the flank of Britain's vital sea-route was thrown away".[2] With the arrival of reinforcements on the British side in men and material, the British seized the initiative and effected a speedy conquest of Italian East Africa.

In addition to fighting the British, the Italians had to cope with the rising of the Patriots in Ethiopia. Maintenance of internal order became a heavy burden for the Italians. As the British offensive mounted the Patriot movement gained in impetus until it had become a powerful force. British victories affected the morale of the Italian forces and the Patriots with British help were able to put in more and more effort as Italian morale deteriorated. Italian forces were thus hard put to repel British offensive and at the same time to keep internal order.

The campaign in Italian East Africa involved men of many countries and races. The victories gained by Indian soldiers testified to their good training, their fighting spirit and determination to meet the challenge they were called upon to face and no less to the good leadership and sound judgement of officers who commanded them. It should not be forgotten that both the 4th Indian Division and the 5th Indian Division whose operations have been treated in this narrative consisted both of Indian and British battalions whereas at some places forces from Commonwealth and Empire countries had an important part to play. It was a joint venture and though the extent of participation in various battles varied it was in a real sense a joint victory.

---

[2] *Ibid. p.* 448.

APPENDICES

APPENDIX I

ORDER OF BATTLE OF 5TH INDIAN DIVISION
(After reorganisation on 27 September 1940)

5th Indian Division (Maj. Gen. L. M. Heath, CB, CIE, DSO, MC).

9th Indian Infantry Brigade (Brig. A.G.O. M. Mayne, DSO).
    2 West Yorks
    3 Mahratta
    3 Royal Frontier Force Regiment

10th Indian Infantry Brigade (Brig. W. J. Slim, MC)
    1 Essex
    4 Baluch
    3 Royal Garhwal Rifles

29th Indian Infantry Brigade (Brig. J.C.O. Marriott, CVO, DSO, MC).
    1 Worcesters
    3/2 Punjab
    6 Royal Frontier Force Rifles

Divisional Tps
    25 Field Regiment RA
    28 Field Regiment RA
    20 Field Company RIE
    2 Field Company RIE

APPENDIX II

ORDER OF BATTLE OF GAZELLE FORCE
On being formed on 16 October 1940

HQ Gazelle Force   (Col F.W. Messervy)

   1 Horse
   One Troop 'P' Battery RHA
   One Troop 28 Field Regiment RA (18 Pdrs)
   4 Ordnance Workshop Section
   170 Cavalry Field Ambulance (less det)
   1 Motor Machine Gun Group SDF
     (2, 4 and 6 Coys)

APPENDIX III

ORDER OF BATTLE

Troops in the Sudan as on 20 January 1941

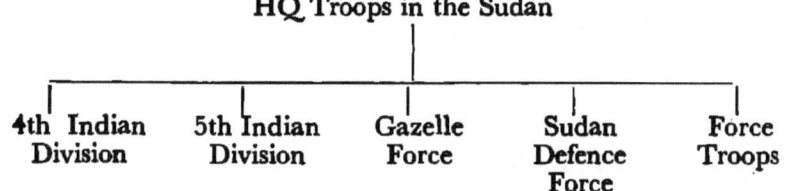

Force Troops

Cavalry

    B Squadron 4 Royal Tank Regiment
    1 French Spahi Squadron

Artillery

    Coast Defence Battery (East Africa)
    4 Field Regiment (Signal Section and Light Aid Detachment)
    68 Medium Regiment (less one battery) (Signal Section and Light Aid Detachment)
    One Survey Troop, 4 Survey Regiment
    Anti-Aircraft Defence HQ (from HQ 2 Heavy Anti-Aircraft Regiment)
    25 Heavy Anti-Aircraft Battery
    41 Light Anti-Aircraft Battery
    1 Light Anti-Aircraft (Breda) Battery
    2 Light Anti-Aircraft (Breda) Battery (less one Troop)
    1 Light Artillery Battery, Sudan Regiment (less one Troop)
    1 Anti-Aircraft Company, South African Defence Force
    2 Anti-Aircraft Company, South African Defence Force
    3 Anti-Aircraft Company, South African Defence Force
    4 Anti-Aircraft Company (Steamers), South African Defence Force
    5 Anti-Aircraft Company (Stores), South African Defence Force

Engineers

    CRE North Sudan
    CRE South Sudan

2 Bridging Section Sappers & Miners (less detachment)
10 Railway Construction & Operating Company
8 Army Troops Company Sappers & Miners
   One Section 6 Army Troops Company Sappers & Miners
16 Workshop & Park Company Sappers & Miners
7 Artisan Works Company
8 Artisan Works Company
514 Field Survey Company

Infantry

2/5 Mahratta Light Infantry
2/6 King's African Rifles

Signals

Detachment 3 HQ Signals
1 Company Sudan Defence Force Signals
2 Company Sudan Defence Force Signals
21 Infantry Brigade Signal Section

Pioneer & Labour

1201 Indian Labour Company
1202 Indian Labour Company
1203 Indian Labour Company
1204 Indian Labour Company
1209 Indian Labour Company
1210 Indian Labour Company
1211 Indian Labour Company
1212 Indian Labour Company

Supplies & Transport

HQ RASC Sudan
68 Medium Regiment RASC Section (Med).
29 Reserve Mechanical Transport Company
    (RASC No. 233)
34 Reserve Mechanical Transport Company
    (RASC No. 120)
1 Cypriot Pack Transport Company
2 Cypriot Pack Transport Company
A Company Cape Mechanical Transport Corps
B Company Cape Mechanical Transport Corps
C Company Cape Mechanical Transport Corps
D Company Cape Mechanical Transport Corps
E Company Cape Mechanical Transport Corps

55 Supply Depot Section
 51 Petrol Section Indian Petrol Depot
  2 Cattle Stock Section RIASC
  3 Cattle Stock Section RIASC
 16 Cattle Stock Section RIASC
  9 Cattle Conducting Section RIASC
 10 Cattle Conducting Section RIASC
  3 Cattle Conducting Section RIASC
  8 Cattle Conducting Section RIASC
  1 Base Supply Depot (Type A) RIASC
    Transit Supply Depot (Port Sudan)
 10 Field Bakery
 10 Field Butchery & Command Supply Depot
    HQ 20 Supply Personnel Company
100 Supply Personnel Company
101 Supply Personnel Company
103 Supply Personnel Company
104 Supply Personnel Company
106 Supply Personnel Company
107 Supply Personnel Company
 51 Detail Issue Depot
 52 Detail Issue Depot
  1 Petrol Depot
  3 Motor Ambulance Section
  6 Motor Ambulance Section

Medical

 21 Indian Field Ambulance
 16 General Hospital
 32 General Hospital
 53 General Hospital
 10 Indian General Hospital (less three Sections)
 11 Indian General Hospital
 14 Combined Indian General Hospital
 15 Combined Indian General Hospital (less two Sections)
 16 Indian General Hospital
 30 Indian General Hospital
 11 Motor Ambulance Convoy (less one Section)
  1 Sudan Ambulance Train
  2 Sudan Ambulance Train
  3 Sudan Ambulance Train
  2 (Egypt) Ambulance Train
 11 Bridge Staging Section

- 11 Indian Staging Section
- 12 Indian Staging Section
- 19 Indian Staging Section
- 4 Indian Depot Medical Stores
- 7 Indian Depot Medical Stores
- 8 Advance Depot Medical Stores
- 1 Anti-Malaria Unit
- 2 Anti-Malaria Unit
- 1 Mobile X-Ray Unit
- 4 Mobile X-Ray Unit
- 2 Field Laboratory
- 6 Field Laboratory
- 10 Convalescent Depot

Ordnance

- HQ 1 Advanced Ordnance Workshops
- Detachment 4 Base Ordnance Workshops
- 1 Advanced Ordnance Depot IAOC
- 1 Ammunition Depot IAOC
- Oil Cooker Repair Section
- Tent Repair Section

Miscellaneous

- Detachment 2nd Echelon (Indian)
- 11 Reinforcement Camp
- 31 Rest Camp
- 32 Rest Camp
- 2 Indian Base Army Post Office
- Stationery Depot
- 202 Air Liaison Section
- 205 Air Liaison Section
- Area Pay Office
- 8 Field Cash Office
- Indian Field Accounts Office
- Sudan Provost Company
- 260 Field Security Section
- 261 Field Security Section
- 264 Field Security Section
- Indian Field Security Section
- 2 (Indian) Field Censor Section
- 51 Middle East Commando
- Armoured Train
- 42-44 Mess Units

APPENDICES

Detachment Movement Group
1 (Indian) Prisoner of War Cage

4TH INDIAN DIVISION

5th Indian Infantry Brigade (Brigadier W. L. Lloyd, CBE, DSO, MC)

HQ 5 Indian Infantry Brigade
5 Indian Infantry Brigade Signal Section
5 Indian Infantry Brigade Anti-Tank Company
5 Indian Infantry Brigade Light Aid Detachment
1 Royal Fusiliers
3/1 Punjab Regiment
4/6 Rajputana Rifles

7th Indian Infantry Brigade (Brigadier H. R. Briggs, CBE, DSO)

HQ 7 Indian Infantry Brigade
7 Indian Infantry Brigade Signal Section
7 Indian Infantry Brigade Anti-Tank Company
7 Indian Infantry Brigade Light Aid Detachment
1 Royal Sussex
4/11 Sikh Regiment
4/16 Punjab Regiment

11th Indian Infantry Brigade (Brigadier R.A. Savory, DSO, MC)

HQ 11 Indian Infantry Brigade
11 Indian Infantry Brigade Section
11 Indian Infantry Brigade Anti-Tank Company
11 Indian Infantry Brigade Light Aid Detachment
2 Cameron Highlanders
1/6 Rajputana Rifles
3/14 Punjab Regiment

Divisional Troops

HQ 4 Indian Division Employment Platoon

Artillery

HQ 4 Indian Divisional Artillery
1 Field Regiment (Signal Section & Light Aid Detachment)
25 Field Regiment (Signal Section & Light Aid Detachment)
31 Field Regiment (Signal Section & Light Aid Detachment)

Engineers

HQ 4 Indian Divisional Engineers
4 Field Company Sappers & Miners

12 Field Company Sappers & Miners
18 Field Company Sappers & Miners
11 Field Park Company Sappers & Miners

Signals

4 Indian Divisional Signals (and Light Aid Detachment)

Supplies & Transport

HQ 4 Indian Division RIASC

Divisional HQ Mechanical Transport Company RIASC

4 Indian Division Supply Column (Light Aid Detachment)

4 Indian Division Ammunition Company (Light Aid Detachment)

4 Indian Division Petrol Company (Light Aid Detachment)

12 Supply Issue Section
13 Supply Issue Section
14 Supply Issue Section
15 Supply Issue Section

Medical

14 Indian Field Ambulance
17 Indian Field Ambulance
19 Indian Field Ambulance
15 Indian Field Hygiene Section
2 Indian Casualty Clearing Station

Ordnance

17 Mobile Workshop Company
18 Mobile Workshop Company
19 Mobile Workshop Company
20 Mobile Workshop Company
21 Mobile Workshop Company

Miscellaneous

13 Field Post Office
17 Field Post Office
19 Field Post Office
25 Field Post Office
4 Indian Divisional Provost Unit.

5TH INDIAN DIVISION

9th Indian Infantry Brigade

HQ 9 Indian Infantry Brigade
  9 Indian Infantry Brigade Signal Section
  2 West Yorkshire Regiment
3/5 Mahratta Light Infantry
3/12 Frontier Force Regiment

0th Indian Infantry Brigade

HQ 10 Indian Infantry Brigade
 10 Indian Infantry Brigade Signal Section
  2 Highland Light Infantry
4/10 Baluch Regiment
3/18 Garhwal Rifles

29th Indian Infantry Brigade

HQ 29 Indian Infantry Brigade
 29 Indian Infantry Brigade Signal Section
  1 Worcester Regiment
3/2 Punjab Regiment
6/13 Frontier Force Rifles

Divisional Troops

HQ 5 Indian Division Employment Platoon
  5 Indian Divisional Anti-Tank Company

Artillery

HQ 5 Indian Divisional Artillery
144 Army Field Regiment (less one Troop) (Signal Section & Light Aid Detachment)
 28 Field Regiment (less one troop) (Signal Section & Light Aid Detachment)
J & K Mountain Battery Indian State Forces
  5 Indian Division Ammunition Unit

Engineers

HQ 5 Indian Divisional Engineers
  2 Field Company Sappers & Miners
 20 Field Company Sappers & Miners
 21 Field Company Sappers & Miners
 44 Field Park Company Sappers & Miners

Signals

    5 Indian Divisional Signals

Supplies & Transport

HQ 5 Indian Division RIASC
  20 Supply Issue Section
  32 Supply Issue Section
  33 Supply Issue Section
  52 Divisional HQ Mechanical Transport Section
  14 Indian Mechanical Transport Company
  15 Indian Mechanical Transport Company (less 28 Section)
  29 Indian Mechanical Transport Company

Medical

    3 Indian Casualty Clearing Station
  10 Indian Field Ambulance
  20 Indian Field Ambulance
    7 Indian Field Hygiene Section
  12 Indian Field Hygiene Section

Ordnance

  22 Mobile Workshop Company
  23 Mobile Workshop Company
  24 Mobile Workshop Company
  25 Mobile Workshop Company
  26 Mobile Workshop Company

Miscellaneous

  15 Field Post Office
  23 Field Post Office
  24 Field Post Office
    5 Indian Divisional Provost Unit

APPENDIX IV

ESTIMATED ORDER OF BATTLE OF ITALIAN NORTHERN ARMY ON 10 APRIL 1941

(Showing units liquidated and those still to be dealt with.)[1]

Unit	Prisoners Checked	Location	Remarks
ITALIAN TROOPS			
Savoy Grenadier Div (less MG Bn)	3,005	Liquidated	Twenty officers taken at Massawa.
44 CCNN	534	Liquidated	Eighteen officers taken at Massawa.
136 CCNN	854	Liquidated	Twelve officers taken at Massawa.
150 CCNN	623	Liquidated	
170 CCNN	302	Liquidated	Seven officers taken at Massawa.
11 Legion CCNN	814	Liquidated	Nine officers taken at Massawa.
5 Legion	114		.
Marines and miscellaneous coastal troops	3,584	Liquidated	Taken at Massawa.
COLONIAL TROOPS			
1 Col Div		Liquidated	Commander and staff taken at Massawa.
BDES.			
2 Col Bde (4,5,10, 151 Bns)	1,050	Liquidated	Went to Ghinda where Eritreans deserted. Forty-seven officers taken at Massawa.
5 Col Bde (97,106 Tipo Bns)	281	97 Bn at Amba Alagi, rest liquidated	Possibly split. Eight officers of HQ taken at Massawa. Many prisoners taken by 4 Div. Very heavy casualties at Keren.

[1] Appx. A to 5 Ind. Div. Intelligence Summary No. 159 of 11 April 1941.

Unit	Prisoners checked	Location	Remarks
6 Col Bde (19, 24, 31, 34 Bns)	927	Liquidated at or on way to Massawa	Thirty-four officers from HQ and all units taken at Massawa.
7 Col Bde (13, 15, 21, 45 Bns)	1	Unknown	Presumably on southern front.
8 Col Bde (102, 108, 110 Bns)	55	102 Bn on Gondar road 110 Bn Amba Alagi.	108 Bn was believed to have deserted mostly.
11 Col Bde (51, 52, 56, 63 Bns)	1,499	Liquidated	Officers from 52, and 55 Bns were found at Asmara. The remainder were found at Decamere where troops were disarmed and sent home by their own officers.
12 Col Bde (36, 43, 103 Bns)	133	Gondar road.	Had probably been split. Prisoners from HQ and 103 Bn had been taken at Adi Ugri, while twenty-eight officers were taken at Massawa. Many prisoners had been taken by 4 Div. The balance was about one to two battalions.
16 Col Bde (22, 23, 47, 53 Bns)	327	Gondar road	Had suffered heavily at Barentu. All except 53 Bn were also reported at Nefasit, but none were identified at Massawa.
21 Col Bde (78, 79, 80 Bns)	227	Amba Alagi	80 Bn lost eight officers at Ad Tecle-

APPENDICES

Unit	Prisoners Checked	Location	Remarks
			san. 79 Bn had not been identified, it had last been reported at Debra Tabor. 78 Bn was all captured at Adigrat.
41 Col Bde (98, 99, 131, 132 Bns)	90	Liquidated	Men were disarmed and sent home by their own commanders at Decamere.
42 Col Bde (35, 101, 111 Bns)	201	Liquidated	35 Bn was identified at Nefasit, and officers of 101 and 111 Bns were taken at Massawa.
43 Col Bde (44, 104, 113 Bns)	81	Gondar road	Probably had many desertions in withdrawal from Om Hagar.
44 Col Bde (105, 107, 112 Bns)	225	Probably Liquidated	Sixteen officers taken at Massawa.
61 Col Bde (50, 57, 85, 141 Bns)	2,228	Liquidated	This brigade was split. HQ was taken in Massawa. 141 Bn was captured complete in Adigrat.
Rizzio's Command (26, 31 Bis, 41)	20	Amba Alagi	No 4 Coy 31 Bis was captured at Quiha.
Unbrigaded (109 Bn)	10	Amba Alagi	Two companies reported dispersed.

ARTILLERY

In all, a total of eighty-five Italian guns had been captured since the beginning of the advance from Keren. The number of artillery prisoners captured by the 5th Indian Division was one thousand one hundred and seventy-eight.

MISCELLANEOUS

The number of prisoners from miscellaneous services was about three thousand.

Units Still to be Dealt With

Amba Alagi Sector

Probable
97 Col Bn
109 Col Bn
110 Col Bde
Rizzio's Command

Possible
All or part of
7 Col Bde
79 Col Bde

Gondar Road Sector

Probable
102 Col Bde
43 Col Bde

Possible
All or part of
7 Col Bde
12 Col Bde
16 Col Bde

Note :—

The number of prisoners is not complete, as many missed the forward check where units were noted, owing to rapid advance. Also the figures do not include those captured by the 4th Indian Division. A very large number must also be added for deserters who went straight home, and for casualties in killed and wounded.

BIBLIOGRAPHY

War Diaries

HQ 4th and 5th Indian Divisions ('G' and 'A' and 'Q' Branches); 5th, 7th, 9th, 10th, 11th, and 29th Indian Infantry Brigades; Gazelle Force; 1 Horse (Skinner's); 3/1 Punjab; 3/2 Punjab; 3/14 Punjab; 4/16 Punjab; 2 Mahratta; 3 Mahratta; 1 Rajputana Rifles; 4 Rajputana Rifles; 4 Baluch; 4 Sikh; 3 Royal Frontier Force Regiment 6 Royal Frontier Force Rifles; 3 Royal Garhwal Rifles and Central India Horse.

Despatches

Despatch by Gen Sir A. P. Wavell, Commander-in-Chief, Middle East, on Operations in the Middle East from Aug. 1939 to Nov. 1940 (published in Third Supplement to the London Gazette of 11 June 1946)

Despatch by Gen Sir A. P. Wavell on Operations in the Middle East from Nov. 1940 to July 1941 (published in Supplement to the London Gazette of 9 July 1946)

Report by Lt Gen Sir William Platt on Operations in Eritrea and Abyssinia, Dec. 1940 to Aug. 1941, dated 11 Sept. 1941 (published in Supplement to the London Gazette of 9 July 1946)

Report by Brigadier H. R. Briggs on 7th Indian Infantry Brigade Operations on the Red Sea Littoral, Feb.-Apr. 1941.

Books

The Abyssinian Campaigns. (H. M. S. O. London); Brett-James, Antony, *Ball of Fire*, (Aldershot, 1951); Butler, J. R. M., *History of the Second World War : Grand Strategy*, Vol. 2 (H. M. S. O. London, 1957); Churchill, Winston S., *The Second World War*, Vol. 1, *The Gathering Storm*, and Vol. 3, *The Grand Alliance*; Collins, Maj-Gen R. J., *Lord Wavell* (Hodder and Stoughton, 1947); *Encyclopaedia Britannica*; *Handbook of Topographical Intelligence, the Anglo-Egyptian Sudan* (1940); *Handbook of Western Italian East Africa*, Vol. 1 General (1941);

Handbook of Western Italian East Africa, Vol. 2 (Communications); Playfair, Maj-Gen I. S. O., and others, *History of the Second World War : The Mediterranean and Middle East*, Vol. 1 *The Early Successes against Italy* (H. M. S. O. London, 1954);

Stevens Lt-Col. G. R., *The Fourth Indian Division* (McLaren and Son)

INDEX

Ab Aures : 80, 90
Abyssinia : *See* Ethiopia
Acqua Gap : 51, 58-63, 67-68, 71, 81, 83-84, 87, 91, 112, 114
Ad Teclesan : 123, 126-27
Addis Ababa : 8, 52, 124, 131-35, 152, 154
Aden : 8, 131
Adi Arcai : 134
Adi Caieh : 133
Adigrat : 133
Adi Ugri : 133
Adowa : 132-33
Agat : 52-53
Agordat : 43-47, 49-53, 56, 58, 65, 81, 122
Aicota : 41-43, 46, 48
Al Al : 85
Alagi Pass or Toselli Pass : 135, 144, 147
Alagi Ridge : 144
Albania : 7
Alomata : 147
Alpini Battalion (Italian) : 84-85
Amba Alagi : 131-38, 142-44, 147-54, 171
Amba Mt. 51, 84, 88, 91
Amien : 41
Anglo-Egyptian Treaty : 3
Anglo-Italian Joint Declaration (Gentlemen's Agreement) : 3
Anseba, the : 80, 86, 90, 120
Anti-Tank Troop R. A. 1st (Independent) : 82, 122, 127
Aosta, Duke of : 7, 150-51, 154
Aqiq 73-74
Arresa : 58, 133
Ascidira Valley : 50, 91
Asmara : 36, 49, 51-52, 85, 87, 97 113, 120, 122-26, 128-32, 154
Asmat Awi Pass : 76
Assab, harbour of : 3
Atbara : 10, 12-13, 25-27, 81
Atzala Valley : 145, 147
Australian Division, 6th : 6

Bab Harmas, Mt. : 80
Bahar : 43
Bald Hill : 136, 142-44, 150
Baluch 4 : 32-33, 107, 115, 117
Balkans : 6-7, 54
Baraka : 12, 43, 50, 52
Barentu : 41, 43-44, 46-47, 49, 58, 70, 81
Beit Gabru, Mt. : 51, 82-83, 86, 91
Belgium : 7
Beresford-Peirse, Major-General Sir Noel : 36, 121
Bersaglieri Battalion (Italian) : 52, 64-65, 84-85
Bhagat, Premindra Singh, V.C., Second Lieutenant : 48
Bhaira Ram, Lance Naik : 57
Biagundi : 48
Bich Hill : 93
Big Hill : 30-31
Big Rock : 107
Biscia : 41, 43
Bloody Hill : 84
Bonetti, Admiral : 130
Brenner Pass : 7
Briggs, Brigadier H. R. (Commander, 7th Indian Infantry Brigade) : 73
Brig's Peak : 51, 53-58, 62-63, 65-67, 71, 86, 88, 92-93, 99, 100-04, 107-08, 114-15
British Artillery : 137, 142, 148-50
British Forces : 5, 7-10, 24, 26, 31-32, 36, 40, 45, 72-73, 79, 90-91, 103-04, 108-09, 120-23, 131-32, 134, 141, 147, 153-54
British Prime Minister : 4, 153
British Somaliland : 5, 8, 24, 26, 153-54
Bump :
  Left, 95, 97, 103; Middle, 97, 102, 111; Railway, 106, 109, 113-15, 117; Right, 97; also *see* Four Bumps
Cairo : 131, 153
Cam Ceua : 76-77
Camerons : 43-44, 52-56, 66-67, 88, 92-93, 102, 112

Cameron Ridge : 51-57, 65, 71, 99, 103, 108
Canabai, Mt. : 65, 118-19
Cantibai : 128
Cannefat : 150
Cape of Good Hope : 9
Carabinieri : 84
Castle Hill : 136, 146, 150
Catholic Mission : 51
Central India Horse : 58, 82-83, 88-89, 117-18, 124-25, 132-34
Centre Hill : 146, 148
Cerasi : 98
Chad Battalion, 3rd : 76-77, 128
Chelamet : 77-78, 80, 127
Chelga : 49
Churchill, Rt. Hon. Winston S : *see* British Prime Minister
Cochen, Mt. : 44-46, 50
Cogai Pass : 80, 98
Coldstream, G. P., Major : 127
Combolcia Pass : 135
Commando, 51st : 83, 86, 88, 137, 141, 144-45, 147
Commando Hill : 141, 145
Corbetta : 136
Crete : 131
Cub Cub : 72, 76-80, 120
Cubcol : 77-78
Cunningham, Lieut—General Sir Alan : 121, 151, 154
Cyrenaica : 154
Dead Tree Hill : 145
Debelai Pass : 78
Debivar : 134
Debra Markos : 131, 135
Debub : 136, 138
Derudeb : 28
Dessie : 135, 138, 144, 147, 151
Di Aiba Pass : 147-48
Dickinson, General D. P. : 27, 153
Dire Dawa : 8, 134
Dog's Head : 33
Dogali : 128
Dologorodoc Mt. and Fort : 51, 87, 89, 91, 99-100, 103, 108—09, 111, 115, 120
Dongolaas Gorge : 51, 84, 87, 112-13
Dugurba : 41
E Atzala Cheros : 147

East Africa Force : 134, 138, 144, 146-47
East Gate Spur : 113-16
Ebibru, Mt. : 98
Egypt : 2, 5-6, 10, 24, 26, 39, 49, 122, 131, 151, 153-54, 156
Elephant, Peak : 136, 142-43
El Ghena : 72
Embremi : 128
Enda Medani Alem : 141
Engiahat, Mt. : 98-99, 119
Enkiabellit : 41
Eritrea : 12, 25, 43, 48-49, 51, 64, 72, 120-22, 126, 130, 132, 135, 153-54
Essex Regiment 1 : 32-34
Ethiopia : 1-4, 8, 10-13, 21, 23, 25, 36, 38, 131-32, 135, 138, 151-56
Falaga Pass : 136-39, 141-45, 147-48
Falestoh : 51, 59-60, 64, 84, 89-90, 103, 105, 109, 120
Field Regiments :
 1 : 60, 68
 25th : 65, 68, 77, 81, 122, 129
 28th, R. A. : 5, 32, 114
 31st : 52-54, 65
 Companies (Sappers and Miners) :
 2 : 116
 12 : 61, 76, 88
 20 : 116
 21 : 32, 98, 116
 Batteries : 28, 32, 53, 79
Fin Col : 146
Flat Hill : 69, 86
Flat Top : 51, 88, 92, 94-95, 101, 108
Fletcher Force : 114, 118-19, 138, 143-45, 147-48
Flit Force : 132-33
Foreign Legion : 78, 98, 119, 128
Four Bumps : 147
France : 4, 7, 9, 24, 155
Free French (Brigade d' Orient & French troops) : 49, 79, 97, 127-30
French Somaliland : 6, 24
Frusci, General : 8, 11, 52, 120
Furze Hill : 145
Gallabat : 10, 12, 25, 27, 31-36, 38, 48-49, 153
Gash Delta : 13, 27, 31, 40; Gash river, 13, 42
Gazelle Force : 27-31, 41-46, 50, 52,

56, 62-63, 67, 69, 71, 81-82, 85-86, 160
Gedaref : 25, 27, 48-49
Gegghiro, Mt. : 98-99
Germany : 1-7, 155
Ghinda : 128
"Gibraltar" : 44-45, 50
Girger : 29
Gojjam : 25, 38
"Golf Course" : 33-34
Gondar : 32, 49, 132, 134-35, 151, 172
Granite, Peak : 107
Graziani, Marshal : 26
Gumsa Mt. : 136, 145
Habi Mantel area : 85, 119
Haille Selassie, Emperor : 1, 38, 135
Haiya Junction : 27
Haldeid : 28-29
Happy Valley : 112, 117
Harar : 8, 134
Hafis : 86
Haurab : 40
Heath, Major-General, L. M. : 32, 121
Highland Light Infantry : 89-90, 99-100, 104, 108, 115, 125
Horse, 1 (Skinner's) : *See Indian Forces*
India : 2, 6, 9
Indian Forces :
  Divisions :
    4th : 5, 36-38, 41-44, 46, 48, 59, 62-63, 66-68, 70, 72, 74-75, 77, 81, 83, 86-89, 91-92, 97, 99, 100-01, 103-04, 111, 114, 118, 121-22, 134, 153, 156, 165, 172
    5th : 26-27, 31-32, 38, 41-42, 48, 67, 81, 86-89, 91-92, 99-100, 103, 105, 108, 110, 112-14, 117, 119-30, 134-38, 142-45, 147-48, 151, 153, 156, 159, 167
  Brigades :
    5th : 6, 41, 44-46, 58-59, 62-63, 67-68, 71, 82-83, 88, 92, 95, 103, 112, 122
    7th : 72, 74-75, 77-78, 80, 86, 90, 97, 99, 115, 119, 122, 127-29
    9th : 27, 48-49, 89, 99-101, 103, 105, 109, 114, 119, 125-26, 128, 147-48, 150
    10th : 27, 32-35, 42-43, 46, 89, 103-04, 107-08, 111, 114-15, 117, 119, 125-26, 128-30, 141
    11th : 41-45, 50, 52-53, 56, 58-59, 62-65, 67-68, 82-83, 88, 92-93, 101, 103, 108, 112, 122
    29th : 27, 41, 46-47, 67-68, 70, 81, 89, 99, 105-10, 114-15, 117-18, 123 126-27, 137, 139, 142-43, 146, 148, 150
  Battalions :
    3/1 Punjab : 56-58, 62, 64-67, 82, 88-89, 97, 114
    3/2 Punjab : 105-07, 109, 115-16, 118, 124, 142-43
    3/14 Punjab : 37, 45, 53-56, 58
    4/16 Punjab : 77-79, 97-99, 119-20
    4 Sikhs : 42-45, 58-60, 63, 67-68, 70, 82, 88-89, 95, 97, 103, 111-12
    1 Horse (Skinner's) : 28-30, 53, 82, 133, 137-38, 144, 147, 150
    2 Mahrattas : 48, 63, 67-68, 82-83, 88, 92, 94, 101-02
    3/5 Mahrattas : 100, 110, 115-17
    1 Rajputana Rifles : 43, 45, 53, 55-58, 65-67, 70, 82, 85, 88
    4 Rajputana Rifles : 60-63, 67-70, 82-83, 88, 94, 101-02
    Royal Artillery Group : 5, 70, 114, 121
    Royal Engineers : 114, 116
    Royal Frontier Force Rifles : 81, 89, 105-07, 118, 127, 142, 146
    Royal Frontier Force Regiment : 29, 100, 109-10, 115, 144-45, 147
    Royal Garhwal Rifles, 3 : 32-34, 102, 104, 107-08, 112, 114, 117-18, 125, 128, 137, 141, 144-45, 147, 149-50
    Royal Tank Regiment, B. Squadron, 4th : 43, 53, 59, 86, 110, 113, 116, 129-30; 6th, 26, 32.
  Companies (Motor Machine Gun) :
    1 : 27, 30, 82, 123, 132-34
    2 : 30, 42, 47, 58
    6 : 28, 29
Italian East Africa : 8, 10, 24-25, 39, 90-91, 153-56
Italian and Italy :
  Forces (Army), 7, 10, 24-26, 28, 30, 32, 38, 40, 44, 46, 48, 50-52, 59, 63-65, 69, 72-73, 80, 82, 85, 87, 89, 98, 106, 111, 115, 117, 119-20, 124, 130-32, 135, 138, 141, 150-54, 169;

Air Force, 30, 42, 113, 135; Navy, 9, 25; Pack Artillery, 65; Aircraft, 73; Cavalry, 83; Artillery, 90, 94, 100, 138, 148; Armed forces, 12; Forces advance, 10, 25-26; Forces withdrawl, 4, 38, 48; Position, 28, 30, 36, 42, 50, 53, 62, 77, 79-80, 85-86, 93-94, 98, 102, 113, 119, 125-26, 134, 138, 141-47; Opposition, 45-46, 93, 102, 125, 151; Resistance, 46, 77; Intelligence, 36; Patrols, 35; Reinforcement, 32; Strategy, 36; Communications, 43, 90, 97-98, 118; Garrison, 43, 71, 73, 75; Possessions, 12; Warships, 25; Somaliland, 8; Battalions, 8, 41, 156; Submarines, 9; Pincer Movement, 26; Counter-attack, 54, 56-57, 61, 65-66, 69-71, 101-03, 108, 110, 141, 146; High Command, 129; also 153, 155

Izel : 82
Jepio, Mt. : 56, 89
Jibouti : 9, 24
Karora : 25, 71-75
Kassala : 10, 13, 25, 27, 31, 36, 38, 40, 48-49, 71-72, 74, 81, 122, 154
Kaukawah : 40
Kenya : 8, 24, 26-27, 151, 153-55
Kerai : 75
Keren : 46, 49-53, 57-59, 63-65, 70-71, 74-75, 77-78, 80-81, 83, 85-87 89-92, 97-99, 103-04, 108-10, 113-15, 118-23, 125, 127, 131, 138, 151, 153-54
Keru : 40-43, 49
Kestrel Force : 82
Khaki Hill : 146, 148
Khartoum : 10, 13, 25-27, 31, 78, 152, 156
Khashm el Girba : 27
King's African Rifles : 8
Kismayu : 36, 154
Kurmuk : 25
Laal Amba, Mt. : 80, 84-85
Laquatat : 43-46
League of Nations : 1-2, 4
Legentilhomme, General : 24
Legion, 11th *CCNN* : 84
Libya : 3-4, 7, 24, 26, 39, 138, 152
Little Alagi : 136, 142-44, 150

Lorenzini, General (Italian): 108, 120
Madruiet : 78
Mai Aghif : 85-86
Mai Aragghez : 86
Mamud : 86
Mansciua : 83, 86
Mai Beicui : 85-86
Mai Ceu : 136, 147-48
Mai Mescic : 133
Marriott, Brigdier, J. C. O. : 123
Massawa, harbour of : 3, 9-10, 25, 36, 75, 80, 122, 126-32, 135, 154, 156
Maula Baksh, Naik : 69
Mayne, Major-General, A.G.O.M. : 136, 138-39, 143-44, 151
Meadowforce : 72-73, 77-78
Mekali Wells : 28, 30
Mendad : 80, 97
Mersa Cuba : 75, 127-28
Mersa Dersa : 76
Mersa Taclai : 72-76, 78-79
Mescelit Pass : 78-80, 97
Messervy, Colonel (later Lieut-General) F. W. : 82
Metemma : 32-35, 48, 52
Middle East : 2-5, 7, 9, 24, 26, 35, 49, 132, 135
Middle Hill: 136, 142-43, 148
Mogareh: 51, 82, 86, 88, 117
Mole Hill: 51, 86, 94-95
Mombasa: 156
Moncullo Fort: 129
Moyale : 26
Mussolini, Benito : 1, 3, 6-7, 155
Myburgh, Lieutenant-Colonel, P. S.: 82
Nacfa : 52, 72, 75-78, 84, 119
New Zealand Division, 1st : 6; Infantry Brigade 4th : 6
Nile, the : 12, 131, 152
Nogues, General : 24
North Africa : 2, 6, 24
Obellet : 80, 128
Om Ager : 47-49
Otumlo Fort : 129
Pathania, Captain Anant Singh : 107
Patriots : 10-11, 25, 35-36, 49, 135, 138, 144, 147-49, 151, 153-56
Pimple : 68, 100
Pinnacle : 100, 109

Platt, Major-General (later Lieut.-General) W : 25-26, 49, 80, 104, 108, 120-21, 123, 153-54
Ponte Mussolini : 50
Points : 51, 130; 66, 130; 649, 40; 900, 85; 1260, 60; 1262, 53; 1422, 67; 1451, 83; 147, 97; 1501, 67; 1552, 89, 105; 1557, 97; 1560, 60; 1565 (Sangar), 60-61, 67-68, 70, 84; 1572, 82, 83, 89; 1616 (Cameron Ridge), 51, 53; 1620, 92; 1643, 84; 1652, 98; 1680, 84; 1691, 84; 1702, 82-83, 89; 1704, 60; 1710, 82-83, 89, 95; 1717, 89, 105; 1760 (Mt. Falestoh), 60; 1767-Mt. Modacca-Mt. Dobac-Mt. Rocciosa area, 84; 1789, 84; 1892, 42; 1967, 98; 1968 (Mt. Beit Gabru), 83; 2084 (Ridge), 97-99; 2129; (7278), 124; 2160 (7269), 124-25; 2182, 86
Pyramid : 136, 138, 142-43, 147-50
Quiha : 133
Rajputana Hill : 122
Ratnagiri, H. M. I. S. : 76, 79
Razor Hill : 100
Red Hill : 116-17, 145
Red Sea : 3, 9-10, 26, 49, 71, 73, 122, 126, 130-31, 155
Rehib : 76
Rhodesian Squadron : 8
Richpal Ram, Subedar : 61, 69
Rome : 7, 26
Roseires : 27
Round Hill : 145
Royal Air Force : 47, 76, 90-91, 111, 144
Royal Fusiliers, 1st : 60, 88, 92-93, 101-02, 107
Royal Natal Carbineers, 1st : 147-48
Royal Navy : 71, 129
Royal Sussex, 1st : 73, 75-76, 78-80, 97-99, 120, 127-28
Rump : 145
Russia : 4
Sabderat : 36, 40-41, 49, 81
Saddle : 51, 86, 93-94, 102
Samanna, Mt. : 51, 84-86, 88-89, 92, 95
Sanchil, Mt. : 51, 53-55, 57, 65, 85-87, 89, 91-93, 99-105, 107-08, 112-13, 115, 117-18, 120

Sandford, Colonel (later Brigadier) D. A. : 38, 152
Sandy Ridge : 136-37, 139
Saraf Said : 33
Sarsareib : 27
Savoy Division: 52, 90, 97, 124
Savory, Brigadier R. A. : 37
Scialaco, Mt.: 53, 85
Senafe : 133
Serobatib : 29, 40
Sheodan Singh, Havildar : 69
Showak : 27
Sidi Barrani : 37
Signal Hill : 129-30
Siuma, Mt. : 82
Skenat : 75-76
Skinner's Horse : 68; see also *Indian Forces*.
Slab Rock: 94
Slim, Brigadier (later Field Marshal), W. J. : 35
Smuts, General, J. C. : 31
Socota : 136, 138
Somaliland Camel Corps : 8
South African Brigade, 1st : 134, 147-51, 153
Sphinx: 51, 60, 83
Suakin: 79
Sudan : 4, 8, 10, 24-26, 31, 36-37, 39, 48-49, 121, 132, 151, 153, 155; Defence Force, 5, 8, 10, 24-25, 27, 32, 78-79, 83, 119, 124, 129, 135, 138, 151, 153; Motor Machine Gun Company, 4th, 78, 80, 125, 129, 136, 141; Detachment 1 MMG Group (light guns), 88-89; Headquarters Troops, 37, 67, 90; Port, 9-10, 12, 25-27, 49, 71-74, 76, 80, 122, 156; Troops in, 161
Suez Canal : 2, 6, 9-10
'Sugar Loaf' (Peak): 102
Swedish Mission : 129
Syria: 6, 10, 24, 131
Tafala, Mt. : 56, 83
Takoradi : 26, 155
Tamanau Gap : 29
Tana Lake: 132
Tanks, "I" : 44-46, 50, 53, 91, 110-11, 116, 113-19, 124
Tantarua: 119
Tegawa: 41

Tchamiyam Wells: 28-29
Tendelai, Gap: 28-30
Tessenei: 41-42, 48, 81
Tetri, Mt. : 84
Tipo Battalion : 52, 64, 72
Togora Pass: 142
Tombe: 130
Tongue: 141, 145
Toselli Fort: 142, 150
Toselli Pass: 132, 134-36, 141, 147-48, 150
Transvaal Scottish, Bn I : 148-49
Triangle (Mt. Corarsi): 136, 148-50
Tunisia: 24
Turkey: 6-7, 24
United Kingdom: 1, 3, 7, 9
Vasentet : 97
Victoria Cross: 48, 69
Vittorio Emanuele Fort: 129-30
Wade's Post: 149
Wadi Athara: 77
Wadi Boo: 130
Wahni: 49
Wakai: 40-41

Wavell, General Sir Archibald : 6, 9-10, 25-26, 31, 36, 49, 121, 132, 151, 153-55
West Yorkshire Regiment, 2nd: 89-90, 100-01, 103, 109-10, 115, 126
Western Desert, Egypt: 36-37, 49, 72, 131
Whale Back: 142-43, 146
White Rock Hill: 89, 100, 149
Wingate, Colonel, O. C. : 38, 151
Wireless Hill: 144-45
Wolchefit Pass: 134
Worcestershire Regiment, 1st: 105, 107, 110, 117-18, 126, 142-43, 146, 148
Yodrud: 28-29
Zahafalan-Zagher-Massawa Road : 126-27
Zeban Minor: 105-06, 114-15, 117
Zeban, Mt. : 51, 87, 89-90, 99, 103, 105-06, 109, 117-18
Zelale, Peak: 51, 59
Zemale, Mt. : 60, 68

INDIAN DIVISIONS WON A FINE REPUTATION IN WORLD WAR TWO

Field Marshal Auchinleck, Commander-in-Chief of the British Indian Army from 1942, asserted that the British *"couldn't have come through both wars (World War I and II) if they hadn't had the British Indian Army"*. British Prime Minister Winston Churchill also paid tribute to *"the unsurpassed bravery of Indian soldiers and officers"*.

Between 1945 and 1947, the Director of Public Relations, War Department, Government of India, published a series of short publications covering the individual histories of the WWII Indian Divisions. They followed a consistent format, having between 44 and 48 pages within illustrated soft card covers. They have an average of 50 monochrome photographic illustrations, and each has a full colour centrespread depicting a scene from the Division's wartime operations (drawn by official war artists). They were printed at various presses in Bombay and New Delhi, and each contains at least one map.

As condensed histories they are useful – particularly those which relate to Divisions for which no other record was ever produced.

The British Indian Army during World War II began the war, in 1939, numbering just under 200,000 men. By the end of the war, it had become the largest volunteer army in history, rising to over 2.5 million men in August 1945. Serving in divisions of infantry, armour and a fledgling airborne force, they fought on three continents: in Africa, Europe and Asia.

This Army fought in Ethiopia against the Italian Army, in Egypt, Libya, Tunisia and Algeria against both the Italian and German Army and, after the Italian surrender, against the German Army in Italy. However, the bulk of the British Indian Army was committed to fighting the Japanese Army, first during the British defeats in Malaya and the retreat from Burma to the Indian border; later, after resting and refitting for the victorious advance back into Burma, as part of the largest British Empire army ever formed. These campaigns cost the lives of over 87,000 Indian service- men, while another 34,354 were wounded, and 67,340 became prisoners of war. Their valour was recognised with the award of some 4,000 decorations, and 18 members of the British Indian Army were awarded the Victoria Cross or the George Cross.

RED EAGLES
The Story of the 4th Indian Division
9781474537520

During the Second World War, the 4th Indian Division was in the vanguard of nine campaigns in the Mediterranean theatre, Egypt, Eritrea, Syria, Tunisia, Italy and Greece. The 4th Division captured 150,000 prisoners and suffered 25,000 casualties, more than the strength of a whole division. It won over 1,000 honours and awards, which included four Victoria Crosses and three George Crosses. Field Marshal Lord Wavell wrote: "The fame of this Division will surely go down as one of the greatest fighting formations in military history."

THE FIGHTING FIFTH
History of the 5th Indian Division
9781474537513

As described in much greater detail in Anthony Brett James's book 'The Ball of Fire', the division saw active service in East Africa, North Africa and Burma.

GOLDEN ARROW
The Story of the 7th Indian Division
9781474537506

The role of this division is also duplicated by a much larger work: the book by Brig. M. R. Roberts. However, this booklet gives a good account of Kohima and Imphal and the crossing of the Irrawaddy. In 1945, the division was flown into Siam, so becoming the first Allied formation to re-enter South East Asia.

BLACK CAT DIVISION
17th Indian Division
9781474537483

This formation was committed to Burma from the early days when the British were in full flight from the invading Japanese. It remained in Burma right through to the end, when the starving remnants of the Japanese Army were making their own desperate retreat.

ONE MORE RIVER
The Story of the 8th Indian Division
Biferno, Trigno, Sangro, Moro, Rapido, Arno, Senio, Santerno, Po, Adige

9781474537490

The 8th Indian Division started its overseas service in the Middle East in the garrisoning of Iraq and then the invasion of Persia to secure the oil fields of the area for the Allies, before moving to Italy in 1943. Landing at Taranto, it pushed up the length of the peninsula in a series of major battles: breaking the Sangro Line, forcing the Rapido and turning the defences at Cassino, breaking the stubborn German resistance at Monte Grande and, finally, forcing the Po River. It won four VCs, 26 DSOs and 149 MCs along the way. During the war the 8th Indian Division sustained casualties totalling 2,012 dead, 8,189 wounded and 749 missing.

TIGER HEAD
The Story of the 26th Indian Division
Arakan, Ragoon

9781474537452

This is a history of the division said later by the Japanese to have been the opponent which they most feared. The 26th held the Allied monsoon line in the Arakan during two such seasons, repulsing every attack launched against it. Later it made a series of leap-frog landings down the coast to clinch the issue in the Arakan. It was the first division to enter Ragoon, invading the city from the sea.

THE TWENTY THIRD INDIAN DIVISION
"The Fighting Cock Division"
Burma, Malaya, Java

9781474537469

The Fighting Cock Division is well recorded in the book by Doulton. This book gives coverage of the heavy fighting at the Kohima Battle, the capture of Tamu, the reoccupation of Malaya in August 1945, and then its strange role on the island of Java – concurrently disarming the Japanese garrison, fighting the insurgent Indonesian nationalists, and caring for 65,000 former internees pending the arrival of a new Dutch administration.

A HAPPY FAMILY
The Story of the Twentieth Indian Division,
9781474537476

One of the few Indian divisions in the 14th Army trained specifically for the war in Burma. Raised in Bangalore in 1942, it commenced active operations in late 1943 and served from Imphal through to the end. It established the 14th Army's first brigade-head across the Chindwin and its second such brigade-head across the Irrawaddy. Its final task was to round up the Japanese in French Indochina.

TEHERAN TO TRIESTE
The Story of the Tenth Indian Division
9781783317028

This History deals with the 10th Indian Div's exploits in Iraq (under Maj Gen "Bill" Slim) its role in the Libyan battles leading up to El Alamein, the following two years of garrison duties in Cyprus and Syria, and finally, its fighting services in the Italian campaign (from Ortona onwards).

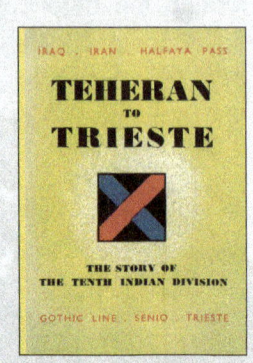

THE STORY OF THE 25th INDIAN DIVSION
The Arakan Campaign
9781783317585

Formed in Southern India in August 1942 for defence of that area in case of Japanese invasion, the "Ace of Spades" Division had its baptism of fire in Arakan in February 1944. It served throughout the remainder of that campaign the climax being the battle of Tamandu. Its victorious fight for the Kangaw roadblock was considered by many to have been the fiercest battle of the entire Burma war, while its liberation of Akyab was the first convincing proof to the rest of the world that the tide had turned against the Japanese.

DAGGER DIVISION
The Story of the 19th Indian Division
9781783317035

Raised in the late 1941, the 19th was the first "standard" Indian Division. Its troops were the first to breach the Japanese defence line in Burma and to raise the flag at Fort Dufferin. It crossed the Chindwin in November 1944, driving on to Mandalay and Ragoon during seven months of continuous fighting. The 19th's exploits are graphically described also in John Masters' personal memoir, *The Road Past Mandalay*.

www.ingramcontent.com/pod-product-compliance
Lightning Source LLC
Chambersburg PA
CBHW060419300426
44111CB00018B/2900